the classical music experience

discover the music of the world's greatest composers

CDs narrated by
KEVIN KLINE

Julius H. Jacobson II, MD

sourcebooks mediaFusion

An Imprint of Sourcebooks Inc.®
Naperville, Illinois

Published by Sourcebooks, Inc.
P.O. Box 4410, Naperville, Illinois 60567-4410
(630) 961-3900
FAX: (630) 961-2168
www.sourcebooks.com

The Library of Congress has cataloged the hardcover edition as follows:

Jacobson, Julius H.
  The classical music experience : discover the music of the world's greatest composers
/ by Julius H. Jacobson II, MD
     p. cm.
 1. Music appreciation. I. Title.
 MT90 .J25 2002
 781.6'8—dc21

                                                                                                2002003403

Printed and bound in the United States of America
              LB 10 9 8 7 6 5 4 3 2 1

A Note about the Audio

The Classical Music Experience was developed with both the reader and the listener in mind. Accompanying the book are two audio CDs on which noted actor Kevin Kline will help you experience each composer, including excerpts from many of the works featured in the book.

These discs offer just a taste, and we hope you'll find lots of things you love and that you'll want to hear more. So Sourcebooks MediaFusion and Naxos, the world's leading classical music label, have formed a revolutionary partnership that will allow you to hear all the music featured in the book through their website at Naxos.com. Here's how:

Logon to www.naxos.com/cme

Input 1402203187 and the password: classicalmusic

Then register with your name, email, country of origin, and a unique password of your choice.

You will then be able to have complete access to the music featured in this book.

NAXOS

sourcebooks
mediaFusion

An Imprint of Sourcebooks Inc.®
Naperville, Illinois

This book is dedicated to the late Arthur Cohn, a great musicologist and a patient who became a close friend, my mentor in music, and finally the person who told me to write this book.

CONTENTS

ACKNOWLEDGMENTS

As this work has progressed, I have been astonished by the alacrity and diligence with which my friends have come forward with suggestions, emendations, and advice, all based on an experience and knowledge of music, arts, and letters far superior to mine. Like my noble editor, Jon Malysiak, and my agent, Allan Wittman, they have enabled me with their help and sustained me with their encouragement. I cherish them all and do not list them individually because, like Abou ben Adhem's, each of their names should lead all the rest.

Nevertheless, I simply cannot omit my wife, Joan, without whose encouragement, judgment, musical instincts, and not least of all, knowledge of grammar, this book would never have reached fruition.

INTRODUCTION

This book is intended for those with little or no knowledge of classical music. As a surgeon, and not even an amateur musician, my only qualification is that I have been an avid listener of classical music since my teens. It has been one of the great pleasures of my life. I believe this to be the first book of its kind—largely a discussion of a beginning basic repertoire (those compositions most often heard at orchestral or chamber music concerts) with excerpts of each on the accompanying compact discs. The knowledge and personal experience of the listener inevitably colors their reactions to music. I have shared mine with you along with some medical stories and trivialities that I think you will enjoy. The lives of the composers are inextricably bound up with their work. When you remember that Beethoven was deaf when he wrote his Ninth Symphony, and that Brahms was in love with Schumann's wife, something extra is brought to the learning experience. You listen differently, and that listening is enriched!

The genesis of this book came from two people. One was a companion at a dinner party who said, "I want to learn something about classical music." I was unable to find what I considered a proper book for her. The other was an eminent musicologist and a grateful patient of mine, the late Arthur Cohn, who had been guiding me in widening my musical tastes. It was his suggestion that I write this book. His thought was that a book on classical music written by a non-musicologist might serve an unmet purpose for the neophyte listener. This book is dedicated to him. My hope is that you, too, will become a lover of classical music. If I can accomplish this, I shall have improved the quality of your life just as surely as I do with successful major surgery. The idea of the accompanying compact discs is mine, but requires an apology at the outset. Reducing the music to excerpts is the only way that they can accompany the book at reasonable cost. I have arbitrarily chosen forty-two composers and a selection of their works. Some I love. Some I like less, but they have all taught me valuable lessons about music. Opera is omitted, except for Wagner, who had a profound impact on composers who came after him.

To give you only a short sampling of great masterpieces is just plain mean. Tantalus was punished by the gods by being confined to Hades forever. When he went to drink, the water disappeared; when he tried to pick a piece of luscious fruit from a tree, the wind moved the branch just beyond his grasp. These musical excerpts will *tantalize* you, but later you can rectify this at the local music store. The complete performances are easily found, often at low cost, because the works are so popular.

Tantalus, although the son of Zeus by a mortal, was allowed to eat with the gods. One day they even condescended to attend a banquet at his palace. Tantalus hated the gods, and to show how easy it was to fool them, he had his only son, Pelops, boiled in the stew so that the gods would become cannibals. But the gods were not fooled. Tantalus's eternal punishment was also meted out for stealing nectar and ambrosia—the food of the gods—from the heavens, and giving them to men.

A chronological order of composer's lives is adhered to because, not unexpectedly, it mirrors the changes in musical styles and content that occurred. While you can skip around, you may come upon a term or concept, that was discussed earlier. When you are well under way, test yourself by randomly listening to the various tracks and discovering which you can identify.

I am convinced that the development of taste in classical music is very much akin to learning to look at paintings. You begin by liking the representational pictures that are easy to understand, and then progress to the more difficult and abstract. Music is the same. At first you are captivated by the romantic lush themes of Tchaikovsky, then by the geometry of Bach, and eventually, *maybe,* you will develop a liking for Schoenberg, Ives, and Shostakovich, with a whole wonderful world in between. What you listen to is purely for your own pleasure, but—as in any form of appreciation—effort is required on your part. The more you know, the more pleasure you get. My advice is to read the text first, then listen to the appropriate material on the compact disc, then read the text again. As a great internist, Sir William Osler, put it for the physician, "Go from the book to the bedside and back to the book."

This book is about listening to music. Since sound comes to us through the ear, I think you will find it interesting to learn more about the ear. The magnificent drawing following is by Max Brödel, the most outstanding medical artist that ever lived. He was on the faculty of Johns Hopkins Medical School, my alma mater.

The vibrations of sound first pass through the ear canal. This causes the drum membrane to vibrate. Attached to the drum membrane is the first of three tiny bones called ear ossicles. The vibrations of the drum membrane cause these bones to vibrate one to another. They then transmit vibrations to the cochlea, shaped like a snail, which is lined by hairs of different lengths. Each of these individual hairs vibrates to specific sound frequencies, and triggers nerve impulses that are then transmitted to the brain. This is our hearing apparatus. In the last century, an entity called "Boilermaker's Disease" was recognized. The din present in the boilermaking shops destroyed quite specific sections of these hairs, which explains the loss of hearing at certain frequencies of the men and women who worked in these shops. A similar loss has been found in some of the generation who have grown up listening to amplified rock music. Please remember this and be careful about too heavy a hand on the volume control. You can do yourself real harm.

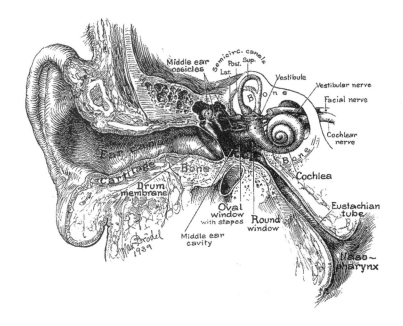

Notice the Eustachian tube that passes from inside the throat to the ear. This is what allows you to compensate for changing pressures in an airplane. Lastly, look at the semicircular canals that are oriented in three different planes and filled with fluid. These are the equivalent of an elegant, biological gyroscope. The nerve impulses from these structures tell you whether you are right side up or upside-down, or leaning to one side or the other.

part one

Palestrina, Giovanni da (1525–1594)

"It is the confession, not the priest, which gives us absolution."

disc one
tracks 2–3

Palestrina is our first composer, and his selection represents what's good for your education rather than a vehicle for instant gratification. Virtually every major composer from Haydn and Mozart to Schubert studied harmony from the textbooks of Johann Fux (1660–1741), which were based on the music of Palestrina, who represented the paradigm of multiple-voiced music (polyphony). Even today, conservatories offer a course in counterpoint based on Palestrina's models. With all that, there must be something to him!

I will be straightforward about my lack of musical erudition. A confession is in order. I chose Palestrina for you because a musical education without knowing about the "Homer of Music" or the "Legendary Saint of Music," as he has been called, would be like a surgeon not knowing about Semmelweis. My confession is that his music has bored me in the past, causing me to have given it short shrift. However, choosing a passage for you from among his major works entailed a lot of listening, and I subsequently became enthralled.

Ignaz Philip Semmelweis's (1818–1865) contribution to medicine and surgery was monumental. In his day, the well-to-do had their babies at home, while the poor had theirs in the hospital. "Puerperal" fever (also called "childbed" fever) was a scourge in the maternity wards, at times accounting for a mortality rate as high as 25 percent. There were two obstetrical services, identical except that medical students were taught in one and midwives in the other. The students' wing had two to three times the maternal mortality than that of the midwives'.

Over the strenuous objections of the Professor of Obstetrics, Semmelweis began to investigate the cause. The epiphany came when one of his friends, a pathologist, died from an infection that clinically resembled puerperal fever. He had cut himself during an examination of a woman who had died from the fever. Semmelweis reasoned that students were possibly carrying something from one woman to another when they examined them during labor. He promptly instituted among the students a regimen of hand washing with soap and water between examinations. The mortality rate in the student wing promptly fell well below that of the midwives' wing!

Joseph Lord Lister, the father of sterile technique and modern surgery said, "Without Semmelweiss, my achievements would be nothing."

Giovanni Pierluigi da Palestrina (1525–1594) received his early musical education as a choirboy in Rome. Tradition says that when puberty took its inevitable toll, he became a tenor. At the age of nineteen, he was appointed organist and singing teacher at Palestrina, a cathedral town in the Alban Hills about twenty-five miles from Rome. This is the first instance of a composer being renamed for where he lived. At any rate, he worked hard at his music, found time to find a girl, and married her.

It didn't hurt his career when his local mentor, the Bishop of Palestrina, was elected as Pope Julius III. He took Giovanni to Rome with him and saw that he was well-placed. Rome had its ups and downs. Pope Julius died in 1555 to be succeeded by Pope Marcellus II, who held the position for only three weeks before he, in turn, died. This mass was written at Marcellus's request (more on this later). The new papal successor, Pope Paul IV, didn't like having a married man in his choir, and dismissed him. Nevertheless, Giovanni went from one prestigious position to another, with the ultimate accolade of history changing his name to Palestrina.

As you may well know, Martin Luther began the Protestant (protest) Reformation in 1517 by tacking a manifesto of ninety-five theses (propositions for debate) on the door of a church. This led the Catholic Church to establish a Counter-Reformation in order to cleanse the church of abuses. The Council of Trent, an ecumenical council, was set up to bring disparate factions together, both from within and outside of the Church. I have attended many committee meetings that seemed interminable. None has ever held a candle to this one, which lasted eighteen years, from 1545 to 1563. The musically pertinent dicta that came out of this were that musical instruments were not to be used to accompany church music, and that the scripture should be clearly heard at all times. Palestrina managed to circumvent these strictures by creating an orchestra out of the voices without sacrificing the words. He composed 106 masses, and is said to have "saved" church music.

Hans Pfitzner (1869–1949) might be a more popular composer today were it not for his embrace of Nazism. As the conductor Otto Klemperer put it, he was "certainly not a philo-Semite." Pfitzner's masterpiece is considered to be the opera *Palestrina*, in which the ghosts of Palestrina's ancestors visit Palestrina, disillusioned because the Council of Trent is on the verge of excluding polyphonic music from the church. They dictate *Marcellus* to him as he takes it down in writing, note by note.

For the Renaissance audience, the mass occupied the same importance as did the symphony in the eighteenth century and the opera in the nineteenth century. A mass is the principal daily service of the Catholic Church that culminates in the story of the Last Supper. A High Mass, performed on the most important occasions, is known as a "Missa Solemnis," and as such contains twenty or more individual sections attended by no-holds-barred ceremony.

The structure of a mass can be divided into two parts. The first, called the "ordinary," is present in every mass, and consists of five or six sections, each of which has its own unvarying text and are therefore most often set to music. These sections are as follows:

Kyrie	a simple prayer	"Lord have Mercy, Christ have mercy"
Gloria	a long hymn	"Glory to God in the highest"
Credo	beliefs beginning with	"I believe in one God, the Father almighty"
Sanctus	another hymn	"Holy, holy, holy, Lord God of hosts"
Agnus Dei	another prayer	"Lamb of God…have mercy upon us"

The remaining portions of the mass are the "proper" ("appropriate" would have been a more suitable word) because this varies according to the event of the day that is being celebrated, and the particular time of year. Music has the great ability to heighten the meaning of words. Just as playwrights have exceptional problems with the second act, and symphonists with the final movement, the most difficult portion of a mass is the *Credo*. This is because, as it is longer than the others, it has many more words.

While Palestrina is the earliest composer whose work is described in these pages, fragments of musical pieces going back to ancient Greece are extant. For example, the first Olympics awarded music prizes. Music was highly developed during the Roman Empire. Christianity became its official religion, and a sophisticated body of liturgical music had already been composed by the time of Rome's fall, nominally in 476 ad. During the Middle Ages, this music was preserved and enhanced by the church. Plainchants (Gregorian) accompanied the masses.

The first towering composer to arise in the early Renaissance was Josquin des Pres (1440–1521) whose music for masses is quite beautiful. His innovations centered on multiple voices (*polyphony*) declaiming the words with a readily understandable, and yet powerful, rhetorical quality. You will find his *Missa "Hercules Dux Ferrarie"* worthy of ownership along with many nonliturgical works. Martin Luther said of des Pres, "He is a master of the notes; others are mastered by them." This musical Michelangelo has been called "The Father of All Music."

Another early musical form that you should be familiar with is the *madrigal*, which dates from the sixteenth century. These are songs written for four to six voices, unaccompanied by instruments, and usually based on poetry. As examples, find works of Don Carlo Gesualdo (1560–1613) and Thomas Weelkes (1576–1623), particularly "As Vesta Was from Latmos Hill Descending." Gesualdo's claim to nonmusical fame is based upon his single sword thrust that did away with his wife and her lover. One need not be proficient in spatial relations to imagine how the lovers were positioned when he happened upon them.

Selections from Purcell's opera *Dido and Aeneas* should also be sampled. There are many CDs available of collections of early music. Browse among them and be adventurous!

Disc One, Track 3—*Missa Papae Marcelli* (*Mass of Pope Marcellus*), "Gloria"

The *Missa Papae Marcelli* is considered Palestrina's best work. Knowledge of the history and the structure of the mass will enhance your listening pleasure as you consider what he achieved. Our selection is the "Gloria." At first listen, just let the music wash over you as you go about your other activities. Later, listen again more intently.

There is no instrumental accompaniment. Do you miss it? Pay attention to the intonation of the words even though they are in Latin. Focus on how the multiple voices interact, sometimes giving support to the voicing of the words and sometimes speaking different words that remain intelligible in both sets of voices. This is polyphony at its peak. Just keep in mind, melody is horizontal and harmony is vertical. The harmony here is absolutely superb, and yet melody does come through, although it is certainly not prominently featured. The overall effect of tranquillity and religiosity may enthrall you, too!

CHAPTER TWO

Bach, Johann Sebastian (1685–1750)

"I really can't think of any other music which is so all-encompassing, which moves me so deeply, and which, to use a rather imprecise word, is valuable beyond all its skill and brilliance for something more meaningful than that—its humanity. I would tire of a repetition of lush Tchaikovsky melodies day in and day out."

—Glenn Gould on
Johann Sebastian Bach

disc one
tracks 4–7

f I were to be stranded on a desert island—equipped, of course, with electricity or a plentiful supply of batteries—and restricted to listening to the music of a single composer, Johann Sebastian Bach would easily be my first choice. In terms of sheer productivity, "J.S." was a wondrous worker, as evidenced by his prodigious musical output. I find, in Bach's music, new subtleties with each listen.

His work falls into the Baroque period. Somehow, listening to Bach or Telemann evokes the feeling of the architectural style. Listen and you will know what I mean.

Bach stood five feet, seven-and-a-half inches tall and was built like a bulldog. He was hard-headed, pugnacious, and was frequently involved in disputes with authorities and students all his life. He once called one of his students a *Zippelfaggotist,* a phrase that referred to a bassoonist who produced sounds like a nanny goat. Tempers flared. The bassoonist and this composer of countless sublime religious works had to be separated as they rolled on the floor attempting mutual mayhem. Perhaps surprisingly, Bach was also a devout Lutheran. He lived in a period when heaven and hell were not abstract concepts, but fearful truths. Nonetheless, his religiosity did

Baroque—referred originally to a misshapen pearl, but applied specifically to a florid style of architectural decoration that arose in Italy in the late Renaissance and became prevalent in Europe during the eighteenth century. It referred to flamboyant bad taste, but has acquired the reverse meaning of dignity and precise craftsmanship. Musically, it was the period in which instrumental music began to rival vocal music. Politically, it was the time of absolute monarchies, Louis XIV epitomizing it with the Versailles Palace; the mantle of the artistic patron passed from the church to the king and the aristocracy. It is also the age in which the scientific method came into being: Newton experimenting with his gravity and physics, Harvey discovering the circulation of blood, Kepler determining the elliptical motion of planets, and Leeuwenhoek looking through a microscope and seeing bacteria for the first time. There is little wonder that the music of the period found new frontiers as well.

not stifle his sex drive, as evidenced by his twenty children, making him to my knowledge the most fecund composer ever. Nine of his children survived him. Four of them followed in his footsteps as composers of note, but their father's near elevation to musical deity eclipsed them. The complexities of raising this many children were simple compared to the writing of his *Die Kunst der Fuge (The Art of the Fugue)*.

Bach died at Leipzig in 1750 and was interred at St. John's Church. In 1894, the church was renovated and the body had to be moved. There was some confusion as to which of three skeletons was Bach's, and eminent anatomists were called in to help. Scrupulous measurements were made, and a facial mask was constructed and compared with an existing portrait. An absolutely certain identification resulted, abetted by the knowledge that Bach had been buried in an oak coffin. The other two were pine!

Disc One, Track 5—Brandenburg Concerto No. 3 in G Major, BWV 1048

There are six Brandenburg Concertos, named after Christian Ludwig, Margrave of Brandenburg, who in 1718 rather casually commissioned Bach to write them. They were completed two years later, and delivered along with a dreadfully obsequious note. It is annoying to remember that the genius Bach all but prostrated himself before a man that history would have completely ignored had it not been for his connection to the masterly composer. The Margrave's orchestra was too small to play them, and Bach knew it. (Maybe this was Bach's method of retaliation?) As a result, they were never played at Brandenburg. After the Margrave's death in 1734, the manuscript was sold for a pittance. Mankind is fortunate that it survived. Each work is scored for different instruments, but all are in the *concerto grosso* form, which simply means that groups of solo instruments—string, wind, or keyboard—alternate with the orchestra as a whole. Thus, the word *grosso* refers to multiple instruments of the same type, as contrasted with a solo instrument.

Here is an excerpt from the first movement of the Third Brandenburg Concerto, an extravagant, unrestrained, and joyful piece, replete with physical energy, dancelike forward motion, and almost pagan ecstasy. The passage selected is scored for three violins, three violas, and three cellos that at times are contrapuntally arrayed against each other within the group, and at times between the groups. Unlike the other

Brandenburgs, it falls outside the *concerto grosso* tradition since there are no solos. Another unique feature of this particular Brandenburg is that a harpsichord plays the continuo line. The opening ensemble passage lasts for the first twenty seconds, ending with a downward scale, and a pronounced finishing beat.

A strange thing about the Brandenburgs is that you are easily able to identify any member of the six as a Brandenburg, but it will require a great deal of close listening before you can separate one from another, even though each is scored for quite different combinations of instruments. Therefore, the excerpt accompanying the book will give you a sense of familiarity when you listen to the rest, and yet each is quite different from the other five.

Spend some time listening repeatedly to the entire movement, and identify which instrumental group is dominant at a particular time. If the amount of sawing up and down and back and forth were applied to a forest, there would be plenty of firewood for the winter. Nonetheless, do you agree that there is nothing faintly boring about the music, although it requires more effort and attention on your part than will some of the other pieces you will encounter in this book?

Disc One, Track 6—Toccata and Fugue in D Minor for Organ, BWV 538

When you listened to our sample of the Brandenburg Concerto, you may have enjoyed it even though you couldn't easily identify a main theme. Why? Because the instruments simultaneously played multiple melodies so entwined that no single melody stood out to leave you with a recognizable tune. Music that contains multiple voices is known as *polyphonic*. Historically, the development of polyphonic music is particularly important because it required that musical notation be developed to write it down. In other words, a spaghetti-like mass of intertwining lines demands a script if it is ever to be played the same way twice.

The single word that best describes this extravaganza of the soul is *soaring*. You have heard this piece if you've seen *Fantasia*, the Walt Disney animated motion picture of 1940 that was re-released in the '90s and is probably responsible for introducing more people to classical music than any other film. It is the only selection in this book to be discussed twice, first for the organ, as it was originally composed, and then in a transcription for a full symphony orchestra. I will leave it for you to judge whether to classify it as two separate pieces of music or the same in two different settings.

A toccata is a short demonstration piece for a keyboard instrument. The word *toccata* is the past participle of the Italian *toccare*, "to touch," in this case referring to a keyboard piece that is "touched" rather than played—in the sense of such rapidity that nothing is dwelt upon, the notes being left as soon as they are sounded. Often the toccata is a prelude to a fugue, a composition in which three or more voices enter imitatively one after the other, each giving chase to the previous voice that "flies" before it. I suppose it is similar to a difficult crossword puzzle that is extremely satisfying when solved. In the word puzzle, each letter must fit down and across. In the fugue, each note must fit with the other notes sounding simultaneously (down) and with the melody line preceding and following (across). Bach, in his genius, made the notes fit perfectly in all dimensions—at each point in time and over time. In truth, because of the multiplicity of distinct musical lines in many of Bach's compositions, he crafted the equivalent of multidimensional crossword solutions.

In the fugue, counterpoint is king. Melody is juxtaposed to melody simultaneously in sometimes dizzying combination. As you can perhaps imagine, writing a fugue is a labor of Einsteinian complexity; though one could argue that composing an academic fugue is not so difficult an accomplishment as composing an artistic one. With that said, the more concentration expended in the listening, the greater the reward.

If we strictly adhere to our definition of toccata, the question then arises, "Is an 'orchestral transcription' a misuse of the word?" Not so! The transcription relates to the medium, not to the structure, of the music. Though, for clarity, the transcriber takes the structural differences into account.

Musical forms serve the psychological needs of the listener. The introduction of a new melody, the going elsewhere, and the return to the familiar are comforting and natural, as is the progression of rhythm from fast to slow to fast, or a shift of volume from loud to soft to loud. This is known as "ternary form." Since most classical songs adhere to this pattern, it is also known as "song form." Defying this standard pattern puts the composer at risk of the sobriquet "modern" or the scathing comment "I can't make head or tails of that music," just as a painting by Constable might be compared to one by Mondrian.

The old Scottish name **"Kist of Whistles"** (box or chest of whistles) was a term of derision dictated by Calvinist piety.

The organ is a fascinating instrument. It is, in essence, a series of whistles of different lengths connected to a bellows with mechanisms to control the amount and strength of the wind going through one or many pipes at the same time.

Refinements within the pipes allow them to imitate all the wind instruments of the orchestra as well as mimic the strings. An organ has multiple keyboards for the different registers. Unlike the pedals on a piano, the feet play a true keyboard. Bach is thought to have been the finest organist who ever lived. He apparently could do more with his feet on the pedals than most organists can do with their hands on the keys. The organ is a natural for churches. Few other places are large enough to house one (some movie theaters have them, most notably the Radio City Music Hall in New York City.)

The toccata portion of this piece occupies the early minutes. It is less rigid in form than Bach's usual work, and probably evolved as he was sitting at the keyboard improvising its astonishing flourishes. To me, its opening is a clarion call worthy of heralding something as consequential as the Ten Commandments, but the fugue is as convoluted as a bowl of noodles. The fugue starts with a complexity that is beyond analysis without years of musical education, but requires none to appreciate. At the end, the toccata returns to finish the piece. If you want to test the bass of your hi-fi system, pump up the volume and listen to organ music!

Each time you listen, you will hear something more. This is music that you'll want to come back to, just like that box of chocolates in the cupboard.

Recommended Listening
Toccata and Fugue in D Minor for Orchestra BWV 538

A sense of the structural elements—harmonies, rhythms, supporting lines, instrumentation—apart from melody is necessary for the appreciation of classical music. As you will discover, Tchaikovsky was a gifted melodist and orchestrator, but after you have listened to his music for a while, it will come to resemble a hit parade of richly developed popular songs. This is why Bach wears so well in comparison to Tchaikovsky, although it may require much more listening for you to fully appreciate this.

The discussion of the fugue form under the Toccata and Fugue for Organ used the metaphor of a crossword puzzle. In *Die Kunst der Fuge*, Bach accomplishes one of the select intellectual *tours de force* of mankind (rather like playing sixty games of blindfold chess simultaneously and winning them all). To give you a further idea of its sheer complexity: it begins with four fugues, two of which present the subject, the other two present the subject backwards, then there are counter-fugues where the pitches are transposed upside down and combined with the original music. Think of putting the musical score in front of a mirror and then rotating the score in all directions while coming up with a cohesive work. Bach didn't adhere to rules—he made them.

Repertoire is the French equivalent for the English word "repertory," meaning a stock collection of frequently performed pieces.

You have just heard the Toccata and Fugue in D Minor played on an organ. Now, I advise you to hear what an orchestra—in an orchestration composed by Leopold Stokowski—can do with it. I feel it is important for you to be able to compare an identical work arranged for different instruments. You will find that the orchestra adds a great deal. The organ can't compete in volume and breadth, but it adds sepulchral and liturgical qualities that seem proper in a church, while the orchestral version fits the concert hall. Repeat listening to the organ version and then the orchestral version. Then start paying attention to the various voices in the fugue and how they weave together. Unless I'm very mistaken, you will return to this music repeatedly, both for the pleasure it gives you, and the sense that you hear more and more with each listen.

Bach eclipsed all the great musicians of his day, including Handel, Vivaldi, Couperin, and Alessandro and Domenico Scarlatti (1685–1757). Handel and Bach were born the same year, as was Domenico Scarlatti. Scarlatti composed 550 keyboard sonatas, which are a delightful staple of the piano repertoire.

Bach was particularly fond of the works of Domenico's father, Alessandro Scarlatti (1660–1725). In the same way you have increased your perceptions by listening to the Toccata and Fugue played by an organ and then a symphony orchestra, I believe you will enjoy *Sonatas for Keyboard* by Domenico Scarlatti, which can be obtained in harpsichord, piano, and organ versions. *The New Penguin Guide to Compact Discs* by Edward Greenfield, Robert Layton, and Ivan March [Penguin Group London, 1988] is a valuable book to consult in making choices of the many recordings.

Recommended Listening
Passacaglia and Fugue in C Minor, (arr) for Orchestra

Monumental is the best description for this work, which was originally written for the organ. My recommendation is another orchestral transcription by Leopold Stokowski. You should by now have already heard the equally monumental Toccata and Fugue for the organ, as well as its orchestral transcription. Get a recording of each in both the organ and orchestral versions, and compare one to the other. The music is the same, but I would venture to guess that you will find each version a quite different listening experience.

> The experience of listening to music is, to a considerable degree, what you bring to it. Make it a point to listen to something you particularly like at the end of a busy work day and again when you wake up the next morning. You will find the difference fascinating. I did exactly that with this music. I had spent a long day in the operating room on a difficult case, and was concerned about the patient's eventual well-being. The result of the evening listen was relaxation and banishment of anxiety. The morning experience left me exhilarated and raring to go. I confess that the experiment was flawed. I had called the ICU before the morning listen to find that the patient was doing splendidly—vital signs were stable, urine output excellent, and the endotracheal tube had been removed.

My personal preferences are for the orchestral transcription of the Toccata and Fugue and the organ rendering of the Passacaglia and Fugue. Nothing, in my opinion, equals the deep bass register of the organ for the Passacaglia, but you will have to hear that rendition to compare.

The first massive chords in a deep bass immediately give you the key to the passacaglia form (the "g" is not pronounced in Italian so the pronunciation is *pass-a-cal-ia*.) These deep-throated sounds never stop throughout the entire performance. It is known as a ground bass, which tells it all. Quite typical of Baroque music is the use of a so-called "basso continuo," where a harpsichord or a lute plays a steady accompaniment, often embroidering on the lowest single line of the written music, much as a jazz musician takes a theme and runs with it.

Figured bass refers to a musical shorthand where numbers in the bass line at the bottom of a score indicate the chords for whichever instrument doing the continuo part is instructed to play, with the expectation of embroidering around them.

I confess that for years I thought the word "continuo" referred to an instrument called the continuo. You might say, and possibly make a musicologist wince, that a passacaglia is the "ultimate" in the use of the basso continuo.

Bach composed only one other work in the passacaglia form, Chaconne for Violin, which is equally famous. The chaconne and the passacaglia both originated in early Spanish dances. My understanding is that the passacaglia keeps a bass theme (basso continuo) consistent throughout the entire work, but a chaconne allows the repeating theme to move occasionally to higher registers.

The differences are actually more complex, and the discussions of them remind me of the interminable bickering at gourmet dinners about the distinctions between a sorbet and a granité. The form was dying out when these were written. It has been suggested that Bach wrote no more because he felt he could never equal or surpass these firstborn.

When you have a chance, listen to all of the Passacaglia, and then please listen again, concentrating on nothing but the passacaglia theme. It is stated as a solo in the first sixteen notes (count them: da-dum, da-dum, da-dum, da-dum, da-dum, da-dum, da-dum, da-dummm,) lasting for twenty-eight seconds. The exact same theme is then repeated twenty more times. From the eleventh to fifteenth repetition, Bach moves to a higher register with less volume, but the notes are the same. The effect is lighter, and the plodding sensation has departed. The passacaglia theme in the bass gets louder, and is particularly easy to follow in several spots. At repetition sixteen, the plodding deep rendition returns, and is continued to the end.

Now listen once again, paying particular attention to the upper registers above the passacaglia theme. Bach has written a new variation of the theme with each repetition of the bass. In the midst of all this, the fugue, derived in part from the passacaglia theme, starts soaring above the passacaglia theme itself that has endured in the deep bass.

I think you will agree with me that Bach was quite a fellow, twenty children and all. This is music that you should enjoy more with each listening as its structure becomes ingrained. In this passacaglia, the constant repetition of the bass theme becomes a part of you akin to the street noises of a big city that you automatically discount but, were they to suddenly stop, you would sense the void. I hope you feel this. If so, you are making real progress. If not, listen again with your attention focused on the structure, both high and low, which to me recalls my geometry classes. Suddenly, I remember, "In a right triangle, the square of the hypotenuse equals the sum of the squares of its sides."

CHAPTER THREE

Handel, George Frideric
(Händel, Georg Friederich)
(1685–1759)

"Raphael paints wisdom,
Handel sings it…"
—Ralph Waldo Emerson

disc one
tracks 7–9

Georg Friederich Handel was born in Saxony (Germany) to a barber-surgeon and his wife, but lived in England from the age of twenty-six. When he left Saxony and his former employer, the Elector of Hanover, to go to England, it was with the definite understanding that it was only for a *short* trip. Upon arriving in England, he met with great success, including a stipend of £200/year from Queen Anne. When she died, the new monarch was none other than

Handel dropped the umlaut from his name when he went to England, but the pronunciation "Hendel" remained, and so it was sometimes spelled.

George I, the former Elector of Hanover. There is an apocryphal tale that Handel wrote the *Water Music* to propitiate his old boss but, to say the very least, their first meeting must have been rather strained.

1. The barber-surgeons did things with their razors such as opening abscesses and bleeding patients (thought then to be therapeutically valuable). They found themselves in competition with the established physicians, who were called doctors (much the same relationship as chiropractors and MDs today.) The doctors refused to let the barber-surgeons into their guild! As their surgical skill increased, the barber-surgeons stopped shaving beards and became surgeons. The doctors were then willing to welcome them into their societies (no longer guilds) but now the surgeons refused to join.

To this day, the aspiring surgeon in Great Britain is called "Dr." after medical school graduation. Upon completion of surgical training, his title becomes "Mr.," and he is proud of it. The female surgeon is called "Miss," married or not. Nonetheless, well into the nineteenth century, a physician's wife could be presented at court, a surgeon's wife could not. The same distinction was given to a barrister's wife, but not to that of a solicitor's.

2. When the barber-surgeon was shaving a beard he put a bowl against the patient's neck to catch the lather. This "barber-bowl" looks like a soup bowl with a circular cutout in the rim to conform to the neck. As the practice of surgery advanced, the shape of the barber-bowl was found to have general utility. It remains, in modified form, in every hospital room today; it is now called a kidney, or emesis, basin.

I once visited Mr. [sic] Able, a distinguished cancer surgeon, in his London Harley Street office/home where he was kind enough to show me some of his four hundred barber bowls. They were produced in many materials such as pewter, tin, silver, and majolica, and clearly demonstrated the transitional changes in shape from the barber bowl to the emesis basin. I have two porcelain barber bowls in my own collection.

In 1711, Handel moved to London, where he was catapulted to instant fame when, in his first opera, *Rinaldo,* an aria was begun with a flock of sparrows released inside the opera house. He went on to write nearly fifty operas, which have largely disappeared from the repertoire, but many lovely arias have survived. All of Handel's operas are in Italian and are based on classical or mythological themes. The singers sang, but there was no character development or action on the stage. They adhered to this rigid and static form just as the cowboy films do to theirs. The artificiality of Handel's operas became apparent to the London operagoers when contrasted with John Gay's *The Beggar's Opera*, with its popular tunes sung in English. Kurt Weill later modified this into *The Three Penny Opera.*

Even though few composers were so eulogized in their lifetime, Handel managed to guard his privacy, and precious little is known about his personal life. He never married, and whatever sex life he had he kept to himself. Handel has the distinction of being the first composer to be the subject of a biography, written a year after his death. He went blind in 1752, but this did not stop him from playing the organ or composing. He even maintained his reputedly good sense of humor. At one point, his surgeon suggested that an eminent blind organist participate in one of his concerts. Handel burst into laughter and said, "Mr. Sharp, have you never read the Scriptures? Do you not remember, if the blind lead the blind, they both fall into the ditch?"

Modern viewers have a difficult time adjusting to the sight of women singing men's parts in these old operas. These roles were originally written for the *castrati*—men who were castrated as children so that they would grow up with exquisite voices. This practice, in order to provide adult male sopranos and contraltos, was justified by the Roman Catholic Church's interpretation of an injunction by St. Paul to the effect that women should keep silent in church (1 Cor. 14:34). Castrati were first admitted to the Sistine Chapel in 1599.

Disc One, Track 8—*Water Music*

From the *Daily Courant* of July 19, 1717:

On Wednesday Evening, at about 8, the King took Water at Whitehall in an open Barge, wherein were also the Duchess of Bolton, the Duchess of Newcastle, the Countess of Godolphin, (etc.) And went up the River towards Chelsea. A City Company's Barge was employed for the Musick, wherein were 50 Instruments of all sorts, who played all the Way the finest Symphonies, composed express for this Occasion by Mr Hendel, which his Majesty liked so well, that he caused it to be plaid over three times in going and returning.

One can surmise the pageantry involved with Handel's *Water Music* from the above quote. There is an anecdote that "his Majesty" didn't like violins, and told Handel on that particular day to score it for woodwinds and brass. I don't believe it. The river mentioned is, of course, the Thames. Should you get to London and have decent weather, I heartily recommend that you take the standard tour boat, which goes down the Thames to the Naval Museum at Greenwich.

The *Water Music* has various versions divided into three suites, comprised of nine sections. The first is a minuet, the second a bouree, and the last a hornpipe, a dance by British sailors aboard ship. Handel's instrumental music has a lot of what I think of as "sawing" in it; by this I mean the violin bows going back and forth like a hand-saw. I don't mean to denigrate it, but there is a certain monotony that Bach escapes completely. If you like what you hear, get "The Arrival of the Queen of Sheeba," *The Royal Fireworks Music,* and *Alexander's Feast.*

Disc One, Track 9—"Hallelujah Chorus" from *Messiah*

The word "oratorio" derives from the Latin *oratio,* which means "prayer." An oratorio narrates a story (usually, but not always, with a religious context) set to music, and told by two or more singers. Oratorios are performed without costume, not intended for a stage, are not part of any church service, and are in the operatic genre. They are also meant to occupy a full evening's, or afternoon's, entertainment. Handel is sometimes credited with inventing the form. However, this is not true since other oratorios preceded his by about 150 years. Nonetheless, without doubt, Handel brought the form to its loftiest peak. He composed his first when he was still in Germany. In England, he managed to combine the elements of Italian opera with its arias, German passion plays with their choral commentary, and the English anthem. He also threw in a little French drama.

A few brief definitions of other terms you should be familiar with, describing sacred vocal music:

Cantata—like an oratorio, it is performed by chorus, soloists, and orchestra but is much shorter, almost the equivalent of a one-act opera. Sacred and secular cantatas were composed during the Baroque period. Where the oratorio is primarily Catholic, the sacred cantata is Protestant (Lutheran) in origin, usually based on the gospel of the week, and accompanies Sunday church services. When you begin to explore this genre, a glorious introduction is J. S. Bach's Cantata No. 140. As it begins, the church bells are striking twelve with a completely seductive rhythm.

Motet—essentially a cantata sung unaccompanied by musical instruments (a capella).

Mass—written for both Catholic and Protestant services.

Magnificat—based on actual biblical text and sung at services.

Passion—type of oratorio, based on the events leading up to Christ's crucifixion.

Messiah, based on a text from the New Testament, is the best known and most frequently performed example of this genre. When he wrote it, Handel's popularity with London audiences was rapidly declining, but he was still adored in Ireland. To orient you, twenty-five years had passed since the following newspaper quote about the *Water Music.*

From the *Dublin Journal* of April 10, 1742

Yesterday Morning, at the Musick Hall…there was a public Rehearsal of *Messiah,* Mr. Handel's new sacred Oratorio, which in the opinion of the best Judges, far surpasses anything of that Nature, which has been performed in this or any other Kingdom. The elegant Entertainment was conducted in the most regular Manner and to the entire satisfaction of the most crowded and polite Assembly.

The first public rehearsal of *Messiah* took place on April 9, 1742. At the first public concert, on April 13, ladies were asked not to wear hoopskirts and gentlemen to refrain from sporting swords, so large was the expected audience. The review from the same paper:

Words are wanting to express the exquisite Delight it afforded to the admiring crowded Audience. The Sublime, the Grand, and the Tender, adapted to the elevated, majestick and moving Words, conspired to transport and charm the ravished Heart and Ear.

Later, at its London premiere, some say King George II was so moved that he stood up early in the "Hallelujah Chorus," and remained standing. Since decorum dictates that when the King stands, everyone must follow, this tradition has endured. To this day, the audience stands during the "Hallelujah Chorus."

The words of the "Hallelujah Chorus" are:

Hallelujah! For the Lord God omnipotent reigneth.
The Kingdom of this world is become the kingdom of our Lord, and of His Christ;
and He shall reign for ever and ever.
King of Kings, and Lord of Lords, Hallelujah!

Can you imagine, given these boilerplate biblical phrases, being assigned the task of writing accompanying music for them that would endure for over two hundred and fifty years? Handel succeeded and, if humankind doesn't destroy itself, there is no doubt that seven hundred and fifty years from now, performances of the *Messiah* will remain an absolute staple of the Christmas season.

This is pure homophonic music; the melody is king with the instruments and other voices serving it. The sheer joy imparted in these few minutes is entirely due to the music, except for the word *Hallelujah!*

Following the success of *Messiah*, Handel's London following improved. He began to write opera again, but after three decades of writing Italian dialogue, he switched to English. An absolutely charming product of that effort was *Semele*; a recording of this won a 1994 Grammy Award. You will relish Jupiter wooing Semele and incurring Juno's wrath!

CHAPTER FOUR

Haydn, (Franz) Joseph
(1732–1809)

"If it soon comes without much difficulty, it expands, but
if it does not make progress, I try to find out if I have
erred in some way or other, thereby forfeiting grace;
and I pray for mercy until I feel that I am forgiven."

disc one
tracks 10–12

Joseph Haydn, called "Papa Haydn" by his intimates, was born in an area of Austria with a large immigrant population consisting of Austrians, Moravians, Magyars, Croats, Czechs, and Hungarians. There is still a hot debate as to who gets credit for his ancestry. He came from an artisan background. His mother, who wanted him to be a priest, was happy when he was recruited to a church choir school in Vienna. He received some musical education, but alas, when his voice changed, an adolescent prank was used as an excuse to throw him out. He scraped together a living by entertaining at parties and dance halls, and taught himself music theory largely by studying the work of Joseph Fux, an Austrian composer known for his theoretical work on counterpoint.

Haydn had the good luck of getting a job teaching the daughter of one Metastasio, the most famous librettist of his day. This daughter was also taking lessons from a great singer who was, at the same time, giving lessons in composition to Haydn in return for menial tasks (scut work as we say in medicine). These connections finally led to Haydn's appointment, at the age of twenty-six, as composer and musical director to a Viennese noble, Count Morzin. While employed with the count, he composed his first symphony (Hob I:1).

Haydn is unquestionably the father of the symphony. He composed 104 of them, in contrast to Mozart's forty-one; Beethoven's, Schubert's, and Bruckner's nine; Tchaikovsky's six; and Brahms's paltry four. Haydn's music is easy to listen to, melodious and very pleasant, but it is neither grand nor rousing. Somehow it fails to grip the soul. One wonders if the reason for this is the staid life he led, or the fact that most of his works were written on commission for nobles who wanted something "nice" to be played at some event. The great exception to this is the truly rousing German national anthem, *Deutschland über Alles*, that derives from the Anglican hymn "Glorious Things of Thee Are Spoken."

Haydn should not be derogated, however, because of the type of music he wrote. As you will hear, it is easy and pleasant music to listen to, with infectious melodies, and rhythms that almost make you want to keep time. I had a good deal of difficulty in selecting the symphonies I wanted you to sample. You will derive great pleasure from listening to Haydn's entire symphonic output. Perhaps comparing Haydn to Beethoven in popular terms would be like comparing a watercolor to an oil painting.

The venerable titles of the "Father of the Symphony" and "Papa Haydn" generate a picture of conservatism that is totally unfair to his persona. Haydn was, in fact, a feisty little man at constant odds with those around him. He was a genuine innovator who was always departing from the norms of the times. Once, when bored by a musical grammarian, he said, "What nonsense this is! —I wish somebody would write a new minuet instead of bothering with such pedantries." He never lost his love of practical joking, which dated back to when he was expelled from the church choir for cutting off the pigtail of the boy in front of him—during Divine Service, no less!

Disc One, Track 11—Symphony No. 94 in G Major "Surprise"

Your disc features an excerpt from the second movement (andante) of Haydn's Symphony No. 94, written roughly at the time of Mozart's death. You will recognize the main theme as none other than "Twinkle, Twinkle, Little Star." The "surprise" (*Paukenschlag*) is a sudden crash heard approximately thirty seconds into the piece. It is completely out of context in the course of this intentionally simple tune. You will hear it again, albeit less jarringly, throughout.

Haydn did a number of innovative things like this in his work, such as quick-tempoed instead of elegant minuets, counterpoint to make the instrumental parts equal, and striking new combinations of instruments within the orchestra. Perhaps here, in the midst of the repetition of this lovely and restful theme, he wanted to wake up the snoozers in the audience, or frighten the little old ladies.

The full orchestra then enters. A gentle "Twinkle, Twinkle" melody comes back, but now instead of the crashing chords, Haydn raises the sound level by ending with a real *fortissimo*. The gentle theme is repeated in variations until the decibels are turned up again. After this, the alternation of soft and loud (*piano* and *forte*) continues with the whole orchestra banging away until the movement ends with a delightfully fetching and sweet variation.

Mozart used the same melody twelve times in an ingratiating piece called Variations on "Ah, vous dirai-je, maman" for Piano, K. 265. The song is a French nursery rhyme. I don't know whether "Twinkle, Twinkle, Little Star" has precedence over it. The so-called Theme and Variation Form is a common one, and each variation is approximately the same length. Very often composers will alternate one theme with another (A-B-A, or A-B-A-B-A...) In this movement, it seems to me his variation is soft (*piano* = P) to loud (*forte* = F), so that one could reasonably diagram this movement as P-F-P-F-P, with the few *Paukenschlags* thrown in for fun. I bet you anything he was thinking of his pigtailed classmate at some point during this composition.

Upon his first hearing of this symphony, Charles Ives, whose music is not soft, sweet, or easy, lampooned it by singing "*pret*-ty *lit*-tle *sug*-ar *plum sounds*" and called it "easy music for the sissies." I think you'll disagree.

I recently heard an otherwise knowledgeable talk show host on public television pronounce the first syllable of Haydn as in "new mown *hay*," rather than as in "*Hi* there." It was conspicuously clear that this otherwise well-educated man had never even listened to a classical music station. Doubtlessly, classical music literacy has been lost. Perhaps it is time for schools to go back to giving musical appreciation courses.

Disc One, Track 12—Concerto in E-flat Major for Trumpet and Orchestra

Haydn wrote a great deal of music other than symphonies. I want you to listen to a portion of a concerto that was highly innovative for its time. The newspaper advertisement for the premiere of this concerto by the soloist, Anton Weidinger, told of his "intention to present to the world for the first time, so that it may be judged, an organized trumpet which he has invented and brought—after seven years of hard and expensive labor—to what he believes may be described as perfection. It contains several keys and will be displayed in a concerto specially written for this instrument by Mr. Joseph Haydn, Doctor of Music." Haydn first used a trumpet in Symphony No. 20 and then dropped it until Symphony No. 32. This back-and-forth continues until Symphony No. 93. By then, he was using a fairly consistent instrumentation. Exploring the Haydn symphonies, and not just the named ones, will be both pleasurable and valuable to you in your learning experience.

I'm happy to say that hearing the concerto today with a modern orchestra would be an experience quite different from that of the premiere in 1800. The valve, used in today's trumpets, was not even invented until 1813. The trumpet, as well as a good many other orchestral instruments, has been greatly improved in the ensuing years, and it sounds better. All is not lost; we can still hear the music as it sounded in Haydn, Bach, or Beethoven's time. There are a good many orchestras and chamber music groups that have resurrected the old instruments. The music has a noticeably different sound. It is interesting, not jarring, but to my ear at times less than pleasant. Still there is a satisfaction in knowing "that's the way it was!"

It does no good to have a new and better instrument unless there's music written for it. As in most concertos of the classical period, the orchestra introduces the opening theme before the trumpet has a chance to show its stuff and, at the very end of the movement, it really goes to town. Haydn used the trumpet with the bravura of fanfares as contrasted with later Austrian composers like Bruckner and Mahler, who took advantage of its sweet and poetic qualities. In Handel's *Messiah*, the piece "The Trumpet Shall Sound," in combination with the voice, is truly dramatic.

This trumpet concerto, from the first movement of which you are about to hear, has become the best-known work for this instrument by any composer. Because the trumpet has the highest pitch of all the brasses—and a prominent brilliant sound—it is typically called upon to highlight passages of great majesty. Someday, listen to its offstage call in Beethoven's *Leonore* Overture No. 3, or its use in Bach's *Magnificat in D,* or the aria "Sound an Alarm" in Handel's oratorio *Judas Maccabaeus.*

I loved this piece on first hearing, and hope you do too. In this first movement, the entrance of the trumpet, as in most concertos of the classical period, is delayed until the orchestra has introduced the opening theme of the first movement. It is tossed back and forth between various segments of the orchestra. The trumpet intermittently takes over for solos with a bravura trumpet passage before the full orchestra brings this movement to a close.

I suggest that you delve into other Haydn concertos, particularly the C and D Major for Cello and the Concerto No. 1 in C for Violin and String Orchestra. If you enjoy Handel, Haydn's *Creation* (*Die Schöpfung*) Oratorio is a great piece of music.

Recommended Listening
Symphony No. 100 in G Major "Military"

Haydn composed about eighty of his one hundred and four symphonies during the thirty or so years that he was employed by the Esterhazy family. Twenty-nine of the symphonies have one or more nicknames. Numbers 82 to 87 are known as the "Paris Symphonies," and 93 to 104 as the "London Symphonies."

At first, Haydn had only a small group of musicians to work with, but evidently he had no difficulty convincing his employers that bigger was better. Additional musicians were employed, and still others were brought in from local churches and the orchestras that most towns kept. Haydn's spreading fame attracted virtuoso instrumentalists. As a result, a standard symphony orchestra evolved. It consisted of one or two flutes, two oboes, two bassoons, two horns, timpani, six first violins, six second violins, three violas, two cellos, and two double basses, as well as trumpets. There were no clarinets; Haydn introduced these much later, taking his cue from the twenty-two-year-old Mozart, who was twenty years his junior. Haydn would play the harpsichord to provide a figured bass (pronounced *base*)—usually a large string instrument (bass viol) or cello that played a single bass line of the score while the harpsichord harmonized with it—to the orchestra. Thus, there were approximately thirty players in all. In contrast, the modern symphony orchestra averages about a hundred players.

After the death of his wife, a deeply depressed Prince Esterhazy believed that music could restore his happiness. Consequently, he forbade Haydn to leave the estate. When Haydn was fifty-eight, the Prince died, and the court orchestra disbanded, thus setting Haydn free. He returned to Vienna for a short while until a violinist and impresario, Johann Peter Salomon, lured him to London to compose and perform. Mozart discouraged him, saying Haydn knew nothing of the ways of the world and its languages, to which Haydn replied, "All the world understands *my* language." He went to London, and during that year and a half, composed Symphonies No. 93 through No. 98 in what amounted to a public competition between Haydn and a former student, Ignaz Pleyel. All of London had opinions as to which of them was the better composer. The "Surprise" Symphony won the battle for Haydn.

He returned to Vienna now a comparatively wealthy man. It was then that he took on a new student, Ludwig van Beethoven. He gave his student short shrift, however, because he missed the adulation of his London triumphs, and was in the midst of negotiating his return. Haydn made it back to London for the 1794 season, where a really triumphant reception was accorded the premiere of the "Military" Symphony. It is a fine work but not, by the opinion of history, in the class of Beethoven's "Eroica." You compare the two.

Upon his return to Vienna, Haydn worked for another Esterhazy, Nicholas II. He lived another fourteen years, but never composed another symphony. Number 104, his last, dates from his second stay in London.

The name "Military" is derived from the "Turkish" influence in the third movement, in which a big bass drum is employed, along with cymbals and a military triangle. In Mozart and Haydn's time, the big drum was played with two sticks of markedly different size. The big stick signaled the accents, and the little stick marked the rhythm. The cymbals clashed in time with the big stick, while the triangle tinkled with the little stick.

The second movement begins with a slow dancelike march initially played by the strings. The timpani appear in full force, and the music blusters on. The opening tranquillity is restored, and then alternates with some stomping by the entire orchestra (sans triangle and cymbals.) There is a trumpet fanfare, and a kettledrum roll followed by a relaxation with a repeat of the theme, and a final orchestral crescendo.

Buying Haydn's full 104 symphonies is a bit much, but a good place to begin is with all of the "London Symphonies," which comprise numbers 93 to 104.

CHAPTER FIVE

Mozart, Wolfgang Amadeus (1756–1791)

"People make a mistake who think that my art has come easily to me. Nobody has devoted so much time and thought to composition as I. There is not a famous master whose music I have not studied over and over."

disc one
tracks 13–16

ave you ever considered this? A person requires years of painstaking practice and schooling in musical theory before he is considered a musician. A painter, however, can go out and buy paints, brushes, and canvasses and call himself an artist and be considered one by society—but not necessarily a good one—from day one!

Mozart was a foul-mouthed and socially unattractive person. Yet his music is probably loved and admired more than that of any other composer. Older opinion attributed Mozart's frequent use of obscenities to Tourette's syndrome. More reliable recent scholarship debunks this theory completely. He and his family simply liked to swear! The story goes that Mozart's father, Leopold, was disturbed by his son's refusal to conform to social conventions. Thus, he was particularly delighted to hear Joseph Haydn say these now famous words: "Before God, and as an honest man, I tell you that your son is the greatest composer known to me." Incidentally, the document that contains this quote fetched £138,000 ($210,000) at a Sotheby's auction in May 1993.

Mozart's father, Leopold, was a composer who wrote a treatise on playing the violin; his music is remembered only for a composition that included whistles and pistols, among other instruments. Mozart's sister, Nannerl, was a pianist of real talent. It is to be expected that, with this background, Wolfgang would have been exposed to music at an early age. It was quite unexpected, however, that at the age of three he would go to the piano and begin to pick out tunes. Leopold, although a not very high-minded man, knew he had something special. By age six, Wolfgang and Nannerl were playing for the nobility in the principal cities of Germany. They went to Versailles to be admired by the king and queen—to say nothing of Madame Pompadour—then to London, the Low Countries, and on and on, with only illness intervening at various points. They finally returned home when Wolfgang was approaching the age of ten, after three and a half years on the road. The next decade was occupied with still more concertizing in Italy and throughout Europe. But, more important, they were steeped in musical theory and practice.

The cliché that Mozart sat down to play the piano at age three and from then on pumped out one great musical composition after another is untrue. Mozart's greatest works were produced in the last ten years of his life. This is hardly speaking to venerable old age since he lived only thirty-five years. The age of death hits home. Even though I graduated from high school at a young age, after the Navy, college, a master's degree, medical school, and seven years of internship and residency, I was thirty-two years old before I started a surgical practice—one year older than Schubert, and three years younger than Mozart at the time of their respective deaths. Tom Lehrer, the political satirist and songwriter, used to be able to say, "It's a sobering thought that when Mozart was my age, he'd been dead for five years."

Another cliché that requires exploding is that most great composers were not honored in their lifetimes, and were appreciated only by subsequent generations. Mozart enjoyed the most extreme adulation possible, all the way up to the crown heads of Europe. The myth that he was buried in a pauper's grave is also false. His graveside was unmarked, but that was due to sumptuary laws restricting the elaborate—and expensive—funerals to which the Viennese were "too partial." These laws were ordained by Emperor Joseph II, a truly enlightened despot, who was ten years ahead of the French Revolution in trying to bring about reform to benefit the common man.

Current scholarship holds that Mozart died of rheumatic heart disease with a terminal infection emanating from bacteria that settled on the already diseased heart valves (endocarditis), which spewed forth from the heart with each beat. His passing was memorialized by a huge service in Prague, where his almost completed (his very last composition) Requiem Mass was played. If you have seen *Amadeus*, you observed a final irony: a gargantuan memorial service in Vienna at which the music was conducted by Salieri, a man who was rumored to have poisoned Mozart: yet another myth.

Disc One, Track 14—Serenade in G Major, K. 525 "Eine kleine Nachtmusik"

This serenade for string orchestra is probably Mozart's most popular piece. A serenade is music played at night. (Just imagine the aristocrats in their elaborate costumes dancing gently in a candlelit garden!) Mozart had just finished *The Marriage of Figaro*, probably his most outstanding opera, and was working simultaneously on *Don*

Giovanni. Schubert is reputed to have been the most fecund generator of melody, but Mozart is a close second. Superlatives are particularly dangerous when applied to classical music.

We have here an excerpt of the first movement of "Eine kleine Nachtmusik" *("A Little Night Music"),* which certainly represents the quintessence of Mozart's geniality. You will notice that it is written for a string orchestra *(only strings!).* The single opening theme is varied and embroidered upon during the entire movement. It demands nothing of the listener but to enjoy basking in its gentility. Buy the complete work. The remaining movements are equally outstanding, but of different tempi and feeling.

The range of Mozart's music is profound, and some feel that "Eine kleine Nachtmusik" did more harm than good. Even with all its charm, it is one of his weaker compositions, creating the impression of flighty, facile music, and veiling the immensity of his genius.

Disc One, Track 15—Symphony No. 40 in G Minor, K. 550

In general, the named works of a composer are those most appreciated by the public, and are often the best. If you want to buy the work of a specific composer and are browsing in a shop, your chances of getting something you really like are best if you pick a named composition. While I've found this to be true, I must admit that it defies logic because the publisher chiefly assigns the names, or they are created by happenstance. When Beethoven was asked what his Sonata, Op. 31, No. 2 was all about, he quipped, "Read Shakespeare's *Tempest.*" Thus, for posterity, it became known as the "Tempest" Sonata. Schubert intentionally never completed his Eighth Symphony, thus it is now known as the "Unfinished."

A **sonata** is usually a work for one or two instruments. The sonata form usually has three or four movements: fast, slow, moderate, and fast. The third movement is usually a dance. There are rules for the form of each movement and the relationship of one to another.

Mozart wrote forty-one symphonies. Some names that have stuck are "Paris," "Haffner," "Linz," "Prague," and the very last, "Jupiter."

The "G Minor," as professional musicians sometimes call it, has no real name, yet it is the most popular of all Mozart Symphonies (so much for generalizations). From June 22 to August 11, 1788, Mozart composed his last three symphonies, and eight other pieces of music (K. 542 to 552)—a completely unrivaled feat of productivity, and a devil of a way to spend a summer vacation! These last three symphonies are considered to be his greatest, and this selection is from the first movement of one of them.

The "G Minor" serves as a fitting work for a digression on the analysis of music. Obviously there are the nuts-and-bolts technical factors that must be left to the professionally trained, but there are some things that no one would debate. Just as hunger and thirst are known to everyone, the description of "soaring" for Bach's Toccata and Fugue is intuitive. However, the bulk of musical interpretation varies from listener to listener. No matter how learned the interpreter, there will always be others, equally authoritative, who will differ.

To demonstrate this variance and the fallibility of words, here is a paragraph of quotes regarding the "G Minor" from Jonathan D. Kramer's book, *Listen To The Music*:

Otto Jahn called it "a symphony of pain and lamentation" (1856), while C. Palmer called it "nothing but joy and animation" (1865). Alexandre Dimitrivitch Oulibicheff (1843) wrote of the finale, "I doubt whether music contains anything more profoundly incisive, more cruelly sorrowful, more violently abandoned, or more completely impassioned," while A. F. Dickinson (1927) felt that "the verve of this movement is tremendous. It is…the best possible tonic for the low in spirits." Georges de Saint-Foix wrote in 1932 of "feverish precipitousness, intense poignancy, and concentrated energy," while Donald Francis Tovey wrote at about the same time of "the rhythms and idioms of comedy." Robert Dearling called it "a uniquely moving expression of grief," while H. H. Hirschbach thought it "an ordinary, mild piece of music." While scholar Alfred Einstein found the symphony "fatalistic" and Pitts Sanborn thought it touched with "ineffable sadness," composers seem to have had happier opinions. Berlioz noted its "grace, delicacy, melodic charm, and fineness of workmanship"; Schumann found in it "Grecian lightness and grace"; Wagner thought it "exuberant with rapture."

This diversity of opinion carries over to the conductor's interpretation of the work. One may stress the passion, and another the grace. This of course helps explain the divergent opinions of critics as to particular performances. Be careful of the common human failing to assign the first hearing of the work as the correct interpretative baseline on which to judge future performances.

The salient feature of this piece is the transition between the tranquillity of a placid day and the coming of a storm. The opening theme enchants with its rapid-fire, prodding, and compelling rhythm. It is immediately repeated, but this time the last part of the passage gets a bit rougher. A new theme begins restfully, but it too assumes a more roiled quality. This passage repeats with an insistent urgency. An interlude occurs as storm clouds gather. Our original theme returns, but the storm is coming closer; occasionally rays of sun get through the storm clouds, and so on. *Listen and formulate your own interpretation.* I realize that it is far easier to listen passively, but if you do as I suggest, you'll find you are listening with greater comprehension and added depth to your appreciation.

When you are fortunate enough to listen to the entire symphony, you will also find that the entrancing main theme of this first movement contains some extraordinary variations that remarkably change its feeling, and yet it continues to be quite recognizable.

You would do well to purchase Symphony No. 41 in C (*Jupiter*) as your next Mozart symphonic experience, followed by the named symphonies—"Haffner," "Linz," and "Prague"—along with the nicknameless Symphony No. 39 in E-flat. Mozart's only other symphony in the key of G Minor is Symphony No. 25. To distinguish it from Symphony No. 40, it has been nicknamed the "little G Minor." Both "G Minors" are logically paired on a number of CDs, making them an excellent buy.

Disc One, Track 16—Concerto No. 21 in C Major for Piano and Orchestra, K. 467

Mozart wrote twenty-three piano concertos, one for two pianos and another for three. The latter was written to curry favor with an infamous archbishop, whose sister was Baroness Lodron. The parts for her two children required little more than the repetitious banging of some keys. This is, however, Mozart's most popular piano concerto. He completed it in March 1785, and first performed it in Vienna three days later.

Should you go into a music store and ask for the "Elvira Madigan," chances are you will get it without further ado. We've briefly discussed how pieces of music get their names. This is an odd one. There was a 1967 award-winning movie—named...you guessed it!—that featured this melody. It's bizarre to see a work named almost two centuries after its composition. Frankly, I would hate to see Beethoven's Ninth Symphony lose the name "Choral" in favor of "Clockwork Orange," but stranger things have happened.

You have a sample of the second movement of Mozart's Concerto No. 21 in C Major for Piano and Orchestra on your disc. The first minute or so is a sweet, lyrical but undominating introduction to the main theme. The "Elvira Madigan" theme is repeated three times at intervals. It is as soft and creamy as perfectly ripe Brie, without the rind. In between, you will hear connecting passages hearkening back to the introductory theme. As you listen to the piano, there are no explosive pyrotechnics, but rather the melodies come through without pretentiousness, and you end up feeling warmer for having listened. It is the same in the operating room and at sporting events: the better the performer, the more simple and effortless it looks. A great pianist, Artur Schnabel, summed it up brilliantly: "Mozart is too easy for children, and too hard for artists."

Of all the arts, music is the most directly in communication with the nervous system. Thus, it can evoke response without subjective awareness. Introducing music into the operating room seemed logical for the calming influence it would bring into an otherwise stressful environment. This was soon abandoned. We discovered that the music often took over without our conscious realization. For example, one day the rhythm of a polka was discovered to be dictating the speed of an operation. On another occasion, the lilt of a waltz was completely inappropriate to stanching the flow of a major hemorrhage.

What you have heard is not representative of the symphony as a whole, but a gem in its own right. For example, the first movement has a festive, martial feel to it, completely without the lyricism so evident in the second. The last (third) movement deftly brings about reconciliation between the first two worthy of a world-class diplomat. Get this work and pay special attention to the way in which the movements complement one another. This is the essence of a well-constructed piece of music.

The movement you just heard was marked *andante*. The composer will insert this type of direction at the beginning of each movement to indicate at what tempo it should be played. Most often, Italian words are used, but sometimes German is thrown in there as well.

Here is a table of tempi, from slowest to fastest, that you may find helpful, since people will refer to the *largo* of this or the *andante* of that:

Largo	Very slow
Grave	
Lento	Slow
Adagio	
Andante	Moderate (at a normal walking pace, not to be confused with moderato below)
Andantino	
Moderato	
Allegretto	Moderately fast
Allegro	Fast
Vivace	
Presto	
Prestissimo	As fast as you can (too many young artists choose this speed, even though not at the composer's direction, in order to dazzle you with their virtuosity)

Finally, Mozart's piano concertos Nos. 9, 14, 17, 19, 20, 22–26 should be marked for acquisition, along with Concerto No. 10, which is for two pianos. Violin Concertos Nos. 3–5 can give you a break from the piano. And for a completely new experience, also buy the very popular Concerto Nos. 1–4 for Horn and Orchestra.

Recommended Listening
Clarinet Quintet in A Major, K. 581

A contemporary of Mozart's is reported to have said upon his death, "It is a pity to lose so great a genius, but a good thing for us he is dead. For if he had lived much longer, we should not have earned a crust of bread from our compositions." This sentiment is easy to understand once you have listened to this Clarinet Quintet. It was written in 1789, the year of the French Revolution, and two years before Mozart's death.

As far as I know, Mozart was the first to add the clarinet to a string quartet. One must remember that chamber music is chiefly performed for the pleasure of the players, as contrasted to orchestral music where the interest of the audience dominates. Mozart wrote a later Concerto for Clarinet and Orchestra, K. 622, and had already written Trio in E-flat for Clarinet, Oboe and Violin, K. 498. Beethoven wrote Trio for Piano, Clarinet, and Cello, Op. 11. Some say—heretics all—that Weber surpassed Mozart in two concertos (Op. 73 and Op. 74).

The earliest mention of the clarinet is found in an order dated 1710. The clarinet is a single reed instrument with five pieces, a cylindrical bore, and seventeen keys. It possesses the widest dynamic range of the woodwind family, extending from a faint whisper to a real "pay-attention" fortissimo. Its agility rivals that of the flute. The clarinet comes in a variety of sizes that play different levels of the musical spectrum.

No mention of the instrument would be complete without noting the primary role it has had in ragtime and jazz. The latter is imitated (especially the opening for solo clarinet) in George Gershwin's *Rhapsody in Blue,* Igor Stravinsky's *Ebony Concerto,* and Leonard Bernstein's *Prelude, Fugue, and Riffs.*

The Mozart Clarinet Quintet is profoundly beautiful, but as light and pleasant as cotton candy. The entire quintet is about thirty-seven minutes long. This sampling will be sufficient for you to appreciate its absolute beauty.

The strings play the lilting first theme until the clarinet comes in for a short flourish, before the melody is reclaimed by the strings. The clarinet shows its facility in its low register, and soon after repeats this in its high register. The repeat is sublimely gossamer in texture and craftsmanship.

CHAPTER SIX

Beethoven, Ludwig van
(1770–1827)

"I carry my thoughts with me for a long time…I turn my ideas
into tones that resound, roar, and rage
until at last they stand before me in the form of notes."

disc one
tracks 17–21

Beethoven is the Shakespeare of music, who generated the most powerful body of music ever brought together by one composer. He was a small man with a leonine head that housed true genius, but he was personally unkempt and possessed deplorable social habits. His quarters were in such distressing condition that he could not keep servants. In the words of one visitor to Beethoven's apartment:

> Picture to yourself the darkest, most disorderly place imaginable—blotches of moisture covered the ceiling; an oldish grand piano, on which the dust disputed the place with various pieces of engraved and manuscript music; under the piano (I do not exaggerate) an unemptied chamber pot....The chairs, mostly cane-seated, were covered with plates bearing the remains of last night's supper.

The only thing that mattered to him—and the world—was his music. With Beethoven, it was a matter of the world adapting to his desires. Mozart and Haydn were flattered to be invited to an aristocrat's dinner table, whereas Beethoven felt he deserved to be seated next to the host. This formidable and irascible man never married. His life was an affluent one, but tragic in that he began to lose his hearing at age thirty. He never heard many of his finest masterpieces. This, however, was less devastating than you might think. Most musicians can "hear" a score in their head as they read it, and there are some who prefer to read it rather than listen.

Beethoven stood at a turning point in musical history. He was the last of the Classical and the first of the Romantic composers. By Romantic, I mean music of the post-Classic period—after Beethoven—in which more attention is given to the expression of feeling and emotion than to the observance of form. Although this will become more meaningful later, keep in mind that Beethoven's work builds on the foundation of Haydn and Mozart, and was a profound influence on Wagner.

In contrast to Mozart, who wrote his three crowning symphonies in three weeks, the major theme of the slow movement of the Fifth Symphony went through a dozen transitions over a five-year period. For a marvelous fictionalized version of Beethoven's life, I commend you to read *Jean Christophe* by Romain Rolland (Paris, Modern Library, 1938).

The word symphony is derived from Greek, and means "sounding together." Symphonies, as the form has evolved through the last two centuries, generally consist of four movements. Typically, the first movement dictates the overall character of the piece. It is usually fast (for example in allegro speed) while the second movement is slow and lyrical. The third is often a dance, minuet, or scherzo (an Italian word meaning "joke") while the fourth is rapid and upbeat, usually the longest, and the most important to the composer because he is making his final statement. (Composers have most trouble with their final movements, just as playwrights commonly have problems writing the second act, and, as mentioned in the chapter on Palestrina, the Credo is the bugaboo in composing a Mass.) Generalizations have exceptions, but the above pattern holds true in the majority of symphonic works. This combination of tempos and emotion has withstood the test of time with even the most modern composers, although it has become fashionable to talk about the symphonic form having outlived its usefulness. To quote the composer Aaron Copland, whom you will come to know later, "It is still the form in which the composer tries to come to grips with big emotions."

The great majority of classical music is written in one form or another, whether it be symphony, concerto, or sonata. These forms serve a useful function in that they predefine the work for the audience, laying down certain ground rules within which the work can be judged. An analogy might be made to a football game; the spectators know that the game is divided into four quarters and that there are four downs before the team has to give up the ball to the other side, unless they have brought the ball ten yards down the field. The forms are not immutable, just as the football game can go into overtime, or the team may not get four downs if the ball is fumbled or a pass intercepted. As we listen to the individual works, you will learn a bit about musical forms and discover that this knowledge increases your pleasure.

Up until now, I have purposely avoided being pedantic, but I feel that a "big brother" talk about proper listening is in order. The only way to listen properly and truly get maximum pleasure out of what you're listening to is by obeying the magic word: CONCENTRATE.

On May 25, 1993, at a concert of the New York Philharmonic Orchestra, its permanent conductor, Kurt Masur, stopped the orchestra one minute into a performance of Charles Ives's *The Unanswered Question* because of coughing in the audience. In his best Germanic accent and grammar, he admonished the audience to stop coughing, which it did, and then the orchestra played the entire piece from the beginning. His words of wisdom in his Germanic grammar were, "We are all never coughing on stage, and do you know why? Because we concentrate so much to perform, we don't feel like coughing. Just concentrating makes us healthy, so if you are listening with the same concentration to our music-making, you would enjoy it and will forget to cough." Subsequently, he complimented the New York audiences by saying, "Compared with every great city, New York is one of the best. But," he added, "it is also one of the best coughing audiences."

Arcangelo Corelli (1653–1713) was more diplomatic than Masur. He was playing a cello solo before a large audience at a cardinal's home when he became disturbed by talking. He subsequently laid down his instrument. When asked if something was wrong, he said only that he feared he was interrupting the conversation.

All of us find our attention straying from time to time. Music as a background to dinner or conversations is lovely, but you are not *listening*. Reading while music is playing is fine, but you are not *listening*. This also applies to program notes in a concert program, or the brochure that came with the disc, or even this book.

There are a few simple aids that can help avoid lapses in concentration if you feel yourself slipping (but are not to be used at public performances, please):

1. Close your eyes.
2. Tap to the beat of the music.
3. Pretend that you are the conductor and wave your arms!

As you listen to more and more music, test yourself by tuning into a classical music station. If you recognize the piece, it will give you tremendous satisfaction; identifying the composer is almost as good. You will confuse Mozart with Haydn; Mahler with Wagner; Vivaldi, Telemann, Couperin, and Bach with one another and a good many other composers whose last names end in "i," but never Vivaldi with Tchaikovsky, Bach with Mahler, or Beethoven with Schoenberg. It can be very satisfying to see what you've learned, and it will increase your thirst for more.

Disc One, Track 18—Symphony No. 5 in C Minor, Op. 6

This excerpt is from the first movement of Beethoven's Fifth Symphony. You are immediately immersed in the most famous four notes in all of classical music in the most frequently performed symphony. Beethoven described these four notes as "Destiny (fate) knocking at the door." Coincidentally, the rhythm of these four notes—dot, dot, dot, dash—spells out "V" in Morse code, and they came to stand for VICTORY during World War II. An irony that seems to have been lost is that during World War I, German music was not played at all in Britain.

Such a short group of notes is called a *motif*—or motive. In this symphony, this motif is akin to the individual stones in a mosaic picture. Each stone contains the same four colors, but the colors can vary in proportion and intensity. Here, the musical counterpart of the colored stones is that the four notes in the motif are varied in intensity, duration, length, and rhythm, played in higher or lower registers, and by assorted instrumental combinations. Fix the concept of motif firmly in your mind, as a basic building block of intelligent listening will then be in place. One of the delights of music is the variation in feeling and emotion that can be wrung from the same few notes.

In the first five seconds, the four-note motif is repeated twice, then followed by the same eight notes, but this time played at first gently, softly, and then again with gusto. The pattern is repeated softly, but played by different instruments, and then with increasing volume until a horn plays the four notes to announce a second theme that is lyrical, gentle, and bucolic. The first section of the movement ends, and is then repeated.

This first section is called the exposition. It identifies the part of the movement in which the initial themes are presented. Music, like this sentence, has punctuation marks in going from one section to another. These are called cadences. Sometimes you will sense an incomplete ending—the equivalent of a comma—which is known as an "open cadence." In this particular case, it was heralded by the horn playing the fate motif, signifying that the first theme presentation had concluded, and the second theme was about to start. You will also hear two "closed" cadences, followed by a pause that tells you, as forcefully as being hit over the head, that this particular section of the movement is DONE. *Spend some time reviewing these cadences in the two halves of the exposition.* Once you become aware of cadences, you will start to appreciate the structural elements of individual sections.

The two themes are modified, savaged, and revived, but remain changed forever. Observe how gradually notes are subtracted from the four-note motif so that they come in clusters of threes and then twos until finally only a single plaintive note remains, which is dolefully repeated. These have been called the "chords of despair." Resuscitation efforts have been successful, and the "fate" motif returns with some force, but is somehow drained of its original vitality. There follows a melancholy oboe passage, which you expect to lay the groundwork for trouble. The big surprise here is that the lyric theme comes back as beautiful and unruffled as it was in the exposition, until it inexplicably mutates into the "fate" theme.

Normally the coda is a short section that tells you in forceful terms that you are finished. But Beethoven was unconventional, and often did not adhere to the classic forms, resulting here in a coda that is longer than usual. At the conclusion of this movement, we still don't quite know where we stand. It remains for the next three movements to tell us.

This combination of power and gentleness define this symphony which, despite overexposure in the world's concert halls, never loses its ability to thrill every time. The extraordinary feature of Beethoven's Fifth is that each movement is quite different, yet the *destiny knocking* rhythm is interwoven as a major component in each. In your further reading, you will see the term "cyclic" or "cyclic form" which applies to portions of an earlier movement appearing in a later one. This symphony consists of motifs that are repeated with variation throughout the work; thus it is motivally constructed music, not "cyclic."

Up until the time of Beethoven, each symphonic movement was a complete entity ending with a closed cadence. In Beethoven's Fifth, *for the first time*, the third movement ends with an open cadence, making it incomplete until you get to the fourth movement (as in a TV news program where there is almost always a teaser inserted before the commercial break so you won't zap to another station.) The symphony ends with a *forty measure cadence*, a superstar of final cadences. I urge you to get the complete symphony.

We shall listen to a good deal more of Beethoven's work, though still only a tiny fraction of his prolific output. It is difficult to know what to buy when confronted with the thousands of titles available at any music store. You will not be sorry if you buy all of his symphonies. There is a particularly fine collection of all nine conducted by Leonard Bernstein. It is a fair generalization that Beethoven's even-numbered symphonies are *pastoral* and soothing in feeling. His Sixth Symphony, the most popular of the evens, is named the "Pastoral," while the odd-numbered symphonies are scrappy and tense. One might exaggerate to make the point by comparing the evens to frolicking pussycats meowing and the odds to roaring lions.

It is interesting to note that concerts in Beethoven's day were ever so much longer than in our time. The first performance of Beethoven's Fifth Symphony was on the same program as the premiere of the "Pastoral" (Sixth Symphony), and the entire Fourth Piano Concerto.

Disc One, Track 19—Symphony No. 3 in E-flat, Op. 55 "Eroica"

Unlike Mao's abject failure, the "Eroica" was surely a "great leap forward" for symphonic development. Not only is it loaded with completely unprecedented musical gestures, it is twice as long as any previous symphony. (Beethoven wanted it played at the beginning of a concert before the audience became weary.) More important, its entire conception was different from anything that came before it. It was the turning point in music between the eighteenth and nineteenth centuries. Subsequent composers could not ignore it; the radical changes in symphonic form of the nineteenth century are directly traceable to it.

The "Eroica," which translates from the Italian as "heroic," was composed in 1803, and presented for the first time in Vienna in 1805. Its original dedication was an homage to Napoleon Bonaparte, rather strange when you think about it because Austria and France were at war half the time. Beethoven hated the obeisance constantly being paid to the Viennese aristocrats and, by some accounts, thought seriously about moving to Paris. Had this come about, a dedication to Napoleon wouldn't have hurt.

The following is a quote from a letter written by Elisabeth (Bettina) Brentano, a German author who knew Beethoven and Goethe. The two distinguished men were out walking:

There came towards them the whole court, the Empress [of Austria] and the dukes. Beethoven said, "Keep hold of my arm, they must make room for us, not we for them." Goethe was of a different opinion, and the situation became awkward for him: he let go of Beethoven's arm and took a stand at the side with his hat off, while Beethoven with folded arms walked right through the dukes and only tilted his hat slightly while the dukes stepped aside to make room for him, and all greeted him pleasantly; on the other side he stopped and waited for Goethe, who had permitted the company to pass by him where he stood with bowed head. "Well," Beethoven said, "I've waited for you because I honor and respect you as you deserve, but you did those yonder too much honor."

Nonetheless, when Napoleon declared himself king, Beethoven destroyed the title page, and changed the title to *Sinfonia eroica, composta per festiggiare il Sovvenire di un grand Uomo (Heroic symphony, composed to celebrate the memory of a great man)*. Beethoven's fury on learning of Napoleon's coronation is attested to by the autographed title page in the Vienna musical archives, which shows a ragged hole where Bonaparte's name once stood. I'm not going to summarize the movements except to say that the second is a funeral march that Beethoven had considered contributing for use at Bonaparte's funeral.

Historical classifications are ordinarily useful, but fuzzy guideposts for making sense of polyglot changes. To the contrary, keep in mind that this symphony unequivocally demarcates the end of the Classical period and the beginning of the Romantic. The most common pattern of symphonies is to present two themes in the opening movement. Beethoven's fecundity overflowed; in this symphony there are no fewer than six. Most symphonies up to this time lasted twenty to twenty-five minutes or less. This is twice that length.

Do you recall how Beethoven used four notes as a motif to tie and build new structures in his Fifth Symphony? Focus on the rhythm of three notes played in repetition, and observe how they entwine the whole selection. I hope your finances aren't being strained, but this is another absolute must.

Make it a duty to listen to the *Egmont* Overture, which was clearly a labor of love in support of his very close friend Goethe, who wrote the drama on which the music is based. Egmont was the governor of Flanders who was put to death in 1568 by the invading Spaniards. If you buy it, look for a pairing with the *Coriolanus* Overture as well as the Overture to Beethoven's only opera, *Fidelio*. Beethoven knew the works of Shakespeare well. The *Coriolanus* tells the tale of Shakespeare's play in musical terms. One facet to observe is its muted ending that to me is more telling than the usual crescendo finish. *Fidelio* is the essence, in musical terms, of the individual's right to freedom, and the integrity involved in fighting for it in the face of political oppression. The *Fidelio* Overture reminds me very much of his Fifth Symphony in thematic material, and in the emotions it evokes, praise indeed for a work lasting seven minutes. I really wish this book were more inclusive so that you could hear, immediately, the *Egmont, Coriolanus*, and *Fidelio* Overtures.

Disc One, Track 20— Symphony No. 9 in D Minor, Op. 125 "Choral"

The phrase "bang for the buck" originated in the defense industry. If such a parlance were used in music, this symphony would be an intercontinental missile! You may be familiar with the nonchoral part of the fourth movement from the 1971 film, *A Clockwork Orange,* where only Beethoven's Ninth could temporarily soothe Alex the Droogie. In my opinion, the use of the Ninth accounts for much of the film's success. In Japan, there are so many performances of this symphony at year's end that the piece is affectionately known as the "Ninth Pollution." The performance of this work conducted by Leonard Bernstein in Berlin soon after the Berlin Wall went down is one of the most awe-inspiring moments in musical history.

The end of the fourth (last) movement burst the bounds of musical history. It was the first time a symphony ever included a chorus, a departure that gave the work its popular name. Verdi, perhaps the preeminent figure in nineteenth century opera, and the composer of *Aida* and *La Traviata* among many others, admired the symphony, but didn't like the choral portion, which, in essence, is a *de facto* fifth movement. This is entirely understandable, Verdi's *métier* being opera. Brahms, as we shall learn, delayed writing his first symphony for almost fifty years because he was reluctant to have it compared to Beethoven's Ninth. As a result, the prolific conductor Von Bülow dubbed Brahms's First Symphony, "The Tenth."

The length of the entire symphony is approximately sixty-six minutes. You get much less than this on your disc. Nevertheless, this sample is most important since it is the beginning of the choral portion, and as stirring as any of the rest. Beethoven toyed with the idea of composing an alternative "instrumentale finale" for use when a chorus was not available. The concept seems a good one for obvious reasons, but was never carried out.

I wish you could hear right now the lovely introspective pastoral sections of the third movement and, for that matter, the entire symphony. This is a work you absolutely must own! Save some money by purchasing any one of numerous boxed sets of all nine symphonies.

Bear in mind that Beethoven was completely deaf when he composed this symphony. Thus, it represents the triumph of the human spirit, which is the general theme of the poem *Ode To Joy* by Friedrich von Schiller, with whom Beethoven had a profound spiritual affinity.

Johann Christoph Friedrich Schiller (1759–1805) was one of Germany's greatest dramatists, literary theorists, and poets; his life exemplified the victory of spirit over adversity. He was ennobled in 1802, hence the use of **von** Schiller in the above reference. You should note that it is **van** Beethoven; this reflects his grandfather's Belgian origin. Personally, I have been grateful to Schiller for an aphorism that I think about often when frustrated by this or that in daily activity, whether it is a clerk who doesn't care or a bureaucratic hospital administrator. To paraphrase the German—***Against stupidity even the gods are powerless.***

Fidelio, Beethoven's great and only opera, was the most important transitional step to the "Ninth." Both works have the same essential message—All Men Are Brothers. This symphony is historically important, for it really ushered in the entire field of musical drama. We shall discuss this further when we turn to Wagner.

Now for the "Choral" (last) movement of Beethoven's Ninth Symphony, known as the "An Die Freude" ("Ode To Joy"). After a short orchestral flourish, the singing begins. This passage stirs the soul with its combination of voice, melody, and pulsing rhythm. The drum and glorious choral passages usher in the famous melody familiar from *A Clockwork Orange.* I repeat, Beethoven's audacity in putting a chorus into a symphony represented a startling innovation for music of his time.

Disc One, Track 21—Sonata No. 23 In F Minor, Op. 57 "Appassionata"

This placement of the "Appassionata," (in an impassioned style), our first sonata and first solo piano selection, will give you a point of reference for the revolution in piano composition achieved by Chopin and Liszt. Rather than paraphrase, I will quote from Karl Haas's book *Inside Music*. This is a valuable book to own when you are ready to dig into musical theory sans musical notation.

> The most basic definition of a sonata is a musical composition for any instrument, such as the piano, harpsichord, organ, violin, cello, or any instrument of the woodwind or brass family. Each of these can appear unaccompanied, although most frequently the piano is involved. From the middle of the eighteenth century on, the piano part attained the same importance as the other featured instrument. For example, a sonata for flute and piano is vastly different from a flute piece with piano accompaniment. That difference lies in the implementation of certain principles of formal structure…

The pattern of exposition, development, and recapitulation must, by definition, be adhered to in the first movement of a sonata, but not necessarily in the two or three movements that follow. Listen to it once or twice to gain familiarity, and then again as many times as you need to so that you may dissect out the definition of the theme, its development, any digressions, then the summary—or recapitulation—and coda. Whether you can do it or not doesn't make a bit of difference in that your listening will be sharpened either way.

The "Eroica," the "Appassionata," and the "Waldstein" piano sonatas represent a royal line of pieces written in the 1803–1805 period. One of my great favorites of this same period is the so-called "Triple Concerto" (Concerto for Piano, Violin, Cello and Orchestra in C Major, Op. 56). It has gained less stature among critics than it clearly deserves. It is dangerous to identify the best part of such a glowing work, but the third movement, a polonaise, is a paragon of the form. In it, the cello is the crown prince of the solo instruments. Beethoven never wrote a cello concerto, so effectively this is it. You will appreciate my leading you to it!

A bit of perspective is in order. Mozart and Beethoven contend with each other for greatness. When war and strife predominate, as is the case with the *Eroica*, Beethoven wins hands-down. However, let the economy be good with a sustained period of peace, there's no beating Mozart.

Recommended Listening
String Quartet in F Major, Op. 59. No. 1 "Rasumovsky"

A quartet can be written for any four instruments or voices. However, a string quartet typically consists of two violins playing "first" and "second" parts, a viola, and a cello (also called violoncello). You will find, incidentally, that "piano quartet" is an illogical appellation as it pertains to a quartet written for piano, violin, viola, and cello.

You will be pleasantly surprised to find what a breadth of emotion, volume of sound, and intricacy of detail can be produced by four instruments, even though they are all of the same family. Pay close attention to the way a specific melody is passed back and forth among the instruments, and how the other instruments interact. Keep in mind that chamber music was written largely for the pleasure of the players. Charles Avison (1709–1770), an English composer and organist, described it as "a conversation among friends, where few are of one mind."

Beethoven wrote seventeen string quartets. He, Bartok with six, and Shostakovich with fifteen, are considered exemplars of the form. They fall into his early, middle, and late work periods, and are divided as such. The seventeenth is called the "Great Fugue," and was originally composed as the last movement of the thirteenth. It is considered an apotheosis. The early quartets (Op. 18, Nos. 1–6) are easy listening. The middle quartets (Op. 59, Nos. 1–3, Op. 74 and 95) took a new path, and met with some resistance because of their break with existing tradition. The late quartets (Op. 127, 130–132, 135, and the "Great Fugue," Op. 133) were a radical departure from anything that had gone before. They anticipate the modern music of the twentieth century, and are quite difficult to listen to and understand. Musicologists agree that these last quartets represent the zenith of Beethoven's genius. They were the last works of his life, and at the time he wrote them, he was stone deaf.

The Rasumovsky Quartets are from Beethoven's middle period. Their melodies are lovely, and the interaction of the instruments is readily comprehended. With each listen, you will grow more appreciative of Beethoven's genius. The most startling thing to me about these String Quartets is that the impact is as distinct as in his symphonies. Spend time getting to know them in order to fully appreciate the individual instruments playing as a unit and reacting with one another. After listening to the big symphonic works, you will be amazed that four stringed instruments can do so much and, in their way, compete with the hundred or so instruments of a major orchestra.

The complete Beethoven String Quartets will be an excellent addition to your—I hope by now—growing library. Buying them in a boxed set saves money. As stated above, the late quartets are quite modern, and you may not be ready for them, but be courageous and give them a listen. The Beethoven Sonatas (5) for Cello and Piano, and the Sonatas (10) for Violin and Piano (including the famous "Kreutzer"), the Trio No. 4 for Piano, Violin, and Cello, and Trio No. 6 ("Archduke") will be worthy additions to your collection.

Recommended Listening
Concerto in D Major for Violin and Orchestra, Op. 61

This will be a real treat for you! The use of superlatives is particularly dangerous when describing classical music because you'll inevitably come across a piece you like even better. With that said, I know of no piece of music with such beautiful melodies that are sustained for the full length (three movements lasting forty-five minutes) of the composition. Incidentally, the critics lambasted the initial performance for, among other reasons, the repetitious melodies!

Are you asking, why so much Beethoven? The answer is that these pieces are the touchstones of classical music, and there is no doubt at all that you will be bewitched on first hearing. Not all classical music has this instant appeal, which is not to denigrate those works that don't. The vogue at teaching institutions—and a good one—is to start with a core curriculum of what everyone must know, and then let the student go on from there to specialize, depending on inclination and talent. These Beethoven selections are the reading, writing, and arithmetic for you. As you acquire more knowledge, they will serve as your measuring rod.

I think of the concerto as a symphony with a soloist. There are two possible reasons for using the concerto form. The first is that the composer feels that the contrast between the orchestra and the soloist will add something to the total effect. The second is to show off the soloist, who can play more difficult music with more skill than is possible for the orchestra alone. Musical forms, while not necessarily important to the listener, are very important to the performer, who has to develop the relationships and contrasts within the limits of the form. One of Beethoven's great strengths is his willingness to break with the forms that represented the rigid wisdom of his day. Thus, he is characterized as serving as the bridge—a better term might be pathfinder—between the Classical period and the Romantic period that followed. In actuality, as epitomized by the string quartets of his last period when he was deaf and near death, Beethoven presaged some of the free tonality and unfamiliar rhythms associated with Modern music.

Franz Clement was the soloist at the premiere of this violin concerto. He had been a child prodigy and retained a prodigious memory, once rendering a complete transcription of Beethoven's opera, *Fidelio*, for piano without a score. He later became the concertmaster and conductor of the Vienna Opera, and conducted the first performance of the "Eroica." Be that as it may, he was not without ego, and it is felt that this was in part responsible for the bad reviews of the first performance on December 23, 1806. Apparently, he played a solo piece of his own composition between the first and second movements of the concerto while holding the violin upside down. Beethoven punned on a note written on the score "Concerto par Clemenza pour Clement" and was inveigled into producing an alternative solo keyboard version for his pianist friend Muzio Clementi, an interesting composer himself who once had a one-on-one piano-playing competition with Mozart, which I assume Clementi lost. At any rate, the piano version never went anywhere, but in the OPUS catalog, I found that there is a single recorded version of it, as compared to twenty-seven for the violin. This is another work to buy for your permanent collection.

You will eventually listen to the Brahms Violin Concerto, and will later be introduced to a violin concerto by Max Bruch. Each has its adherents for being the most noteworthy violin concerto of the nineteenth century. Once you've listened to all three, you will have the analytical power necessary to form your opinions based upon a solid foundation. More importantly, the synapses (connections between nerves) will be developing in your gray matter (the outer layer of the brain's cerebral cortex), allowing you to make associations, deductions, and comparisons applicable to all the music you hear, whether it be a piano concerto, a string quartet, jazz, or rock. You've actually been forming these particular synapses all your life, whether you know it or not, so their participation in evaluating the question will not be an arduous task.

This reminds me: years ago, a not-so-famous conductor who spoke seven languages was referred to me because he was having a series of mini-strokes (transient ischemic attacks—in medical parlance, TIAs.) During these attacks the right side of his body became weak, and he could not speak. We determined that these attacks were the result of a narrowing of the main artery (carotid) that supplies the left side of the brain with blood and oxygen. His loss of the ability to speak told us that the dominant side of the brain was affected.

I took him to the operating room to fix the artery—in plumbing terms, to clean the rust out of the pipe. (I consider myself a high-class plumber.) The operation (a carotid endarterectomy) passed uneventfully, but during the course of such surgery, it is necessary to stop blood flow for a short period. This is always worrisome because deprivation of oxygen can cause brain damage. However, at the completion of the operation, I was confident of a good result.

When the patient awoke, he could speak well, but only in his native German! Keep in mind, language function resides in a thumbtip-sized area named after its discoverer, Broca-C. You can imagine my chagrin but, fortunately, each day or two thereafter, another language came back. He left the hospital with no deficits and had no further mini-strokes. The complexity of the brain never ceases to amaze me, and yet, I've held it in my hand. The extraordinary thing about this case to me is not only that language is centered in a tiny part of the brain, but also within this area there were seven levels of imprint! But I digress…

This concerto is another work in which there are no gaps between beautiful melodies. In the recording I've been listening to, there is no pause between the second and third (last) movements. At a concert, such a departure from the norm can get you into trouble with premature applause. Between movements, the orchestra comes to a rest for a short period; at that time there is no way of knowing whether the work has been completed. When at a concert, look in the program for the piece's number of movements, because *one does not applaud until the final movement is completed.* It can be embarrassing to do otherwise. I have a recollection of a piece by Hector Berlioz in which the orchestra just stops before the end, and then finishes up. A rule: don't applaud until the entire audience is doing so. Contrary to this, when at the opera, it is perfectly proper to hiss, shout, and boo at most any time except while the diva is in the middle of an aria, or during operas by Wagner. I'll explain later.

The full concerto takes about forty-five minutes to perform with the first movement occupying twenty-four minutes. As the magnificent opening theme is developed, you will say to yourself, "Where is the solo violin?" It does not even make an appearance until over three minutes into the piece, and is not given full sway until near the end of the movement.

Beethoven wrote only one violin concerto compared to five for the piano, all of which are wonderful. The violin concerto has also been arranged for the piano. While he never wrote a formal cello concerto, the cello has the lion's share of his "Triple Concerto" (Concerto in C for Violin, Cello, Piano and Orchestra, Op. 56). It should be in your collection, along with the "Archduke" trio (Trio in B-flat for Violin, Cello and Piano, Op. 97).

Concerto No. 5 In E-flat for Piano and Orchestra "Emperor"

In Beethoven's time, the piano did not have the volume, dynamic range and control necessary for the virtuosity later displayed by Chopin and Liszt. In point of fact, a Liszt concerto would have been impossible to play earlier in Liszt's career and probably, in part, explains why this greatest of all piano virtuosos took twenty-five years to write it. The corollary of all this is, just as surely as hardening of the arteries follows the excessive consumption of cholesterol, music composed for an instrument must conform to its capabilities. To me, in the "Emperor," the orchestra is the star attraction, just as the piano incontestably subjugates the orchestra in the Liszt concerto.

The reason for this difference is obscured to a considerable degree when the older music is played on modern instruments, which may explain and justify the vogue for original instrument orchestras, chamber groups, and so on. They are both outstanding pieces. You might well prefer the Beethoven. That's not the point! Listen enough times, both to hear and to understand this distinction.

The origin of its sobriquet, "Emperor," remains a mystery. As related in the material presented with the "Eroica," Beethoven had long lost the admiration he had had for Napoleon. In fact, Napoleon's armies invaded Vienna in 1809, and Beethoven's quarters were in the midst of the battle. There is a touching story of his cringing in the basement as the cannons were booming, not out of cowardice or fear, but because he was trying to protect his precious hearing.

The "Emperor" Piano Concerto, Beethoven's last concerto for any instrument, was composed in 1809. He was thirty-nine years old at the time and although he had eighteen years of productive life ahead of him, this is the last time he served as arbiter in that ever-present war between the solo instrument and the orchestra. Its early popularity is explained by the thirst of contemporary audiences for martial music in march time. The dramatic orchestral parts and feeling of forward momentum are certainly reminiscent of the Fifth Symphony, composed just the year before.

This is our last work by Beethoven, so fittingly a tribute is in order. Romain Rolland, a Nobel laureate and the author of the fictionalized biography of Beethoven, *Jean Christophe*, wrote in another of his books, *Beethoven, the Creator* (1927):

He is not the shepherd driving his flock before him; he is the bull marching at the head of the herd...In painting his portrait, I paint that of his stock ...our century, our dream, ourselves…Joy. Not the gross joy of the soul that gorges itself in its stable, but the joy of ordeal, of pain, of battle, of suffering overcome, of victory over one's self, the joy of destiny subdued, espoused…And the great bull with its fierce eye, its head raised, its four hooves planted on the summit, at the edge of the abyss, whose roar is heard above the time…

I suggest that you purchase the Schwann catalog, called OPUS. It is an exhaustive compendium of virtually everything on disc, tape, and LP. Pay particular attention to the number of recordings of individual works, as this usually gives a good idea of the most popular pieces, and those you will likely most enjoy. OPUS also lists the composer's major works with critiques on each of the recorded performances. When trying to locate a piece in OPUS, do so by the musical form. Typical examples are Symphony, Sonata, Quartet, Sacred Music, Serenade, and Trio. There are also separate sections in the back having to do with Collections (Accordion, Ballet Music, China and Japan, Classical Music Favorites, Early Music, and Vocals) plus still another section with the title Movies, Musicals, and TV shows.

If I had to suggest a single volume to answer the myriad questions that inevitably occur as you listen, it would be *The New Oxford Companion to Music,* Oxford University Press, Oxford, 2002.

CHAPTER SEVEN

Schubert, Franz Peter (1797–1828)

"My music is the product of my talent and my misery. And that which I have written in my greatest distress is what the world seems to like best."

disc one
tracks 22–24

Schubert was the only one of the great composers to have been born in Vienna. His ability to conjure up beautiful melody is second to none. He never mustered the courage to meet Beethoven, although they both worked in Vienna. However, he carried a torch and served as a pallbearer at Beethoven's funeral. He was buried next to him—at the age of thirty-one—a scant twenty months later. Had Beethoven died at the same age, he would have written only one symphony. Schubert, on the other hand, had written nine, as did Beethoven in his entire lifetime, although the best known is labeled the "Unfinished." Unlike Beethoven and the other great composers who led comfortable lives, Schubert was never truly a professional composer or musician. While he virtually lived for his love of music, he had to be supported by handouts from friends. He composed all day, and met with his friends for entertainment in the evening. These evenings were labeled "Schubertiade" by his friends—a term back in fashion now for Schubert festivals—and consisted of Schubert playing his own works. Historically, Schubert is classified as carrying the Classical tradition of Haydn and Mozart into the early Romantic period.

Eduard von Bauernfeld, an Austrian playwright, was present at many of these evenings. His description gives you a feel for what they were like:

There were Schubert evenings when wine flowed generously, when the good Vogl sang all those lovely Lieder and poor Franz Schubert had to accompany him endlessly so that his short and fat fingers would hardly obey him any longer. It was even worse for him at our entertainments, only Würstelbälle (hot-dog parties) in those frugal times, but with no lack of charming ladies and girls. Here our 'Bertl,' as his friends familiarly called Schubert, was made to play and play again and again his latest waltz until the endless cotillion was finished and the small, corpulent, and freely perspiring little man could finally take a rest and eat his modest dinner. Small wonder that he sometimes fled and some "Schubertiades" had to take place without Schubert.

Schubert's output was extraordinarily prolific, quite extraordinarily so when one considers his truncated life. While most composers must labor at their compositions, Schubert's work came from an almost divine inspiration. Music poured out of him so quickly that he had trouble getting it down on paper. It is said that he failed to recognize some of the music he had composed a year earlier. His lieder—German poems set to music and sung with piano accompaniment—are almost a genre unto themselves. He composed more than six hundred.

Recommended Listening
String Quartet in D Minor, D. 810 *Death and the Maiden*

The "D" here stands for Otto Erich Deutsch, a musicologist who tried to make sense of the helter-skelter of Schubert's work. Such classifications attempt to put the musical works in chronological order.

Death and the Maiden (*Der Tod und das Mädchen*) was based on a song he had written by the same name. Concentrate on the power of the first four notes—dah, dit, dit, dah—that are repeated twice. The last three notes are coupled together rapidly, and are musically categorized as a "triplet." These four notes are again repeated, and used as the basis of a beautifully lyrical, but assertive and agitated melody, which is varied until yet another theme is introduced. The two melodies are intertwined for the remainder of play. The overall tone is one of insistence. This is imparted, it seems to me, by the repetition of the triplets. In Beethoven's Fifth Symphony, four notes in a reverse order—dit, dit, dit, dah—were also used, and it became the most famous symphony of all time. Compare the two and observe how they differ in effect. One of the fundamental aims of this book is to get you to analyze as you listen. *No more treating music as something that washes over you in the background!*

As you concentrate on *Death and the Maiden*, focus on which instrument, or instruments, are carrying the theme, and try to determine the role of those that are not. Would the rest of the movement have been less effective if the initial four-note sequence had been omitted?

Disc One, Track 23—Piano Quintet in A Major, D. 667 *The Trout*

In our discussion of Beethoven's "Rasumovsky" Quartet it was pointed out that the appellation "Piano Quartet" was a poor term. On the other hand, "Piano Quintet" is a good one because it accurately adds a piano to a string quartet, although the instruments in this string quartet are not standard because a double bass is included instead of the second violin. In fact, the term "Piano Quintet" should only be used when the piano plays with two violins, a viola, and a cello. The genuinely proper nomenclature is Quintet in A Major for Piano, Violin, Viola, Violoncello, and Double Bass, but one doesn't change a name in use since 1819. Schubert used the theme from a popular song he had composed a few years earlier called *Die Forelle* (*The Trout*). The charming song is about catching a trout and throwing it back into the water.

Most chamber music has at least three movements, but more often four. This one has five. The trout theme doesn't appear until the fourth movement, where a set of variations is built upon it. You will reap rich dividends if you listen to the beginning, and then pay attention to each of the variations, making a special effort to determine which instrument is carrying the theme; I think I heard the double bass playing it at one point. I've chosen *The Trout* because it is Schubert's sunniest piece, and demonstrates his unsurpassed ability to create beautiful melodies, and his penchant for chamber music. He wrote it when he was twenty-two and on summer vacation in a small town in upper Austria. His host had eight pretty daughters, whom I suspect had an influence, though possibly not, since current scholarship contends that Schubert was gay.

One of the difficulties in writing a multimedia book like this is choosing what to leave out. The entire *Trout* is one of the great chamber music offerings, and each movement is special. Your sample is from the fourth movement. It was particularly painful to have to omit the first movement because I like it so much. Acquire a complete performance and decide which choice you would have made.

Following his performance of the piano part in *The Trout*, a lady admirer sent the German composer, Max Reger (1873–1916), a freshly caught trout. In his thank-you note he enclosed a program for an upcoming concert that included Haydn's *Ox Minuet*.

Schubert provides no introductory notes here since the strings immediately introduce the lilting and gentle theme. The piano repeats this theme with accompanying strings. The five instruments share the theme equally at first, but then the magnificent low register of the cello dominates. The tempo becomes quite rapid, and the piano is given a bravura passage against a background in which considerable thumping occurs, while the strings carry the theme more slowly in the lowest register. Sweetness reigns again as both piano and strings have their way to the end with the piano getting a last gasp at the melody.

The Trout is one of the most performed works of the entire chamber music repertoire. Schubert's impromptus (8) for Piano, Octet in F for Strings and Winds, and Piano Sonatas in C Minor, D. 958 and in B-flat, D. 960 can be your next stops in the instrumental sphere. In the voice category, the compelling *Die schöne Müllerin (The Fair Maid of the Mill)* is a towering achievement. I urge you to get the incidental music to the play *Rosamunde*; it lasted only two performances, despite its delightful music.

Disc One, Track 24—Symphony No. 8 In B Minor, D.125 "Unfinished"

The possible confusion between Schubert and Schumann should end once you've heard this. There is only one "Unfinished Symphony" and that is by Schubert. I repeat, Schubert!

Schubert also wrote a mysterious work called the *Gmunden-Gastein Symphony* after two cities where he vacationed. The manuscript has never turned up, but if it ever should, it will certainly have its name changed to the "Lost" Symphony.

After you listen to the beginning of this work you will again realize the tragedy of this "unfinished life." Compound this tragedy with the realization that this gorgeous achievement was never heard by its composer, and was lost to posterity for thirty-seven years before it was played for the first time in Schubert's home city of Vienna.

The earliest use of the word "symphony" was to describe instruments "playing together" as an introduction or interlude to a vocal work. As Italian opera developed and the introductory music assumed a greater importance, the word "symphony" gave way to "overture." As the quality of the overtures improved, they began to be performed in the concert hall independent of their origin. During the second half of the eighteenth century, a style of instrumental music developed for entertainment in the courtyard, garden party, concert room, and private party. Gradually such entertainment became differentiated into two types. One, the garden party variety, consisted of a series of dances strung together to form a coherent whole, known as a suite or divertisement. The second type was intended for performance in a concert chamber. Three or four separate entities (movements) were put together into what was called a sonata with a stature no longer dependant on the garden or the courtyard for its ambiance. The music of both types could be played by as few as four players or as many as twenty. Haydn brought coherence to the sonata form, and expanded the number of players. Hence the symphony, as we know it today, was born. Mozart and Beethoven improved on what Haydn had started by increasing the orchestral dynamics and timbres. They also did away with—or stretched—the rules that Haydn had evolved for the symphony via the sonata form.

Leading up to this were people such as C.P.E. Bach, Johann Sebastian's second son, who honed the structure. The possibilities of music are so boundless that the listener feels an instinctive pleasure in reading that, as in a nineteenth century novel, there is a beginning, a middle, and an end. The terms for these in music are exposition, development, and recapitulation. (At times there is also an introduction and a coda, or both.)

Why was the "Unfinished" never finished? Much theoretical rubbish has been written, based on some scribblings Schubert did on the very beginning of the third movement, but the truth is that no one will ever know. The most gracious explanation is that he felt he could never improve on what he had. Much more likely is that he only lived to be thirty-one and never got around to it.

It took about forty years after Schubert's death for him to be fully appreciated as the first of the Romantics or, as Harold Schonberg, long-time music critic, Pulitzer Prize winner, and author of *The Lives of the Great Composers*, described him, "the first lyric poet of music."

As the symphonic form developed, it had four movements: the first for the intellect, the second a lyric respite for the heart, the third for the body (dance), and the fourth for the spirit. The "unfinished" product here consists of two movements. You get to hear only a snippet of the first movement. It starts out so softly that it can hardly be heard. Then comes a theme you will love (transcribed by Romberg in his operetta as "Song of Love.") Some strident chords follow, then a restatement of the theme you will surely recognize. The contrast of the pleasing followed by the disagreeable seems to be an essential component in the music of "big emotions." If everything you ate was sweet you would soon cease to get much pleasure from sweetness. The musical terms that explain the need for this contrast are consonance and dissonance. Why Schubert chose to make the consonance and dissonance so repetitive provide the intellectual stimulus a first symphonic movement is meant to provide. It will be valuable for you to listen to the rest of the symphony to see how he resolved the obvious conflict of sweet and bitter. When you do, you will realize at the end of the second (and last) movement, even if you didn't know its name, that the symphony is "Unfinished." I'm certain you'll wish you could hear the last two movements it would have had, had it been finished. But be grateful for what has been left to posterity—it was almost lost!

CHAPTER EIGHT

Berlioz, Hector (1803–1869)

"To render my works properly requires a combination
of extreme precision and irresistible verve,
a regulated vehemence, a dreamy tenderness,
and an almost morbid melancholy."

disc one
tracks 25–26

Berlioz was born thirty years earlier than Brahms. He was profoundly influenced by the Beethovian symphonic style, but he took the orchestra to previously unexplored heights in the production of new sonorities. The *Symphonie fantastique* was a forerunner of the tone poem credited to Liszt, and anticipates the programmatically inclined works of Mahler, Strauss, and Tchaikovsky.

From the opera house, Berlioz took orchestration techniques that were entirely unknown to Beethoven, combined them with an extraordinary aural imagination, and used new combinations of instruments for heightened effect. In the ball scene (second movement) of *Symphonie fantastique*, he uses four harps; in the field scene of the third movement, an English horn (a lower-pitched oboe) gives its plaintive, romantic call; in the finale, the squeaky little E-flat clarinet and a whole army of percussion instruments, among them deep bells heard in opera houses, but not previously in the concert hall. In the fifth movement, there are deep horn calls normally given to tubas but considered too bland for Berlioz. Instead he used two ophicleides (a painfully flatulent precursor of the tuba), an instrument of the bugle family invented for use in army bands during the Napoleonic wars. Get a version as Berlioz scored it, and then one with modern orchestral instruments. I feel certain you will be able to tell the difference.

Christened Louis-Hector Berlioz, he was born in France near Grenoble, the son of a prosperous physician and a pious Catholic mother who was certain that the stage and concert hall were a way station to hell. His father directed him toward medicine, but Hector learned to play the flute and guitar—never the piano—and started to read books on musical composition. At the age of eighteen, he was sent to Paris to study medicine where, instead, he became an opera fanatic. He finally matriculated to the Paris Conservatory when he was twenty-three, a very late age. Despite this belated start, his first teacher, LeSueur, who was Napoleon's court composer, assured Hector that he was a genius. Fittingly, Hector's heroes were Beethoven, Goethe, Shakespeare, Victor Hugo, and himself.

When he was twenty-three, Berlioz attended a Paris performance of *Hamlet*. Ophelia was played by Harriet Smithson. The performance was in English, which Hector could not speak. I must conclude that it was not Ophelia's diction that entranced our Hector, but rather he was head-over-heels in love. He deluged Ms. Smithson with letters, but she would have none of him. Still desperate, Berlioz decided to conquer her by writing a great symphony. Eureka! It was this *fantastic symphony* that tells of a desperately smitten young musician of "morbid sensibility and ardent imagination" who tries to kill himself with opium. Instead of death, he hallucinates as the scenes of the symphony unfold. He sees her for the first time in a wave of passion for his unrequited love ("Reveries—Passions"); sees her dancing at a ball ("Un bal"); soothes himself in an open field ("Scène aux champs"); then murders her, marches to the guillotine, and is executed ("Marche au supplice"—the fourth movement and ours); finally his corpse attends a Witches' Sabbath during which the witches mock his beloved ("Songe d'une nuit de Sabbat"). Anticipating Wagner's *leitmotif*, Berlioz has a melody for Ophelia/Smithson that he called an *idée fixe*, whose transformation is fantastic to listen to as it moves from the beautiful young thing to the old hag.

Harriet did not attend the premiere, but Hector—all of twenty-six years old—found an interim pianist to whom he became engaged. At this point, after failing four times, he won the coveted Prix de Rome, a three-year sojourn in Rome, by writing an orthodox cantata. Our Hector was desperately unhappy in Rome, separated as he was from his pianist, who in his absence managed to find and marry a rich piano maker. Berlioz was so incensed by the marriage that he set out for Paris disguised as a chambermaid with a gun beneath his apron, vowing to kill the pianist and her mother. Good sense prevailed, and he returned to Rome, having composed on his travels the overture to *King Lear*. Nevertheless, influenced by his Italian sojourn, he subsequently managed to compose two pieces of music I commend to you—*Harold in Italy* and the *Roman Carnival* overture.

Berlioz returned to Paris at age twenty-nine, and produced a concert featuring the *Symphonie fantastique*. Guess who showed up? Harriet Smithson. Berlioz is said, by the poet Heinrich Heine, to have bewitched Harriet as he played the timpani. They were wed in Paris less than a year later, after he cajoled her with a suicide threat. They had a child. Harriet turned into a jealous shrew and they separated, but he continued to support her until her death. He then went on to marry a singer.

Berlioz was never accepted by the French establishment, but was a darling of the avant-garde in other European countries. He went to Vienna and Russia, where he was lionized, and is credited by Rimsky-Korsakov with setting the music of Russian nationalism in motion. He was also championed by Liszt and Wagner. He could not get a teaching job at the Paris Conservatory, but was made a librarian instead. In addition, he was a successful conductor and augmented his income as a critic; his reviews are said to have been superb. Most composers are expert on one instrument or another. Berlioz was not. His instrument was the orchestra.

He had a short-lived local triumph when he received a commission to write a Mass for the Dead. *Requiem* was performed upon the death of an Algerian general in 1837 at Les Invalides, with royalty in attendance. Berlioz was granted the Babylonian forces he requested: one hundred ninety players, a chorus of two hundred ten, plus four brass choirs in the chapel corners, and sixteen kettledrums. In view of the establishment's dislike of him, Berlioz feared sabotage by the conductor, and sat next to him. Just prior to an apocalyptic entry of the brass, the conductor quite deliberately put down his baton to take a pinch of snuff. Berlioz leaped up, snatched the baton, and marked the beat. The brass entered on time.

Requiem received tremendous acclaim by the critics and public alike, but his enemies in the establishment did not relent. From 1856 to 1858, he wrote his wonderful opera *Les Troyens* (*The Trojans*), but only the last half was finally premiered in 1863. Alas, he could not attend the performance because of what sounds like the "turista," but modern scholarship points to ulcerative colitis. In fact, *Les Troyens* was not staged as Berlioz would have wanted until the 1960s. His wife and son died in 1862. With his loved ones gone, Berlioz lived as an unsought-after recluse in Paris until his death at the age of sixty-six. Within two years, the Paris establishment deified him. Still, not everyone shared this newfound posthumous adoration. Mendelssohn, our next composer, wrote: "One ought to wash one's hands after handling … his scores."

It is not easy music.

Disc One, Track 26—*Symphonie fantastique*, Op. 14

To paint this musical picture, Berlioz demanded a 220-piece band. He was as practical in this as in his lovemaking. This fourth movement of the *Symphonie fantastique* depicts our young composer's march to the scaffold. It starts with the drums in the distance, and then combines with a huge Napoleonic marching band. The condemned, standing in a small cart (while the onlookers shout obscenities and throw rotten vegetables) is being pulled toward the guillotine with the band marching behind. At around a half-minute, the somber, tortured, and violent first theme (*idée fixe*) makes its appearance. (Listen for the ophicleides.) It is repeated three times, first soft, then loud, and again soft before the justly famous, powerful, bombastic "March To The Scaffold" is heard three times. All the while, tension is building insistently. There is a short respite, and then massive chords indicate that his neck is being placed across the block. Unexpectedly, our soon-to-be-departed hero conjures up a brief vision of his beloved, which is depicted by a snatch of the Ophelia/Smithson theme (*idée fixe*). The horrible moment arrives with a drum roll, and the fatal theme is intoned by a clarinet. The blade falls, and the head tumbles into the basket.

You must listen to the first movement in order to fully appreciate the *idée fixe* theme heard in every movement. The last movement is the greatest Halloween event of all time, complete with hobgoblins and an uncanny *Dies Irae*. Pay particular attention to the witches' sabbath dance, and how it is combined and followed by the measured cadence of the *Dies Irae*, a chant from the Mass for the Dead. Had he written this into a witches' dance one hundred years earlier, he would have been excommunicated; two hundred years earlier he would have been incinerated! Berlioz outdoes anything produced by the Hollywood horror movie contingent. It is an absolute must-have, and a complete break from everything you've heard before. The orchestra becomes a sound effects machine as the witches dance around the graves.

Above all, annex *Les Troyens* to your music library, and follow it with a collection of his overtures, especially *Harold in Italy* and *Romeo and Juliet*. Beyond these, there is a whole Berlioz world to investigate. Were Hector my child, the phrase "Grow up!" would have been hissed day in and day out. Once you've been captured by his music, you will be glad he didn't. He also wrote magnificent prose. His memoirs make a good read.

A must for your acquisition, and education, is Franz Liszt's *Totentanz (Dance for the Dead)* which exploits the *Dies Irae* theme in a way that, quite unbelievably, makes its use in the *Symphonie fantastique* sound comparatively like music for a tea party. The cheerful (!) fourteenth century fresco in Pisa, titled *The Triumph of Death* is musically described in *Totentanz,* and deals with the Black Death in medieval Europe.

CHAPTER NINE

Mendelssohn-Bartholdy, Felix (1809–1847)

"People often complain that music is too ambiguous, that what they should think when they hear it is so unclear, whereas everyone understands words. With me it is exactly the opposite…the thoughts that are expressed to me by music I love are not too indefinite to be put into words, but on the contrary, too definite."

disc one
tracks 27–28

Countless newlyweds have walked down the aisle to the "Bridal Chorus" from Wagner's *Lohengrin* and marched back triumphantly to the strains of the "Wedding March" from Mendelssohn's *A Midsummer Night's Dream,* composed when he was sixteen years old. It was a supreme musical accomplishment for anyone so young, truly rivaling Mozart in its precocity. Mendelssohn was a genuine child prodigy, born with a silver spoon in his mouth that he used superlatively well.

Notice the variations on Mendelssohn's name. On his birth certificate, he is identified as Jakob Ludwig Felix Mendelssohn. He was the grandson of a great Jewish philosopher, Moses Mendelssohn (1729–1786). Though the family was proud of its heritage, the dual factors of German anti-Semitism—which might affect Felix's career—and a desire, in keeping with nineteenth-century liberalism, to mark the emancipation from the Ghetto, the children were baptized in their youths as Lutheran Christians. The name Bartholdy was that of a family property. When a maternal uncle from that area, who had embraced Protestantism, left a large fortune to the Mendelssohns, they decided to embrace the name Bartholdy, hence Felix Mendelssohn-Bartholdy.

Somehow my memory is transported back to my graduate school days and celebrations honoring the one-hundredth anniversary of Mendelssohn's death. Centenary celebrations introduce a bias toward greatness. Mendelssohn was considered the heir to Handel in the oratorio form and the successor to Haydn, Beethoven, and Mozart in the symphony. He was categorized, along with a handful of others, as a composer of supreme genius. The pundits no longer give him this rank, but it has never been lost by the general concert-going public. Wagner's anti-Semitism is thought to have been a factor in his denigration of Mendelssohn's compositions. Wagner's musical opinions became sacrosanct in Hitler's Germany, with the result that it was forbidden to play Mendelssohn's music in the Third Reich. After listening to enough works by the various composers, you can begin to establish your own rankings.

Mendelssohn was born the second of three children in Hamburg, but the family moved to Berlin when Felix was two. He was given a rigorous education, with lessons starting at 5 a.m. each morning in languages, literature, drawing, painting, and his beloved music. He and Berlioz were the most classically educated composers we have yet encountered. This is evident in their choice of musical subjects. The *Midsummer Night's Dream* Overture, apart from its originality in harmony and orchestration, reveals a maturity of comprehension and mastery of Shakespearean poetry quite remarkable for a sixteen-year-old. (Perhaps we should work our children more and listen to their complaints less!) His banker-father arranged frequent *musicales* in the home, exposing Felix to the best musical talent in Berlin, and Berlin to Felix's compositions. He became enamored of Bach and, at the age of twenty, he resurrected Bach's reputation and works by giving and conducting the first "modern" performance of the *St. Matthew Passion* after it had lain dormant for almost a century. There is a myth that Bach's music was forgotten, and brought forth anew by Mendelssohn. Bach had four famous musician sons who, along with many others, had continued to champion it. Certainly, this in no way detracts from Mendelssohn's revival of the *St. Matthew Passion* in 1829.

The public concert, as we know it today, was then in its infancy. When some local site was at hand (there were no concert halls), it was used by a composer for the introduction of his own music. The concert by an artist playing the music of others was still a thing of the future. Even in the church, the musician-in-residence played his own compositions; just as the clergyman was obliged to prepare his weekly sermon, the choirmaster composed his cantata.

As he stepped to the podium, he discovered that a similar-looking score had been mistakenly placed there. He conducted the very complex work entirely from memory, but took care to turn the pages of the ersatz score to avoid creating uneasiness in the orchestra, chorus, and soloists. Later in life, a critic said of him, "There is no God but Bach, and Mendelssohn is his prophet."

Mendelssohn was actively sought after as a visiting conductor by most of the great symphony orchestras of Europe. Eventually he was appointed permanent conductor, first in Düsseldorf, and then in Leipzig.

Mendelssohn conducted the Gewandhaus Orchestra from 1835 to 1847 and gave many premières there, including symphonies by Schumann and Schubert. (Among the definitions in a German dictionary for the word "gewand" are "garment, dress, robe, drapery.") The Gewandhaus originally was the hall that housed the "Ancient Market of the Flax and Linen Merchants" of Leipzig. It dates from 1781 when Bach was cantor (*canere* in Latin means "to sing;" the word "canary," disappointingly, comes from a different root) of the St. Thomas School in Leipzig. This history is of particular interest with Kurt Masur dividing his time between New York and Leipzig as guest conductor of both the New York Philharmonic and the Gewandhaus Orchestra. The post of "resident" conductor has been obviated by air travel and been replaced by the "principal" conductor.

The extraordinary musical history of Leipzig had a banner year in 1993 that marked the 300th anniversary of its opera company, the 250th anniversary of the Gewandhaus Orchestra, and the 150th of the music conservatory that was founded by Felix Mendelssohn and Robert Schumann. Here, too, the overthrow of East German communism gathered its initial force in 1988.

This anecdote of Mendelssohn's Gewandhaus stay is worth repetition: Hector Berlioz was a guest conductor. He and Mendelssohn exchanged batons, Berlioz offering a massive cudgel of lime tree covered with bark, whereas Mendelssohn playfully presented his audacious peer with a dainty light stick of whalebone, elegantly encased in leather. The contrast between these two batons accurately reflects the violently conflicting characters of the two composers and their compositions.

The Leipzig stay was the happiest five years of Mendelssohn's life, theoretically enhanced by his marriage to a sixteen-year-old French girl. Apart from his new wife, his life was a frenetic mix of traveling, composing, and conducting; these days he would be known as a "workaholic." He is reported to have had a fantastic memory. Without the score in front of him, he could play a note-perfect Beethoven trio on the piano while singing the principal lines of the violin and cello parts. He once played *Don Giovanni* and *The Magic Flute* for hours to Mozart's son, again without a score at hand.

His frenzied pace eventually took its toll, and he died of a stroke at the age of thirty-eight—soon after his sister, to whom he had been extremely close, died at forty-one of the same diagnosis. The prevalent opinion of musicologists is that Mendelssohn was so distressed by the death of his darling sister that it brought on his own demise. From my perspective, a more reasonable formulation is that they both possessed the same genes that were manifested by the formation of congenital cerebral aneurysms (these tend to rupture at young ages), or premature hardening of the arteries that also cause strokes (check *your* cholesterol!).

Disc One, Track 28—Symphony No. 3 in A Minor, Op. 56 "Scottish"

Now let's turn to the "Scottish" Symphony. Wary of appellations for musical pieces, Mendelssohn removed the "Scottish" from the score when it was first published in 1841. The history of the "Scottish" Symphony begins in 1829, when the twenty-year-old composer made his first highly acclaimed concert tour of the British Isles. (The *Hebrides Overture*, better known as *Fingal's Cave*, had its genesis on this trip. I wish space considerations had allowed its inclusion.) A visit to Holyrood Castle in Edinburgh, where Mary Queen of Scots "lived and loved," and was crowned, gave Felix the idea for the pallid theme of the first movement, which you will not hear until you experience the complete symphony.

A letter to his family is worth quoting:

In the evening twilight we went today to the palace where Queen Mary lived and loved; a little room is shown there with a winding staircase leading up to the door; up this way they came and found Rizzio in that little room…and three rooms off there is a dark corner, where they murdered him. The chapel close to it is now roofless, grass and ivy grow there, and at that broken altar Mary was crowned Queen of Scotland. Everything is broken and moldering and the bright sky shines in. I believe I found today in the old chapel the beginning of my Scotch Symphony.

In our excerpt, which is from the second movement, you will hear a theme with an unmistakable Scottish flavor and lilt. Reportedly, when Robert Schumann heard the music of the "Scottish"—thinking it was Mendelssohn's "Italian" symphony—he commented that it brought forth such a beautiful picture of Italy that it satisfied the listener who had never been there. Borrowing a trick from Beethoven, Mendelssohn put this lively segment, marked in the score "vivace non troppo" (lively, animated, brisk), ahead of the slow (adagio) movement that is the usual speed of a second movement in classical symphonic form. Following a short fanfare, the movement's main theme is introduced, dressed in sprightly enough garb to be used at a country dance. It is then dressed up for the treatment that only a full symphony orchestra can provide. This is undemanding music, where you can readily understand the manipulation of the theme, and the bridges Mendelssohn uses to go from one variation to another, which change from the buttery sweetness of shortbread to the smoky kick of a single malt whiskey.

Recommended Listening
Violin Concerto in E Minor, Op. 64

Discussion of the stellar violin concertos of the nineteenth century inevitably includes one by each of four composers: Beethoven, Brahms, Mendelssohn, and Bruch. Each piece really demonstrates what a violin can do, but you will find in them much more than a solo violin with orchestral accompaniment.

Mendelssohn played the violin and wrote the concerto, with numerous delays, to be performed by his concertmaster in Leipzig. During its composition, the King of Prussia, Frederick William IV, half-ordered, half-cajoled, and half-bribed Mendelssohn to leave Leipzig and return to Berlin to establish a new conservatory that would be the center of the musical arts of the kingdom. Mendelssohn went under protest, but encountered bureaucratic stupidities and hostility from the musicians whom he was supposed to lead. As would be expected under such circumstances, the new conservatory never came into being. Mendelssohn escaped back to the Leipzig he had never wanted to leave. Finally, he had time to compose, and the concerto was completed.

For reasons I don't fully understand, the Beethoven and Brahms are considered more technically difficult for the violinist, in contrast to the Mendelssohn and Bruch that are sought after by both audiences and players. Brahms's concerto, of course, came years later.

The Mendelssohn Violin Concerto represents the very quintessence of nineteenth century Romanticism. The later outstanding stellar counterparts by Brahms, Bartok, and Berg (yet another three Bs) are at times more dramatic and innovative, but the Mendelssohn is the very essence of warmth and sweetness. As is so often the case, hearing only a portion of it can do little more than whet your appetite for the remainder.

The concerto arose from Italian opera, in which a singer would step forward to give a solo performance of an aria meant to be a showpiece for the voice. In the Mendelssohn Violin Concerto, the violinist does exactly this, with the orchestra as an accompanist. The beautiful flowing melody completely dominates with no attempt to impress with virtuoso solo pyrotechnics. Certainly the orchestra has its fortissimos, but they are always supportive, never competitive. There is no need for analysis or erudition. Sit back and experience the sublime and entrancing melody as only the violin can provide.

When you get a chance to hear the entire concerto, you will observe that it is essentially a solo with orchestral highlights. The first movement really shows off the technical prowess of the violin. The second movement, the andante, is no sluggard, and the third and final is a virtuoso piece with both melody and orchestral fireworks. This is still another work to purchase early in your collecting. Speculation is futile, but can you imagine what added musical riches the world would now possess had Mozart, Schubert, and Mendelssohn lived their allotted three score and ten? (As you begin to discuss music with your friends, instead of referring to the number of a movement, throw in an occasional "largo" or "andante" or "scherzo," and you will be accepted among the cognoscenti.)

Mendelssohn was not the most prolific of composers, but there is plenty for you to listen to. His most monumental work is the oratorio *Elijah.* Dominant opinion holds that, of the genre, it is second only to Handel's *Messiah.*

Recommended Listening
Symphony No. 4, Op. 90 "Italian"

The "Italian" is Mendelssohn's most popular symphony, as measured by the number of recorded versions. The Philharmonic Society of London commissioned it in 1832, along with an overture and a vocal piece—an unusual expression of confidence in a twenty-three-year-old. It is listed as his fourth symphony, the "Scottish" being the third. Notwithstanding, the "Italian" premiered long before the "Scottish."

The first movement begins with a declamation by the winds, and then the violins take over, presenting the two themes (exposition). Identify the rousing first theme and the relaxed and leisurely second theme heralded with clarinets and bassoons. (When two themes are of such contrasting character, drama inevitably results.) The themes are brought back and manipulated in wonderful ways (development.) The opening themes are repeated in what is known as the recapitulation. Very often there is a final flourish (coda = tail) to end the movement. This combination of presenting the two (or more) themes, often repeating this introduction, then changing them in a development section, bringing them back, and ending with a flourish is known as the *sonata allegro* form. It was the major contribution of the Classical period, exemplified by Haydn and Mozart.

The "Italian" is an alternately rousing and leisurely symphony that you will adore and find a worthy addition to your growing collection. It is paired with a variety of other great music, so study your choices in OPUS before you make the purchase.

CHAPTER TEN

Chopin, Frédéric (1810–1849)

"When one does a thing, it appears good, otherwise
one would not write it. Only later comes reflection,
and one discards or accepts the thing.
Time is the best censor, and patience
a most excellent teacher."

disc one
tracks 29–30

Chopin was to the piano what Beethoven was to the orchestra. Frédéric François Chopin was born in 1810 in Zelazowa Wola, a small town sixty kilometers from Warsaw, to a French émigré father and a Polish mother. He was sent to a boarding school where he grew up among aristocrats' children. A sensational musical debut at the age of eight—he was labeled the "new Mozart"—garnered him enduring success in Poland. He emigrated to Paris at twenty, taking with him a silver urn filled with Polish soil that accompanied him everywhere except Poland, to which he never returned. In all fairness, Chopin tried to return at one point to see his parents, but was forced to meet them elsewhere due to a Polish uprising against the Russians—*plus ça change*! The urn was buried with him in Paris, where he died at the age of thirty-nine. Although he is buried there, his heart is enshrined at the Saint Cross Church in Warsaw.

In addition to his piano concertos, he is best known for his solo piano pieces that include fifty-five mazurkas, thirteen polonaises, twenty-four preludes, twenty-seven études, nineteen nocturnes, four ballades, and four scherzos, many of which are quite short. These engendered profound respect among his peers, who included Mendelssohn, Berlioz, Liszt, and the writers Heine and Balzac, both for their originality of concept and precision of execution. Chopin blazed new pathways between that heady mixture of consonance and dissonance. His musical colorations were so original, his dissonances so jolting, that even as sentient a listener as his good friend Mendelssohn murmured, "One does not know at times whether [the notes he plays] are right or wrong."

As a man, the image is less complimentary. He was effeminate, overly impressed by fame, a name dropper and salon hopper, always fastidiously dressed in the dandy fashion, a capital snob, neurotic, and stylishly anti-Semitic (excepting his converted friends Mendelssohn and Heine, and the Rothschilds whose sponsorship in the salons of Paris sustained a good deal of his livelihood). Yet his writings reveal another side: a committed Polish nationalist, a loyal friend, charming, ironic, observant, and, lastly, courageous in confronting death.

He had an unusual public career. His approach to the keyboard was fastidious and delicate; no fortissimos for Chopin. This style did not appeal to the bourgeois public who idolized Franz Liszt, the most flamboyant pianist ever. When he was twenty-five, Chopin told Liszt he would no longer give public recitals: "I am not fitted to give concerts. The crowd intimidates me; I feel asphyxiated by its breath…but you are destined for the crowd, because when you do not captivate your public, you have the wherewithal to overpower it." Although he relented at times because of financial pressures, Chopin largely retreated to the salons of the *beau monde* who idolized him and provided him a decent living.

Chopin and Liszt were good friends until mutual jealousy exacted its inevitable price. Before their estrangement, Liszt introduced him to George Sand (née Amandine-Aurore-Lucille Dupin, nicknamed Lucie), the infamous cigar-smoking novelist who called herself by a man's name, wore men's clothes, and would be labeled an ardent feminist today. Chopin was engaged to be married several times (and probably had a homosexual dalliance back in Poland). He resisted Lucie at first, but she was not to be denied. The 1945 movie *A Song to Remember,* starring Merle Oberon as George Sand, is a fictionalized account of their affair, and is well worth renting. Words are said to the effect that she wrote sixty novels and took on half that number of lovers. She left this portrait of Chopin's creative style:

[Inspiration] came on his piano suddenly, complete, sublime, or it sang in his head during a walk…But then began the most heart rending labor I ever saw. It was a series of efforts, of irresolutions, and of frettings to seize again certain details of the theme he had heard…His regret at not finding it again…threw him into a kind of despair. He shut himself up for whole days, weeping, walking, breaking his pens, repeating and altering a bar a hundred times, writing and erasing it as many times, and recommencing the next day with a minute and desperate perseverance. He spent six weeks over a single page to write it at last as he had noted it down at the very first.

Their romance lasted around ten tempestuous years, during which they spent time in Majorca, and summers and winters in Paris at her estate in Nohant. His health was precarious, but she nursed him back to productive work. Eventually, however, she tired of her cadaverous lover, whom she had begun to call "my dear corpse." The inevitable break-up came in 1846, which also marked the end of his creativity. For monetary reasons he was forced to go on a concert tour of England and Scotland that further damaged his health. He died in 1849 of tuberculosis.

Chopin wrote to a friend:

> The three most celebrated doctors on the island have seen me. One sniffed at what I spat, the second tapped where I spat, the third sounded me and listened where I spat. The first said I was dead, the second that I am dying, the third that I'm going to die.

The selection of a single piece of his output for our purposes is particularly difficult. Chopin had a double musical persona, one whose range extended from grand orchestral music to delicate miniatures for the piano. He was aristocratic in demeanor and was the quintessential drawing room dandy. He fitted in elegant salons playing his nocturnes, mazurkas, preludes, and impromptus for the swooning ladies. My reflex choice was the Polonaise in A-flat that almost equals the *Marseillaise* in its patriotic fervor. (After José Iturbi played it in *A Song to Remember*, two million copies of the record were sold!) In fact, the first eleven notes of the Polonaise were the very last sounds to be heard on Warsaw radio before the surrender to the Nazis. Nonetheless, it is his miniaturist persona that dictates my selection of this gem, the Fantaisie-Impromptu. I'm sure you will recognize the theme. Listen to some of his other shorter pieces. I like his two Piano Concertos, but the faultfinders, who should be disregarded, say they are banal.

Disc One, Track 30—Fantaisie-Impromptu in C-sharp Minor

The name for a piece of music is a reflection of its form (i.e., symphony, concerto, sonata, overture, quartet, fugue, passacagalia, mass, and oratorio to give examples of some you have already encountered). A fantaisie is one genre that is free of form, as are impromptus, elegies, études, and nocturnes.

Chopin gives you "whiffs" of emotion in his usually delicate piano music that are as polished and multifaceted as the diamond in an engagement ring. The main theme is repeated only once more, but this time in a lower register. I wish he had used it more often; this is what I mean by the "whiffs" in Chopin's works. You are never bludgeoned.

Schumann, Robert (1810–1856)

"I am but a pure, simple disciple of guiding nature,
and I merely followed a blind, vain impulse
which wanted to shake off all fetters."

disc one
tracks 31–32

magine that it is December 6, 1842, a perfect Sunday afternoon. The Quintet is ready for its first private tryout, and you've invited friends over to play the music. Your wife, Clara, one of the leading concert pianists of the day, is away, and you've asked Felix Mendelssohn to come over to play the piano part, which he has not yet seen. The players assemble, the Piano Quintet is played, and your friends are excited by it, but Felix thinks the third movement needs revision. Robert Schumann lived this vignette. We'll come back to the Quintet after a brief biography that will show a less happy reality than the one depicted on that Sunday afternoon in Vienna.

Schumann was born in Zwickau, Germany, the youngest of five children. His father, a bookseller who impresses me because of his German translation of Byron, died when Robert was sixteen. Shortly after their father's death, his sister committed suicide. His mother spoiled him rotten, but managed to guide him into law school even though he hoped to become a poet or a composer. He compromised—rather cleverly—by settling on the desire to create poetic music. Law school in Leipzig and Heidelberg were washouts because of high living and a lack of application. Robert returned to Leipzig to study piano with Friederich Wieck, who took him into his home to live with him and his daughter, Clara. She was nine years old and Wieck's star pupil. Robert adored Wieck as a marvelous teacher, father figure, and host. Nevertheless, he eventually sued him to gain Clara's hand (they say law school is an excellent background for anything!). In addition to studying the piano, he helped found and edit a music journal. Of Chopin, he wrote: "Hats off, gentlemen, a genius." He was also a champion of Berlioz and Brahms. (At one point, Brahms lived in the Schumann household and fell in love with Clara too—a love that lasted a lifetime!)

Musical publications aver that Schumann's hand was crippled by a brace that he applied to his right fourth finger to increase the span of his hand to ten notes on the piano. This does not ring true. I concur with other medical opinion that suggests syphilis as the cause (another Schumann and Schubert common denominator).

He continued writing for his musical journal, and composing frenetically. At twenty-three, he suffered his first nervous breakdown, and attempted to jump out a window. The fits of depression, combined with tremendous spurts of productive work, would seem to fit the diagnostic category of "manic-depressive" psychosis.

The relationship between Robert and Clara was at first that of an adopted uncle and child. As the years went by, she blossomed, and he succumbed to her allure. He proposed marriage, which her father opposed in view of Schumann's mental problems. As mentioned earlier, Robert finally sued his future father-in-law. After prolonged humiliating legal proceedings, Herr Weick lost; the marriage took place. Schumann was twenty-seven, and she was one day short of her twenty-first birthday.

It was a good marriage. Clara was one of the foremost pianists of her day and provided both psychological and financial support, giving Robert the time to compose. He referred to her, not self-deprecatingly, as the guardian angel of his genius.

Clara Schumann (1819–1896) was a child prodigy at the piano and a highly successful concert pianist throughout Europe. She composed some charming piano music and songs, although these were largely written after Robert's death; clearly, she sacrificed her composing to her husband and eight children. She wrote in her diary when she was twenty: "I once thought that I possessed creative talent, but I have given up this idea; a woman must not desire to compose—not one has been able to do it, and why should I expect to?"

The feminist movement in music has made Clara one of its pillars, but points to Hildegarde von Bingen (1098–1179) as the first known woman composer; her works were written in a twelfth century religious community. Feminists are most proud of the French composer and pianist Cecile Chaminade (1857–1944), who built a thriving career with music she wrote and performed herself. Lest you think feminism in music is a recent movement, note that the 1893 Columbian Exhibition in Chicago had a Woman's Building. Over a six-month period, seven orchestral compositions and fifty-five chamber music works by women were performed there.

Schumann composed 140 songs in 1840, the first year of their marriage. Among these were *Frauenliebe und -Leben* (*Woman's Love and Life*) and *Dichterliebe* (*A Poet's Love*).

Schumann's lieder are less melodic, but truer poetry than Schubert's. The manic-depressive label would seem to correspond with the manner of his output. Most composers work to create music in a multiple of forms at more or less the same time. Not Schumann. His first twenty-three compositions were for solo piano, followed by the songs, and then nothing else. Even though the shadow of Beethoven made symphonic composition difficult for all who followed him, 1841 was the symphony year, followed by 1842, the chamber music year (and the year of our present selection,) the piano quintet, and clearly the masterpiece of Schumann's total chamber music output. (Mendelssohn had him revise part of the third movement by inserting a scherzo.)

Robert and Clara had eight children, five of whom lived. He moved from position to position—Vienna, Leipzig, Dresden, and Düsseldorf—with depressions and irascible outbursts taking their inevitable toll. Clara continued to gain in stature, but Robert's compositions lacked the instant appeal of Mendelssohn. At one of Clara's concerts, he was asked, "Are you musical, too, Herr Schumann?" He started hearing voices, and at the age of forty-four, after another suicide attempt, was pulled out of the Rhine by a fisherman. He had himself committed to an asylum, where he died two years later. The physicians didn't allow Clara to visit him; I do not know why.

Enough of this sad story, except to say that Clara never deviated in her devotion to him, and went on to edit his collected works. Schumann discovered Johannes Brahms, and hailed him as the Savior of German music, rescuing it from the likes of Liszt and Wagner.

Disc One, Track 32—Quintet for Piano and Strings in E-flat, Op. 44

Only an excerpt of the Piano Quintet's second movement is on your disc. Can you not hear Schumann fighting his manic depression? After two minutes of the disconsolate, plodding march, a new theme is introduced, which is lyrical but still not happy. This continues on until the march returns and persists until around five minutes, when real manic animation takes over. You will wish the march would come back, yet when it does, it is even more tortured. The first contentment in the movement finally makes its appearance, and suggests that life may have more to offer. However, depression soon returns, and carries on to the end of the movement. After listening to this piece, would you possibly be surprised that a sister had committed suicide, that Robert had attempted it twice, and that he later died in a mental institution?

You know something more is coming in the next movement, and are eager to see the state of Schumann's psyche. Once again, we lack the complete work. Go back and listen to the Schubert Quintet. Examine them for similarities and differences. You may derive a new level of pleasure from the analysis.

Strauss, Johann Baptist
(1825–1899)

"A waltz and a glass of wine invite an encore."

disc one
tracks 33–34

The Strauss family produced a father and three sons who all wrote splendid waltzes: Johann (1804–1849), Johann Baptist (1825–1899), Joseph (1827–1870), and Eduard (1835–1916). It is Johann Baptist, also referred to as "the younger," who is the most celebrated. He composed one blue-ribbon opera, *Die Fledermaus* (*The Bat*) and a host of others, but of these only *Der Zigeunerbaron* (*The Gypsy Baron*) comes in as a weak second.

In German **"Fleder"** means flutter and **"maus"** is a mouse. A fluttering mouse is, of course, a bat.

Richard Strauss (1864–1949), whom we shall come to know later, is unrelated to the "Waltz family," and composed more serious music. Please be aware that if an album is labeled "Strauss Waltzes" you will probably be buying a hodgepodge of waltzes by a potpourri of Strausses.

Johann Sr. was born in Vienna, and at the age of fifteen became a violist in a renowned Viennese dance ensemble. Riverboats were responsible for the transfer of the three-quarter-time waltz music from outlying country inns to the city. The dance ensemble and others picked it up. Soon Johann Sr. started composing waltzes, and he and his band promptly became the toast of Europe. Vienna developed "waltz-o-mania," and it soon spread in all directions. Johann Sr. traveled, composed, and conducted at a frenetic pace. Nevertheless, he found time to have six children with his legal wife, and five more with a mistress, with whom he eventually lived.

Johann Baptist, or the younger, was the oldest of the legitimate children. He loathed his father and chose to study music, despite—or perhaps because of—his father's vehement opposition. Predictably, during the Revolution of 1848, Sr. backed the Royalists, and Jr. the rebels. Common sense suggests, along with available information, that his love of music and abandonment of his family were more responsible than politics for their division.

Disc One, Track 34—*The Blue Danube*, Op. 314

The Blue Danube Waltz (*An der schönen blauen Donnau*), was a howling success, and the most profitable music publication up to that time. There is a story that Mme. Strauss asked Brahms for an autographed photo of himself. A few days later he presented her with a picture on which he had jotted down the first measure of *The Blue Danube*, below which his signature was preceded by the exclamation "Alas, not by Johannes Brahms!"

In 1872, Johann received $100,000, or today roughly the equivalent of three million dollars, for a concert tour of the United States. On this circuit, he conducted *The Blue Danube* fourteen times. The demand for the published music literally wore out the printing plates! *The Blue Danube* has been so popularized that one can easily forget that originally it was scored for a big orchestra. The orchestral version has much more substance to it than the version to which you have waltzed around the dance floor.

There are many CDs with collections of the "Waltz" Strauss's works. Try them, they are fun! But whatever you do, don't confuse any of them with Richard Strauss, to whom we will soon come.

CHAPTER THIRTEEN

Liszt, Franz (1811–1886)

"My piano is to me what a ship is to the sailor,
what a steed is to the Arab.
It is the intimate personal depository
of everything that stirred wildly in my brain
during the most impassioned days of my youth.
It was there that all my wishes,
all my dreams, all my joys,
and all my sorrows lay."

disc one
tracks 35–36

Liszt was a rogue of monumental proportion. Wives were unsafe in his presence. He became an idol of Europe and the fountainhead of "Liszto-mania," a term coined by the German poet, Heinrich Heine (1797–1856). His last years, however, were spent in Rome as a white-haired abbé wearing a monk's cassock. The Pope even heard his confession. Four ambitions dominated his life (not necessarily in order of importance): [1] to be the greatest piano virtuoso, [2] to commune with as many women as possible, [3] to commune with the Catholic church, and [4] to reform society through art. While his was certainly a life of contradictions, he worked hard and achieved much of what he set out to do. He invented the tone poem, but also composed vulgar trash. He was a womanizer whose students were unsafe from his lechery; he retired at thirty-five to teach, but would not accept fees. He had illegitimate children, and yet completed four of the seven orders required of a Catholic priest, and was made "Canon of Albano" which entitled him to wear the cassock.

Franz Liszt was born in Hungary in 1811. His given name was Ferenc, not Franz. His father worked on the estates of the Esterhazy family who had been, if you'll recall, Haydn's employers as well. His phenomenal virtuosity as a pianist was soon recognized, and by the age of nine, he was studying in Vienna. One of his teachers was Salieri, Mozart's archrival. He also met Beethoven and Schubert. Liszt's family moved to Paris when he was thirteen and already a renowned star of the concert circuit. His father died in 1827, whose prophetic last words are reported to have been, "I fear for you and the women."

In 1830, three men came into Liszt's life that were to have a profound effect: Chopin pointed him toward new horizons of piano composition and capability, Berlioz became his exemplar for orchestral capability and musical form, while the famed violinist Paganini was his paragon of true virtuosity. Liszt decided to become "the Paganini of the piano." To that end, for two years he abandoned virtually everything but piano practice, and achieved his goal. His hand could span ten keys on the keyboard, two more than the great majority of pianists. He wrote much of his music to display his own skill, which made his compositions devilishly difficult for others. He was the first pianist in history to give a concert entirely on his own, unassisted by fellow artists who would carry on as the great man rested. The word "recital" was coined to describe his solo concerts. From all accounts, he was the greatest pianist of all time.

His basic talent, Barrymore-ish good looks, a flair for showmanship worthy of Barnum, love of adoration, and chicanery of a charlatan—all these qualities and a bourgeoisie middle class obsessed with culture were summed together and idolized by the public. He became the first musical superstar. "Lisztomania" burst upon Europe. A story, more than likely spurious, but repeated in the reference books, concerns a countess who retrieved one of Liszt's cast-off cigar butts. She had it mounted in a locket, which she wore next to her heart. His deification beyond superstardom is exemplified by the following newspaper quote of the time: "As the closing strains began I saw Liszt's countenance assume that agony of expression, mingled with radiant smiles of joy, which I never saw in any other human face except in the paintings of our Savior." His talent also served him well with some of the most attractive women of Europe.

In 1834, wearied by the feeding frenzy of the public, he eloped with a wealthy married woman and mother of two, Countess Marie d'Agoult, who, like George Sand, wrote novels under a male pen name. They first went to Switzerland, and then to Italy, and had three children. The middle one, Cosima, will be discussed in the next chapter, but it won't be giving much away to tell you that she learned from fatherly example. Liszt continued to travel widely, giving concerts, and maintained his popularity. The Countess eventually became fed up with Liszt's constant extracurricular activities, and left him in 1844. He then took up with a Russian-Polish princess, Carolyne Sayn-Wittgenstein, who was beautiful, eccentric, and smoked cigars. She was also an author who later did some ghost-writing for Liszt on books about Chopin and Hungarian music. They never married but she remained with him, tolerant of his many foibles.

In 1848, Liszt moved to Weimar, and was appointed Kappelmeister Extraordinary to the ducal court, having given up his performing career. He remained there for a prolific twelve years of conducting, composing, teaching, and lending his powerful name to worthy artistic causes. Among his output were twelve symphonic poems (a term he invented), a host of piano pieces, and piano transcriptions of the great orchestral works of others. The latter were first-rate and helped popularize the originals.

He and Carolyne moved to Rome in 1861, where he took up his orders. He reveled in being called Abbé Liszt. At age seventy-five, he made a grand tour of Europe, glorying in his status as The Grand Old Man of European Music, and hearing his works received with the same enthusiasm they had commanded in his youth. Despite failing health, he insisted on going to Bayreuth to attend performances of Wagner's *Parsifal* and *Tristan und Isolde*. He died of pneumonia on July 31, 1886.

My favorite Liszt anecdote concerns an incident in Rome. He had tried to become a priest, but the church was too aware of his appetites, past and present, to permit this. One day he managed to get the pope to hear his confession, which must have been the granddaddy of all confessions! Before he could finish, the pope, tiring, exclaimed "*Basta* (enough), Liszt; go tell your sins to the piano."

Disc One, Track 36—Concerto No. 1 in E-flat for Piano and Orchestra

Our selection is from the first movement of Liszt's First Piano Concerto. It will live up to the expectations you must have after reading the biographical sketch. It starts with thunderous chords, followed by a beautiful theme, and then the piano part arrives tailored for a virtuoso pianist. The theme is finally repeated again. The remaining movements are equally enjoyable. When you hear the full work, listen for the triangle in the third movement. A nasty critic, Eduard Hanslick, who was fiercely opposed to Liszt's progressive ideas, pounced upon the use of a triangle as an abomination, called the music the "Triangle Concerto," and heaped contempt upon it. Subsequently, it was not played again in Vienna for twelve years.

CHAPTER FOURTEEN

Wagner, Richard (1813–1883)

"But I am totally absorbed in this music.... It is the pinnacle of all that I created up to now.... I fear the opera will be prohibited—if bad performances do not turn the whole thing into parody...only mediocre performances can save me! Perfect performances must drive people mad."

—Wagner on his opera,
Tristan und Isolde

disc one
tracks 37–39

It has been said that more has been written about Wagner than any man who ever lived, except for Jesus and Napoleon. He took the nineteenth century by storm with his undisputed personal magnetism, overwhelming ambition, sociopathic disregard of convention, and a dizzying talent in the creation of both musical compositions and philosophical treatises. As I said earlier, Beethoven was the bridge from the Classical period of Haydn and Mozart to the Romantic period. Further, it is fair to say that Beethoven dominated the first half of the Romantic period and Wagner the last. The first half of the nineteenth century established art as the dominant religion. Wagner assumed the role, in his mind and many others, of its high priest. Perhaps, since he was an egomaniac of the first order, he may even have thought of himself as its god. Was he the genius he thought he was? Whether he was or not, his presence on earth forever changed the capabilities of the orchestra, opera, and the very tonalities of music.

By any account, Wagner was a despicable person. He was a liar, a cheat, a wife-stealer, and a virulent anti-Semite, anti-Catholic, and anti-French. He lived grandiosely within a simple philosophical standard—borrow money and don't worry about paying it back. At the same time, however, he was wonderfully innovative, and wrote stupendous music, though he never learned to play a musical instrument well.

Wagner was born in Leipzig, the home of the Gewandhaus. He was the son of Friedrich Wagner, an actuary, who died when Richard was six months old. A year later his mother married an actor, Ludwig Geyer, who, some scholars say, was Richard's biological father and Jewish. If the latter is true, one might explain Wagner's anti-Semitism and female relationships by the dynamic of the Oedipus complex.

The Oedipus complex, in psychoanalytic theory, is defined as the repressed desire for sexual involvement with the parent of the opposite sex and an intense competition with the parent of the same sex. Its female equivalent is the Electra complex. According to Freud, in a happy childhood, the superego develops and all is well.

The mythological origin derives from the tale of Laius, King of Thebes, who was warned by an oracle that his son would slay him. When his wife, Jocasta, bore a son, Laius hung the baby up by his ankles to die. (Oedipus means "swollen feet," the same root as oedema—more commonly edema—the medical term for swelling.) Oedipus survives, and ends up killing his father and marrying his mother, with whom he had four children.

As a young man, Wagner began to write for the theater and teach himself music. Upon hearing Beethoven's Ninth Symphony, he decided he wanted to become a composer. When he later saw a performance of *Fidelio,* Wagner decided he wished to become a composer of operas. Later in life, he wrote a fictitious story about a pilgrimage to see Beethoven in which he expressed the conviction that "…Music was crying out for the redemption by poetry," which in the hands of Wagner resulted in his most significant contribution, the music-drama. He certainly practiced what he preached.

Wagner matriculated to Leipzig University where he formally studied music. He wrote his first opera in Prague, and in 1833 became a chorus master in Würzburg, and began to conduct opera. He moved to Magdeburg the following year to serve as a conductor, and married Wilhelmine (Minna) Planer. It was a turbulent marriage that lasted until her death twenty-two years later. Wagner conducted in Riga from 1837–39 but had to flee by boat to London to escape his creditors. During the stormy passage, the sailors' singing and their tales of a mythic flying Dutchman later led to the composition of his opera of the same name, *Der fliegende Holländer.*

Wagner next traveled from London to Paris where he stayed around a year, and completed his first opera of consequence, *Rienzi.* He did not take Paris by storm, but did become immersed in its musical scene. Liszt and Berlioz were the only two composers whom he recognized as colleagues; the remaining composers of Europe were, by Wagner's standards, either disciples or enemies. He was befriended in Paris by the greatest opera composer of the day, Giacomo Meyerbeer (1791–1864), who was a Jew. Wagner showed his appreciation eight years later by savagely attacking Meyerbeer in a pamphlet called *Judaism in Music*—such was the man!

Dresden was his next step in 1842 with the jubilant reception of *Rienzi*, and a less wild but approving response to *Der fliegende Holländer.* The latter was the first Wagnerian opera to become a fixture of the standard opera repertoire. In the years that followed in Dresden, he consolidated his position as a conductor, finished another opera, *Tannhäuser*, and began *Lohengrin*, which is considered one of his greatest operas. Liszt conducted the premiere in 1850.

To name only the best-known, Wagner's operas include *Der Ring des Nibelungen (The Ring of the Nibelung)* which consists of four separate operas (*Das Rheingold, Die Walküre, Siegfried*, and *Götterdämmerung*), *Tannhäuser, Lohengrin, Tristan und Isolde, Der Meistersinger, Der fliegende Holländer*, and *Parsifal*.

Before Wagner shattered its traditional structure, the classic opera told its story by periodically switching attention from one to another of its three principal components: speech (recitative), song (aria), and the still dominant music, while the stage sets provided a pleasant background for the audience to admire. Wagner produced an entirely new form of opera that equalized voice, text, music, orchestration, dramatic movement, and design. They form a single entity that he called *Gesamtkunstwerk,* which translates to "total work of art." The music of *The Ring* is absolutely nonstop, never giving the orchestra a rest. Yet I'm told that in Bayreuth the orchestra is hidden from the audience's view in order to avoid any distraction from what appears on stage.

I agree with the opinion that *The Ring* is the largest and most astounding musical work ever produced. Wagner wrote not only the music, but the libretti as well. The story is an allegory concerning the Nibelungen, a dwarfish people, the gods who inhabit "Valhalla," and giants and heroes, to name only a few. The colossal canvas is given cohesion by a few overriding themes—the metaphysical weakness of gold's power, the failure of masculine might, and the regeneration of humanity by feminine love. The redemption is actually achieved not by Siegfried, the swashbuckling hero with his sword, but rather by the self-sacrificing Brünnhilde, who immolates herself.

Even today, a new production of *The Ring* receives media attention. As with Shakespeare, productions of this work are fiddled with in regard to staging and costume. I own a version that dresses some of its characters in dinner jackets and tails. In defense of television, full-length productions of *The Ring*'s component operas are broadcast on successive nights. Not many of us will have the opportunity to see these masterpieces this way in an opera house. The contrast between the music and the man make for a whopper of a schizophrenic love-hate relationship, considering that he has been dead for almost 120 years.

You should be familiar with one term that plays a significant role in the synthesis that Wagner achieved between music and story: the word *leitmotif,* literally "leading motives." These readily identifiable short musical themes associated with individual characters, places, emotions, ideas, and even objects; for example, Siegfried's sword. These motives become an integral part of the music and the plot, often signifying what the characters are feeling. One must study the meanings of the leitmotifs to get the maximum pleasure from a Wagnerian music-drama. Unlike Italian opera, here the orchestra becomes a full partner with the singers and the spectacle.

Wagner's mature years were good to him. He was finally able to marry Cosima, allowing him to settle into happiness and contentment…almost. Twenty-five years after its conception, *The Ring of the Nibelungen* was completed and ready to be staged. His concept of the staging was that of a semi-religious festival with pilgrims coming from the four corners of the world for the experience. The little town of Bayreuth had contributed the land for a theater. With money raised from Wagner Societies, benefit performances conducted by Wagner, and the ever-enamored good King Ludwig II, the theater was built, and the First Bayreuth Festival was held in 1876. Although, as predicted, a worldwide audience materialized, his press was terrible (including Brahms, Tchaikovsky, and that nasty all-powerful critic Hanslick) which caused attendance to decrease and debt to increase. The festival closed, but was reopened in 1882 for the premiere of *Parsifal,* with Wagner in ill health but overseeing it. He died a year later, but his family continues to run the festival, and tickets are both expensive and hard to get.

Furtwängler, the great conductor, was known to buy eight tickets for the four consecutive performances of *The Ring* cycle. He would alternate, attending the first half of a performance before going to dinner. The next night, he would have a leisurely dinner, and then see the second half. Someone who had attended long ago told me that formal dress was mandatory, and that any clapping or display of emotion by the audience was strictly prohibited—in great contrast to the near anarchy of the customary opera setting.

A facet of Wagner's life I have glossed over for the huskier appeal of his sexual activities was his revolutionary fervor. He produced a barrage of incendiary essays tying art to politics. His support of an insurrection in 1849 resulted in his having to flee Dresden for Zurich. He was forced to leave there because of another love affair, this one with Mathilde Wesendonk (1828–1902), a German poet. He went on to Paris where *Tannhäuser* was met with some violence, but also admiration. He continued to go from pillar to post, hounded by angry creditors, almost sinking under his debts, until he was saved by the nineteen-year-old King of Bavaria, Ludwig II. Space and energy don't permit a full recounting of Wagner's infidelities and conquests, but an inkling is given by the following anecdote. One evening, the relevant parties assembled to hear Wagner read the completed libretto of *Tristan und Isolde*. To quote Victor Borge: "He read it aloud to his wife, his mistress, his mistress's husband, his future mistress, and his future mistress's husband. They all said they liked it." I'll leave it to you to sort it out. *Tristan und Isolde* has subsequently gained the reputation of being the most perfect romantic opera (Wagner hated the word opera and called his works music-dramas) of all time.

Wagnerism quite literally became a cult, with anti-Semitism one of its tenets. Adolph Hitler, a Wagner fanatic, declared fifty years after Wagner's death, "Whoever wants to understand National Socialistic Germany must know Wagner." This association has led those who love Wagner's works to be apologetic. Should Wagner be held guilty for atrocities that began fifty years after his death? In 2001, there was an understandable brouhaha in Israel when Daniel Barenboim, the conductor of the Chicago Symphony Orchestra, chose to present Wagner's music. Indeed, one would have to be completely insensitive not to appreciate the feelings of Holocaust survivors toward a man whose philosophy countenanced the cause of their personal tragedy. But should this preclude the performance of his sublime music?

Disc One, Track 38—Isolde's "Liebestod" from *Tristan und Isolde*

This selection, "Liebestod" (Love-Death), is an orchestral rendition of Isolde's final aria in the third and final act of his opera *Tristan und Isolde*. Most often it is preceded by the "Vorspiel" (Prelude).

To set the stage, it is 1865 and Hans von Bülow, one of Richard Wagner's most faithful supporters, is conducting the premiere performance of *Tristan*. Cosima, von Bülow's wife and Liszt's illegitimate daughter with Countess d'Agoult, is at home caring for her daughter, Isolde, who was born two months before, during the first rehearsal of the opera. Hans does not know that Richard fathered Isolde. Mina, Richard's estranged wife, was living in Dresden and did not attend the premiere. (I don't know how I managed to track all of this when I find it difficult to keep even my wife's family relationships straight.) Twenty years later, to Cosima he wrote: "Really I had nothing new to say after *Tristan*."

The story of the opera revolves around unrequited love: Tristan has been sent to fetch Isolde by sea for marriage to the King of Cornwall. Unknown to both Tristan and Isolde, each is loved by the other. The impending marriage makes the situation impossible. A servant substitutes a love potion for an intended death-draught, thus kindling their love to an irresistible flame. They arrive in Cornwall only to have their passion discovered. Tristan is mortally wounded and taken to his home. Isolde follows in time to hold him in her arms as he dies, and then she dies, never having consummated their love.

The "Liebestod" (Love-Death) is the orchestral transcription of the last scene. You will hear pure undiluted emotion expressed in a way quite different from the beautiful themes with their variations that we have been hearing. The love is there. Tristan dies and then Isolde dies. These can be recognized as separate events. The ending leaves the feeling that they will be together again. You will find no breaks in Wagnerian music to let you know that a particular episode is over, and another is about to begin. No tonal (key) center exists that gives you the comforting sense of return to a home base.

Before going on to the further samplings of Wagner's music, I'd like to give you my perspective by comparing Tchaikovsky, the exemplar of listenability, with Wagner. Tchaikovsky gives his listener instant gratification, but Wagner will in the long run give even more, although there is nothing instant about him.

Has hearing this work helped you draw a distinction between Wagner the man and Wagner the composer?

Disc One, Track 39—The "Bridal Chorus" from *Lohengrin*

This melody from the opera *Lohengrin* is as familiar as "The Star-Spangled Banner," but you are probably unfamiliar with its source. The setting is a fairy tale in which an anonymous knight, Lohengrin, arriving from the sea via a chariot pulled by a swan, comes to save Queen Elsa. This music accompanies their march up the aisle to the ceremony. Remember that Mendelssohn one-upped Wagner on the way back with his Wedding March from *A Midsummer Night's Dream*.

Recommended Listening
"The Ride of the Valkyries" from *Die Walküre*
"Prelude" from *Das Rheingold*
The Sailor and Spinner's Choruses from *Der fliegende Holländer*

"The Ride of the Valkyries" opens the third act of the *Die Walküre*. The plot is too convoluted to encapsulate. Suffice it to say that there are eight wild and angry maidens on their winged steeds traveling through a storm, with their weapons flashing in the glitter of lightning, and their eerie laughter mingling with the crash of thunder. Enjoy!

The Prelude to *Das Rheingold*, the first opera of the four in *The Ring*, is an extraordinary work. The first 136 bars are variations on a single chord. It starts with such low volume that you will not be sure that the sound source is turned on. That changes! The story is chock-full of symbols (leitmotifs) that are beyond summation. Among them is a sword buried to the hilt in an ancient tree, a dragon that must be slain, a magic helmet that allows the wearer to change form, a circle of fire only a fearless hero may pass through, and the Ring itself, forged from magic gold by the Nibelung dwarf.

The Flying Dutchman was Wagner's first attempt at a total musical drama. You will be swept up by the rousing lilt of the Sailor's Chorus, followed by the Spinner's Chorus.

CHAPTER FIFTEEN

Smetana, Bedřich (1824–1884)

"By the grace of God and with his help
I shall one day be a Liszt in technique
and a Mozart in composition."

disc one
tracks 40–41

Smetana is one of the three Czech composers who have risen to composer stardom. You will later be introduced to Antonín Dvořák, and I leave it up to you to discover Leoš Janáček on your own. Of the three, Smetana is considered the most important in his native land, while the outside world gives this credit to Dvořák.

Smetana was born in Bohemia, which is now a part of the Czech Republic.

On January 1, 1993, Czechoslovakia was divided in two. The Czech Republic and Slovakia emerged. While this may be puzzling to the outsider, the division was peaceful in contrast to the carnage that has accompanied the breakup of Yugoslavia. The Slovakian one thousand krone banknote—worth approximately $3.30—bears Smetana's head.

In September 1993, I was invited to Banska Bistrica, Slovakia, to present a paper before the Slovakian Surgical Society. I was elected to an honorary membership in that society, and gained a walloping intimacy with slivovitz, a plum brandy.

The major city and capital of Slovakia is Bratislava. There, within a few blocks in the "Old City," I saw the birthplace of Johann Hummel (1778–1837), a notable composer and pianist (who is listed properly as an Austrian since Bratislava was part of Austria at the time of his birth) and buildings in which Mozart performed at the age of six, Beethoven gave a piano concert in 1796, Liszt performed nineteen recitals, and another commemorating a Dvořák appearance.

Smetana's driving passion was nationalism. His music was banned during the Nazi occupation. This is particularly ironic because his native language was German, though he tried hard throughout his life to improve his fluency in Czech. (It should be remembered that Czechoslovakia had long been dominated by Austria, and had its own history of an unsuccessful uprising for independence in 1848.)

To place him historically, Smetana was thirteen years younger than Liszt, whom he never met but revered throughout his life. When he was twenty-two, Smetana dedicated his first piano composition to Liszt, and sent him a copy of the score. In the letter accompanying the manuscript, he asked for a financial contribution to help him start up a music school. Liszt sent the money!

At one point in an active conducting career that included a five-year stint in Gothenburg, Sweden, Smetana was conductor of the opera house in Prague. An autobiography by Rimsky-Korsakov asserts that Smetana tried to sabotage, by poor performance, operas by Russian composers given in Prague. It is not clear whether he was anti-Russian or simply did not like Russian music. I like to think it was because he foresaw the future Russian occupation of Czechoslovakia.

His death was particularly sad when the ravages of syphilis took its toll. He was forced to give up his beloved opera conductorship, became deaf, and died in a mental hospital. It is sobering to think about biographies of future artistic greats where AIDS may well replace syphilis, and cut off productivity at even younger ages.

Smetana left a legacy of operas and chamber music. The only opera to survive in the repertoire outside his native land is *The Bartered Bride*. He is best-known in the United States for our selection, "The Moldau." It is one of a cycle of six symphonic poems collectively called *Má vlast (My Homeland.)*

Disc One, Track 41—"The Moldau" (Vlatava) from *Má vlast (My Homeland)*

The Vlatava (Moldau, in German) River runs through central Prague, one of the most beautiful cities in Europe. Magnificent architectural triumphs are everywhere. One should not miss the Saint Nicholas Church because it epitomizes the Baroque with gold leaf emblazoned everywhere. I attended a concert of Baroque music there. The acoustics are superb.

This selection follows the last as a means of giving you both a change of pace and an introduction to your first tone poem, a popular musical form of the Romantic period that tells a story or describes an incident or a scene.

Music can impart the warmth of a caress or the lash of a whip. At the same time, it preserves a degree of freedom for what you bring to it; the caress may become a gentle kiss or the lash enhanced to a scourging. Onomatopoeia is the term, defined by grammarians and used by poets, to describe a word that sounds like what it is meant to represent (buzz, clip-clop, ping-pong, croak, cuckoo); an analogous tool in music is the tone poem, used when the music is meant to tell a story.

This musical piece carries you down the river. You will hear the water flowing and gurgling among the pebbles and rocks at one of its source rivulets, the rivulets join to become a tributary stream, the streams unite, and gradually the resplendence of the full-fledged river emerges (a splendid theme) as it flows along its banks, sometimes pastoral and sometimes with boulders roiling up the water. Along the bank there is a rowdy and thunderous peasant wedding. It flows on to pass nymphs dancing at its bank, then the river is once again by itself as the music ends.

Get the complete recording and finish the trip! Its fourth section, entitled "From Bohemia's Meadows and Forests," has an exquisitely beautiful sunrise. I must reemphasize that your interpretation is as good as anyone's; my peasant wedding may be your carnival. I suspect we both agree that the Moldau has not yet reached Prague.

CHAPTER SIXTEEN

Bruckner, Anton (1824–1896)

"They want me to write in a different way. I could, but I must not.
Out of thousands I was given this talent by God, only I.
Sometime I will have to give an account of myself.
How would the Father in Heaven judge me
if I followed others and not him?"

disc one
tracks 42–43

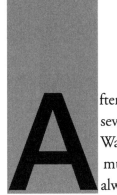After hearing *Parsifal,* Bruckner, hardly a callow youth at the age of fifty-seven, fell on his knees before Wagner and said "Master, I adore you." Wagner, being Wagner, was not taken aback. Thus, to quote the great musical analyst Sir Donald Francis Tovey, Bruckner's "symphonies always began with *Rheingold* harmonic breadths and ended with *Götterdämmerung* climaxes." To better appreciate the quote, go back to the chapter on Wagner or listen to the first 136 bars of variations on the E-flat chord from the Prelude of *Rheingold.* Tovey, one of the greatest musical scholars of all time, is correct!

Bruckner wrote nine symphonies. He wrote his first when he was almost forty, but didn't like it. This is not counted as one of the nine, but rather is known as the Symphony No. 0 (later dubbed by him "Die Nulte"). I once read a play in which the characters were identified by numbers, instead of names. The anti-hero was called ETAOIN SHRDLU, which is defined in the *OED* as "the letters set by running a finger down the first two vertical banks of keys on the left of the keyboard of a Linotype machine, used as a temporary marking slug but sometimes printed by mistake." This seems an apt description of Bruckner; he displayed no charismatic qualities except those reflected in the symphonies and his *Te Deum.*

A short little man like his hero Beethoven, Bruckner was a childlike rustic Austrian who worked as a schoolteacher and organist. He began writing church music, having come under the sway of the Cecilian Movement (shades of the Council of Trent), and wrote a Requiem in the Cecilian-favored contrapuntal style.

St. Cecilia (St. Cecilia's Day is November 22nd, for those of you who have a birthday on that date) has been known since the fifteenth century as the patron saint of music. The Cecilian Movement pushed for the reform of church music, taking as its credo that the Gregorian chant was the true genre of church music. They looked with favor upon our old friend, Giovanni Pierluigi, better known as Palestrina.

Bruckner also wrote a number of well-received masses before starting on the symphonies that were subsequently tarred by the anti-Wagnerites (another old friend, the critic Hanslick) of conservative Vienna. Bruckner though had a little pepper in him. He is quoted as saying of Hanslick: "I guess Hanslick understands as little about Brahms as about Wagner, me, and others. And the Doctor Hanslick knows as much about counterpoint as a chimney sweep about astronomy."

I think the most poignant anecdote about Bruckner is told by the famous and affluent conductor, Hans Richter, who directed the first performance in Vienna of Bruckner's Fourth Symphony: "The thaler [a coin worth a few pennies] is the memento of a day when I wept. For the first time I conducted a Bruckner symphony, at rehearsal. Bruckner was an old man then. His works were hardly performed anywhere. When the symphony was over, Bruckner came to me. He was radiant with enthusiasm and happiness. I felt him put something in my hand. 'Take it, and drink a mug of beer to my health.' It was a thaler." (Richter, not wanting to offend the composer, kept the coin, and had it attached to his watch chain.) The "old man" was fifty-seven years old.

The name Richter provides an excuse to tell a story that, in a roundabout way, affected my finances at a stage in life when it made a difference. Willis Potts was a pioneer pediatric surgeon in Chicago who had conceived and perfected one of the early "blue baby" (congenital heart disease) operations. In doing this, he developed a surgical clamp, with a single row of fine teeth in each of its jaws that allowed him to clamp atraumatically and stop blood flow in the two arteries that were to be joined together during an operation. A German super-instrument maker named Richter had invested much work on the clamp. He secured permission from Potts to patent the design.

The Korean War started. Numerous injuries to blood vessels were encountered, and the "Potts" clamp was the best instrument to use for their repair. The army ordered two for every base hospital in the world. Richter, a Germanic perfectionist, could not keep up with the orders, and would not license the design because he honestly felt that no other manufacturers could assure proper quality. As a result, other instrument companies broke the patent by such measures as putting two rows of teeth in each clamp-jaw, or one row on one side and two rows on the other. These alternative designs were not as good.

Later I showed that very small (1/50th of an inch) blood vessels could be sewn together successfully by using a microscope to enable the surgeon to sew accurately, so-called microsurgery. A double microscope, now residing in the Smithsonian, had to be developed (so that the assistant could see to help the surgeon) along with a host of new instruments of the size and delicacy needed for this fine work. In view of the Richter experience, I refused to have any of the new designs patented. This work led directly to coronary bypass surgery and the reimplantation of limbs and other applications across the spectrum of surgery, including the much-heralded reimplantation of Mr. Bobbitt's appendage.

I feel I did the right thing, but oh, those royalties! (The term "royalty" dates from the reign of Queen Anne in England, when book printers had to pay the Crown a sum for each copy printed.)

Fame and position came, but Bruckner's music was much abused by conductors who, finding the symphonies too long, took it upon themselves to make alterations. Bruckner responded, as the insecure will, by constantly revising his work. As a result, the multiple versions of the symphonies that are extant are in chaos. Because of this, the Bruckner symphony that you might hear next week may bear the same number when you hear it six months from now, but be considerably different.

Bruckner's First Symphony, first performed in 1868, provides the best example of this tendency toward indiscriminate revising. The success of this piece accounted for his moving from Linz to Vienna, where he remained for twenty-five years. While there, he prepared an entirely new score of the work—the so-called "Vienna version," as opposed to the original "Linz version." It is intriguing to note that when revising a symphony, Bruckner's usual practice was to start with the Finale and work backward from there. The differences were in the detail. He left the melodies and rhythms alone even though hardly a bar remained untouched.

As stated earlier, Bruckner admitted to writing nine symphonies. They are of a pattern with tremendous bursts of sound using, more often than not, virtually every instrument in the orchestra at the same time, with a predilection for brass and percussion. His symphonies, because of their bombast, will be an acquired taste. It is said that Bruckner was to the symphony what Wagner was to the opera. After listening to this selection, it becomes quite evident that Wagner was certainly a profound influence.

Close your eyes, and really concentrate as you listen to a Bruckner symphony. Everything is there! Tying it together as a unified entity is something that I cannot do. As a non-musician, I enjoy them but don't understand them. There are fine themes, interesting rhythms, rich orchestral sonorities—in short, everything a symphony should have except, to me, cohesiveness. I've listened intensively to all nine symphonies over a one-week period to select the snippet for you. This has been the most difficult choice in the entire book, at least up to this point.

Disc One, Track 43—Symphony No. 2

Bruckner is known for the beauty of his scherzos. They are usually gentle, and avoid bombast (except Symphony No. 9). This selected excerpt from the scherzo of Symphony No. 2 does not need an apologia since you will be captivated by it on first contact.

Scherzo is Italian for "joke" or "game." Historically, the third movement of the larger forms (symphony and string quartet) was a minuet. Haydn was the first to replace this with a scherzo, but it was Beethoven who firmly established it as an alternative to the minuet.

It has a lyrical and rhythmic theme punctuated by splendid bursts of energy and creativity typical of Bruckner, but it is somewhat easier on the listener than most of his symphonies. It contains a rousing beginning, bugles sounding, a pastoral piping theme, bombast, Beethoven-like flourishes, Schubertian melodies, and Wagnerian orchestral control. How can such panoply not enamor you?

Make it a point to listen to the scherzo from his Symphony No. 1 and compare it to this one. They are different, but very similar in overall shape, instrumentation, and use of melody. The comparison will be most valuable to your further maturation as a classical music buff. Once you've done this, give Bruckner a chance by listening to his other symphonies. If you have a liking for church music, you will find his *Te Deum* special for its exuberance and joy.

CHAPTER SEVENTEEN

Brahms, Johannes (1833–1897)

"It is not hard to compose, but it is wonderfully hard
to let the superfluous notes fall under the table."

disc one
tracks 44–46

The three greats of classical music, also known as "The Three Bs," are Bach, Beethoven, and Brahms. This appellation was coined by the conductor Hans von Bülow to compliment Brahms on his Symphony No. 1. The actual quote translated from the German was, "My musical credo is in the key of E-flat major whose key signature has three flats [b signs]: Bach, Beethoven, and Brahms!" Although Brahms lived during music's Romantic period, he turned back in his composing to the classicism of his masters. He led the most colorful life of the three, growing up on the docks of Hamburg, famous even today for its florid red light district. He helped his family eke out a meager existence by playing the piano in bordellos and dance halls. He never married; his sex life was with prostitutes. These early experiences clearly took their toll. He was quoted years later as having said, "That was my first impression of women…. And you expect me to honor them as you do?" Still, the love of his life was Clara Schumann, the wife of Robert Schumann.

Brahms never attended university, although he once spent a month keeping his friend Joseph Joachim company at Gottingen. He received an honorary degree from Cambridge, and later one from Breslau. For this later occasion, he composed the *Academic Festival Overture*, which was hardly a fitting gesture for such a solemn occasion as it consists of four student drinking songs, "Gaudeamus igitur" being the most famous and stirring. To compensate for this gaffe, he also composed the fittingly sober "Tragic Overture." It is lovely music that you will have to get for yourself.

Disc One, Track 45—*Academic Festival Overture*

The term "overture" can be confusing since it is applied to two types of composition. The first and most common is a purely instrumental (orchestral) piece of music that introduces a work such as an opera or an oratorio. The second type—of which the *Academic Festival Overture* is one—is modeled after the first, but intended for entirely independent performance.

The *Academic Festival Overture* begins with an insistent march. The tension is soon broken by a relaxed theme, only to return to agitation and a foreboding of something new to come. A slightly off-key melody takes over until the rousing main theme begins, and the orchestra shows what it can do in its full strength. The initial agitated march then returns until a lovely, but loud and powerful theme takes over, and undergoes several variations until the march returns, and is gradually given the whole strength of the orchestra. You are allowed to relax briefly before the bombast comes back with a brief respite of a not-so-tranquil melody. Preceded by the fortissimo of fortissimos, the theme of "Gaudeamus igitur" makes its appearance.

The Juilliard School of Music tells me that there are seven sets of words in Latin sung to the music of "Gaudeamus igitur." The first set follows with its English approximation:

Gaudemus igitur, juvenes dum sumus;	So let us rejoice while we are young;
post jucundam juventutam,	after joyful youth and
post molestam senectutem	troublesome age, the ground will
nos habebit humus, nos habebit humus	have us!

Can you think of a more majestic accolade to completing four years of school at any level?

As your classical music library grows, you will probably discover that your collection has multiple renditions of the *Academic Festival Overture* when one would really be enough. Why? Many performances of the main works that were recorded for the long-playing record are being remastered to digital specifications, and transferred to compact discs. The usual length of an LP was forty to forty-five minutes. The record companies know that when people go out to buy music, a disc will have better sales if its full capacity of sixty to eighty minutes is filled with music. This particular ten minute selection is wonderful filler. For a list of further "filler" recommendations, please refer to Appendix A at the back of this book. You'll find some real treasures there, all worthy additions to your growing collection.

Disc One, Track 46—Symphony No. 1 in C Minor, Op. 68

The conductor, Hans van Bülow, labeled this symphony "The Tenth" with the implication that it carried on the torch Beethoven had so wonderfully ignited during the composition of his nine symphonies. So titanic was Beethoven's liberation of musical form from its Classic constraints, that subsequent Romantic composers found themselves self-conscious and uncertain of their own ability. Brahms made remarks to the effect that "writing a symphony after Beethoven is no laughing matter" and "you have no idea how the likes of us feel when we hear the tramp of a giant like him behind us." Brahms worked on this symphony for twenty years. It is considered the greatest first symphony ever composed. He wrote three more. I like to think of Brahms in a famous painting showing him seated at a piano, his short legs barely reaching the pedals, his hands crossing one another at the keyboard in the execution of a typically difficult passage of Brahmsian origin while chewing on a cigar.

Brahms had a sense of humor. At the end of a dinner, the guests were enjoying the bouquet of a particularly fine wine. The host held up his glass and said expansively, "What Brahms is among the composers, so is this Rauenthaler among the wines." Without missing a beat, Brahms retorted, "Ah, then let's have a bottle of Bach now."

I must confess that an unexpected pleasure in putting this book together has been listening to these familiar, towering compositions from a fresh point of view. Some people have a restlessness that impels them to seek the new rather than staying with the proved. I do it with restaurants and find it a mistake most of the time.

When you listen to Brahms, you can turn up the volume and forget the neighbors. Be prudent; too-high levels, especially when listening with earphones, can actually destroy sections of your hearing. (See page xv.)

Brahms's "First" had its premier performance in 1876, fifty-four years after Beethoven completed the "Ninth." It is big, big, big music. You will hear a portion of the third movement. I wish I could have given you the entire last (fourth) movement that, as in Beethoven's Ninth, is the coup de grâce, but, unfortunately for our purposes, it lasts about eighteen minutes. It is much grander, and includes one of the most beautiful themes in the entire symphonic repertoire. I couldn't bring myself to truncate it. *Un poco allegretto e graziozo* is Brahms's instruction on the score with regard to how fast and with what feeling the music should be performed. The Italian translates to "a bit fast and gracefully," if you haven't already figured it out. As you must have concluded, this leaves the orchestral conductor tremendous leeway. There is a quote of Goethe that I like: "One man's word is no man's word; we should quietly hear both sides." Less elegantly in modern parlance: "No pancake is so thin that it doesn't have two sides."

When you read musical reviews, you will find that critics harp on the conductor's interpretation of the instructions, putting forth their own point of view with words like "too fast," "uneven," "stilted," "unsentimental," or even "schmaltzy." My purpose in this note is to urge you to have the courage of your convictions; there is no right or wrong! Also bear in mind that the critic who agrees with you is not necessarily correct. Another pitfall: don't necessarily judge subsequent performances by the first one you heard, or by a recorded ("in stone") performance.

Take some time to listen *repeatedly* to the first half-minute, during which the two major themes of this dance-like third movement are introduced. The first theme, lasting the first quarter minute, suggests to me a contented shepherd boy blowing on a wooden pipe while his sheep graze gently nearby. A nymph is soon seen gliding down a hill toward him. She is so light on her feet that she almost floats. This feeling of graceful descent is the very essence of the second theme. Brahms then spends the remainder of the movement showing the interactions between the "shepherd" and "nymph" themes. They begin to show off for one another, start to be more assertive, tension builds, and they fight as lovers do. Tranquillity returns and a mature relationship develops, each now comfortable with the other. Listen and hear how he varies the moods!

The use of two (or more) themes in a movement is a common pattern. As you begin to listen with added analytical skill, pay attention to the nature of the themes in relation to each other. In the movement we have just heard, the two are both gentle, resulting in a tranquil final product. On the other hand, when the themes are contrasting, the consequence is most often tumultuous and turbulent.

Recommended Listening
Concerto in D Major For Violin and Orchestra, Op. 77

The violin remains an intriguing instrument to scientists who, even today, do not fully understand the mechanism that produces its unique sounds. It is made of slow-growing spruce that improves, as far as sound is concerned, with the aging of the wood. The best trees are found in the southern slopes of the Alps near a village called Cremona (violin capital of the world). There have been many great violin makers, but the the names for you to remember are Antonio Stradivari (1644–1737) and the Guarneri family. Their violins may well fetch a million dollars at auction today.

This concerto is in the key of D Major. The violin has four strings tuned to G, D, A, and E. These are called open strings, which means a finger does not have to be placed on the string to get the pure pitch; the sound is resonant. These technical facets are most helpful to the violinist. Despite this, Brahms's Concerto in D Major is considered very difficult for the soloist. Why? Because Brahms didn't understand the technical problems he created. The conductor von Bülow called the Brahms "a concerto *against* the violin." Actually, Brahms was an accomplished pianist as a child, and at the age of twenty, became the accompanist for a noted violinist, Eduard Reményi. One of his best friends was perhaps the premier violinist of all time, Joseph Joachim. But the bottom line, I guess, is that Brahms simply did not know how to play the violin.

Technically, Joachim helped Brahms a good deal with constructive criticisms during composition. In fact, the cadenza—an elaborate passage or fantasia at the end of the first or last movement of a concerto—at the end of the first movement was written by Joachim. Historically, the cadenza was left to the inventiveness of the soloists, who used it to show off not only their instrumental skills but also their ability to improvise. The composer scoring the cadenza is a relatively recent trend. (Listen to the cadenza of the first movement of Bach's fifth Brandenburg Concerto. It's a real gem and will increase your pleasure in listening to the harpsichord.)

The opening movement of Brahms's Violin Concerto lasts longer than the second and third movements combined. The second movement is slow and lyrical.

Joseph Joachim (1831–1907) is reputed to have been the greatest violinist ever. He formed the Joachim Quartet that performed all over the world for thirty years coming into our century. He was a composer whose works are said to be unfairly neglected. I have a single recording of his, the Hungarian Concerto for Violin and

Orchestra, which is wonderfully schmaltzy (schmaltz is Yiddish for chicken fat but, used musically, implies sentimentality to an extreme.) If you like music of this type (gypsy)—and who doesn't?—I recommend the following: Brahms's Hungarian Dances No. 1 and No. 5; Franz Liszt's Hungarian Rhapsody No. 2; George Enescu's Romanian Rhapsody No. 1; and (taking a back seat to none) Pablo Sarasate's *Zigeunerweisen*. I defy you to listen to this music without bodily movement.

The main theme of the third movement is repeated twice in its opening moments, followed by a short bridge until the full orchestra chimes in with the main theme again. From then on, there is a bit of a battle between the violinist and the orchestra. In most concertos, the orchestra steps aside to let the soloist play. Here they mix it up a good deal by both playing at the same time, sometimes loudly. Another theme is then introduced, followed by the return of the main theme in full force where the violin is allowed to saw away again, culminating in an orchestral flourish at the end of the movement. The lushness of the orchestration is typical of Brahms. I find the rhythmic development fascinating, better listened to than described. Throughout the violin passages, you will hear an unmistakable Hungarian influence.

I'm jealous of the pleasure you will derive from securing the complete work and hearing it for the first time. (That last statement reminds me of a sarcastic professor I once had who told the class he was envious because they knew so little and had so much to learn.)

Other Brahms concertos of note include the "Double" Concerto in A Minor for Violin, Cello, and Orchestra and Piano Concertos No. 1 and No. 2.

CHAPTER EIGHTEEN

Bizet, Georges (1838–1875)

"I shall always take pleasure in being appreciated
only by men of genuine understanding.
I have little use for this popularity
for which people nowadays sacrifice
honor, genius, and fortune."

disc one
tracks 47–49

Commercial sex worker is a term I learned recently at an AIDS conference held at the Harvard School of Public Health. At first I chuckled, thinking that a prissy professor was trying to avoid the use of offensive words in public. But as I thought about it further, I realized it is a better term than the usual synonyms because, particularly in the context of AIDS, it can refer to either sex. Anyway, Carmen was a commercial sex worker in an opera that you must certainly have heard.

Georges Bizet was born near Paris. His real name was Alexandre-César-Léopold Bizet. A favorite godfather took pity and began calling him Georges, a name which ultimately stuck. His father was a hairdresser who graduated to wigmaking, and then taught singing. His mother was a fine amateur pianist. From this background, Bizet matriculated to the Paris Conservatory at the remarkably early age of nine. He won numerous competitions, and while at the Conservatory, at age seventeen, composed his lovely Symphony in C, which I advise you to buy. At nineteen, he won the most prestigious prize of all, the Prix de Rome, and spent three wonderful years in Italy.

He returned to Paris in 1860 and made his first attempt at writing theatrical music. When he was twenty-five, his opera *Les pêcheurs de perles* (*The Pearl Fishers*) was produced, but to negative acclaim. (I have a recording of this opera, and like it very much.) In 1869, he married Geneviève Halévy, a daughter of his former composition teacher at the Conservatory. *Carmen* was his last work, and for it, he was made a Chevalier of the Legion of Honor. He died of rheumatic heart disease at age thirty-six. Think what the world lost because medicine then was still so primitive! Schubert died at thirty-one, Mozart at thirty-five, Mendelssohn at thirty-eight, and Chopin at thirty-nine.

A "strep throat" can lead to an infection that settles on the heart valves (aortic and/or mitral). This results in poor function and eventual death. Rheumatic heart disease has largely disappeared since the advent of penicillin. Please remember this—if the pediatrician prescribes penicillin for your child's sore throat, be sure to give it for the full ten days even if Junior seems fine on day two or three. Discontinuing the medication too soon when treating a streptococcal infection can lead to tragedy.

Disc One, Track 48—Orchestral Suite from *Carmen*

The initial reception to *Carmen* was lukewarm. It was originally presented at the Opêra-Comique where it didn't fit with the usual fare expected by the audience. It was also deemed obscene. A minor French composer, Ernest Guiraud (1837–1892) rearranged it as grand opera soon after Bizet's death. It was this version that swept Europe to become, arguably, the most popular opera of all time. To summarize the plot: outside a cigarette factory in Spain, Carmen—a gypsy girl—is arrested by Don José—a soldier—for causing a disturbance. Seductive promises are made, and he is arrested for allowing her to escape. When he is released from jail, he is welcomed by Carmen, who induces him to join a band of smugglers. Don José must leave their mountain hideaway to attend his sick mother. On his return, he finds that Carmen has become the lover of Escamillo, a bullfighter. In a jealous rage, Don José kills her.

Our music starts with the Prelude to Act I, culminating in the famous *Les Toréadores* (*March of the Toreadors*). This is followed by a magnificently brooding passage that portends the trouble to come more effectively than the printed page could ever do. The *March of the Toreadors* speaks for itself, but you will have to get a more complete version to imagine Carmen's gyrations and the clicking of her castanets!

Disc One, Track 49—L' Arlésienne Suite No. 2: "Minuetto & Farandole"

If Bizet had not gained lasting fame with his opera *Carmen*, it is likely that he would never have made this book, or any book for the classical music novice. But it is my responsibility to see that you come away with a rich underpinning of music that you will take along with you for the rest of your life. I am extremely fond of both of his "Arlésienne" suites and, therefore, exert the author's prerogative to do what I want! The music presented here is from the second suite.

In 1867, Bizet was given a commission to compose some chamber music for Alphonse Daudet's play, *L' Arlésienne (The Girl from Arles)*. Daudet had a profound understanding of music, and both men were stirred by the plot. It tells of a young man named Frédéric's frustrated love for a cold-hearted young woman from Arles—who never appears on stage—and his eventual suicide.

Although a first-rate production was fielded, the audience was bored, having expected a comedy instead of the serious amalgam of music and drama over which Bizet and Daudet had worked so hard. But all was not lost. Another composer, Grieg, whom you will meet shortly, scored the first numbers for symphony orchestra. When this, the First Suite from *L' Arlésienne*, was heard four weeks later, it was a smashing success. Grieg then decided to score another four numbers for a second suite, but he died, and it was left to his friend, Ernest Guiraud, who did a similar service for *Carmen*, to complete the work twelve years later.

Both *L' Arlésienne Suites* are worthy of your collection. The first is the more popular of the two, and has a particularly beautiful opening theme in the prélude. Excerpts from the last two movements of the Second Suite are on your disc.

The first section is a minuet. Note how it has been orchestrated in the pattern of our old friend, the A-B-A design of soft, loud (whole orchestra chiming in), and soft again. Why this is so inherently satisfying is as inexplicable as why the word "beautiful" leaps to mind for one woman and "charming" for another.

The second piece is called "Farandole." A farandole is a dance that originated in the Auvergne, Provence, and northern Spain (the Basque country and Catalonia.) It is danced through the streets by large numbers

Daudet, Alphonse (1840–1897) another *enfant terrible* who wrote his first book at age fourteen. He had the particular ability to register the foibles of the common man or, as has been stated more elegantly, to record "the history of people who will never have a history." His life was a colorful one, but ended sadly with protracted morbidity and death from syphilis. I loathe the man quite unfairly. He wrote a novel called *Tartarin de Tarascon* that I had to read in high school French. My memory of the book was that there were at least a dozen adjectives preceding every noun. I am still rankled by the hours I spent looking up those useless adjectives, and readying myself to parrot back their translation in class.

of people holding hands, to the accompaniment of the pipe and tambourin (a thin, drum-like instrument). This dance dates back to antiquity, inferred by its depiction on ancient Greek pottery. (For some particularly attractive and haunting folk melodies, get *Songs of the Auvergne* by Canteloube.) To me, the title of this piece should be *March and Farandole* because by no stretch of the imagination could the populace be gamboling through the streets to the music at its start and finish (again set A-B-A form). Interestingly, some criticized the work as being too Wagnerian. Nothing, and I repeat, nothing could be further from the truth. Go back and listen to the Wagner excerpts after you have heard the minuet and farandole from the *L' arlésienne Suite No. 2.*

I'm afraid, despite my best intentions, that you won't have the full flavor of the *L' arlésienne Suites,* but certainly enough to titillate you. You know how to correct this.

Once you have become familiar with *Carmen* and the *L' arlésienne Suites* try the opera *Les pêcheurs de perles (The Pearl Fishers).* It is not as instantly appealing as *Carmen,* but few operas are.

CHAPTER NINETEEN

Bruch, Max (1838–1920)

"I stand face to face with the Eternal Energy from which
all life flows, and I draw upon that infinite power.
To contact this Eternal Energy, I must conform to certain laws,
two of the most important being *solitude* and *concentration*.
A composer must sit in the silence and wait for the direction from
a force that is superior to the intellect."

disc one
tracks 50–51

Michelangelo's *David* and Leonardo da Vinci's *Mona Lisa* are undoubtedly among the most famous artworks of all time. Would they still hold this distinction had the artists produced nothing else? I have asked this question many times. The answer is invariably "No." The reasoning is that the art world requires a critical mass of accomplishment before recognition is given to the artist and his work. Certainly the young painter will never get gallery representation unless there are many paintings to be sold! Either the answer is wrong, or Bruch's Violin Concerto is the exception that proves the rule, since it is the only work by this composer that has made it to the big league of frequent concert hall performance; not only that, it is universally identified as one of the greatest violin concertos of all time.

Max Bruch was born in Cologne to a middle-class family. His mother was a music teacher and well-known soprano, so the environment was ripe for his musical education. Max had composed his first symphony by the age of twelve, and won a prize for a string quartet that provided him the means to study piano, composition, and musical theory. He must have learned a great deal quickly since by age twenty, he had composed three operas. Max went on to conduct orchestras in Liverpool and Breslau, ending up with the prestigious position of Professor of Composition at The Berlin Academy, held until his retirement in 1910.

To quote George Bernard Shaw, "He who can, does. He who cannot, teaches." It would be patently unfair to apply this to Bruch since his choral works were thought, in his time, to be among some of the best ever written. The last thing in the world I mean to do is disparage teaching, so another maxim is in order: "If the student does not end up better than the teacher, the teacher has failed." Bruch was an excellent teacher with an effect on a generation of bright students. Be that as it may, this violin concerto, and a cello piece, *Kol Nidrei*, are all that you are likely to hear at a concert. The *Kol Nidrei* is a favorite of mine, and may be a lagniappe when you buy the violin concerto.

Disc One, Track 51—Violin Concerto in G Minor, Op. 26, Second Movement

In addition to containing a mesmerizing display of violin wizardry, this concerto is simply splendid from beginning to end. In my wife's opinion, the second movement, a small portion of which you have on your disc, contains the most beautiful theme in all of music. That's the kind of big statement people make about music based on something they bring to it, which would take a Freud to ferret out. Under any circumstance, evaluate what you hear with my wife's opinion in mind.

You have a few minutes of utter delight ahead, starting with a delicate, gentle, and restful theme with the violin unobtrusively accompanied by varying parts of the orchestra. The dominant theme (my wife's favorite) is first heard in full glory. The first theme is then repeated with more verve, followed by a display of virtuosity. An orchestral crescendo builds up and the full orchestra plays the dominant theme. The violin takes it up again, and never lets go until it satisfyingly fades from hearing. For Bruch, the conductor, to allow Bruch, the composer, to finish with a whimper instead of a roar signifies the true perspicacity of Bruch, the man.

CHAPTER TWENTY

Musorgsky,* Modest (1839–1881)

*You will find his name spelled both Musorgsky and Mussorgsky, not difficult to understand when you think of the conversion from the Cyrillic alphabet (developed by two Bulgarian monks, Cyril and Methodius) to the Latin.

"The artist believes in the future
because he lives in it."

disc one
tracks 52–55

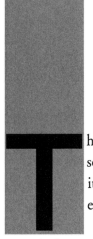

This exercise will be a new musical experience for you. Besides hearing some celebrated music, you are going to be able to compare a portion of it as originally composed for the piano, and then as orchestrated by an entirely different composer.

Modest Petrovich Musorgsky was born of a prosperous Russian family in the village of Karevo, in the province of Pskov. He studied the piano first with his mother, and then in St. Petersburg, where he would spend his life. Adhering to family tradition, he became a cadet. By the time he completed military training, he was an accomplished pianist and composer. Good looks and an amiable disposition combined to make him a popular figure, particularly with women. He also acquired and perfected the military skills of drinking and carousing.

At age eighteen, he began to study with César Cui and Mily Balakirev, and became a driven musician. He left the military a year later to devote himself to music. After some early success, he had a nervous breakdown, which foreshadowed his future life. When he was twenty-two, in 1861, the czar freed the serfs, with the unfortunate result for Modest that his family lost its money. Circumstances forced him to take a government desk job as a clerk at almost starvation wages for the remainder of his short life. After his mother's death, his depressions became more frequent, his drinking increased, and his downhill slippery slide picked up momentum.

By the time he was twenty-eight, a Russian newspaper had begun to speak of a "mighty handful" of St. Petersburg composers dedicated to creating a new form of Russian national music.

St. Petersburg was founded by Peter the Great in 1703 and was the capital of the Russian Empire for two centuries. It was renamed Petrograd in 1914, Leningrad in 1924, then to St. Petersburg again in 1992!

Their tremendous impact has lasted to this day. They shunned the traditional forms of orchestral presentation, such as the symphony and concerto. The "mighty handful" (*moguchaya kuchka*) became the "Mighty Five" and finally, the ultimate accolade, simply "The Five" (Musorgsky, Balakirev, Cui, Borodin, and Rimsky-Korsakov). You will meet Rimsky-Korsakov in a later chapter. Borodin, Cui, and Balakirev will require exploration on your own.

Musorgsky is considered the most talented and innovative of "The Five." Unfortunately, alcoholism attenuated both his life and his musical output. His greatest work, the opera *Boris Godunov*, assures him immortality in the musical pantheon. For sheer drama and pathos, it is unequaled, and should be one of your acquisitions, preferably on video so that you can view the spectacle.

Disc One, *Pictures from an Exhibition*
Track 53—"Promenade" (Orchestrated by Ravel)
Track 54—"Promenade" (Piano)
Track 55—"The Great Gate at Kiev" (Orchestrated by Ravel)

Composed in 1874, *Pictures from an Exhibition* is a suite written for the piano. It describes a promenade through an art gallery exhibiting the pictures of an artist friend. Serge Koussevitzky, a great conductor, commissioned Maurice Ravel to transcribe it for orchestra. This version premiered in 1922.

Up until now, I have avoided the usual technical explanations of musical form. Nonetheless a smidgen is useful here, because you will see the word "rondo" used repeatedly (pun). When one theme is followed by another, and then the first is repeated, the shorthand pattern is called A-B-A. When the first theme alternates between dissimilar themes it is called the *rondo form,* which is what the promenade theme is doing here (like slices of bread in a multilayered sandwich); the pattern becomes A-B-A-C-A-D-A.

You will begin by hearing the initial "Promenade" performed by an orchestra, followed by the original piano version. Variations of this promenade are repeated as the viewer (listener) goes from one picture to another. You will end up hearing, in the Ravel orchestral version, the musical impression of the last picture, "The Great Gate at Kiev," which you will like! Musorgsky was criticized for departing from the academic norms of harmony, as well as for unforeseen transitions and clumsiness of melodic line. These objections have not stood the test of time. Nonetheless, the originality is better heard in Musorgsky's piano version because the work was sanitized in Ravel's rescoring for orchestra, but both are superb.

Explore the complete *Pictures* on your own. The picture titles include such images as "The Gnome," "Ballet of the Unhatched Chicks," "Samuel Goldberg and Schmuyle," and "The Hut on Fowl's Legs." You will have a real adventure discovering the music that goes with such fanciful titles.

part two

Tchaikovsky, Pyotr Ilich
(1840–1893)

"How can one express the indefinable sensations
that one experiences while writing an instrumental composition
that has no definite subject? It is a purely lyrical process.
It is a musical confession of the soul,
which unburdens itself through sounds
just as a lyric poet expresses
himself through poetry."

disc two
tracks 1–3

Tchaikovsky is deservedly the most famous of all Russian composers. His music is lush with beautiful themes. Its romantic character reflects a pathologically sensitive man. He is the composer of the adolescent. The new listener is enthralled, but as knowledge increases, other composers take over. Why? I don't know! Perhaps Tchaikovsky's romanticism simply overwhelms the listener with too much of a good thing.

He was a neurotic and unhappy hypochondriac, nervous in the company of anyone other than close friends. He was also in constant fear that his homosexuality would be exposed. He married a music student but, by mutual consent, the marriage was never consummated, lasted only nine weeks, and ended in 1877 with a legal separation. The *Sturm und Drang* of this experience led him to attempt suicide. Nevertheless, much of his most glorious music was written during this time. For the next thirteen years, he was supported by a wealthy Russian widow, Nadezhda von Meck (whose relationship with another composer, Claude Debussy, will be discussed later.) Again by mutual consent, they never met, and yet carried on an intimate daily correspondence. Tchaikovsky died of cholera in 1893 after having drunk unboiled water. Some modern scholars believe that this was a suicide. Others attribute his death to arsenic poisoning ordered by a tribunal set up to investigate his relationship with a member of the royal family.

Soviet musicologist Alexandra Anatoyevna Orlova writes:

It seemed Tchaikovsky was paying too much attention to the nephew of Duke Steinbock-Thurmor. He was a nice young man, and Tchaikovsky took a liking to him. Whether anything went on between them is unknown; what is known is that the Duke wrote a letter [of complaint] to the Czar and gave it to the Chief Prosecutor of the State, Nikolai Borisovitch Yakobi. Yakobi was a classmate of Tchaikovsky's at the St. Petersburg College of Law. Public airing of the issue could have meant deprivation of all civil rights, exile in Siberia, or worse. All his life,

Tchaikovsky lived in fear of people learning his secret. Nothing could have been worse than exposure…

Yakobi could not very well prevent an official complaint from reaching the Czar. Yet this disgrace, he felt, would reflect not only on Tchaikovsky, but also on the whole College of Law. He decided to call a "court of honor," made up of his classmates—all those still living. Tchaikovsky himself was [among the eight] present….When everyone had left, Yakobi told his wife what had gone on and instructed her never to tell anyone. He called it a "judgment" on Tchaikovsky and said that they had asked for his death. So in one sense it wasn't really suicide, but murder. They condemned him, and they did it in a terrible way. He was to take his own life. And he had to do it in such a way that nobody would know.

Tchaikovsky's music is much more in the classic European style than that of other Russians whom you will come to know. His emotionalism is implicit in everything he wrote. Most listeners respond immediately to the immersion in this sentient hot tub but, after a while, some come to resent it.

Recommended Listening
Symphony No. 5 in E Minor, Op. 64

Although earlier I made the generalization that the first movement of a symphony is usually fast (allegro = "happy" in Italian), the opening of this first movement starts slowly (andante) with an almost funereal dirge. The opening theme is most often described as the "Fate" motif, which is interesting since Beethoven's Fifth begins with "destiny knocking"; the words destiny and fate are synonymous! Once again the opening motif, played during the first nine seconds, is repeated and embroidered upon until a perfectly wonderful flowing dance theme makes its appearance. It is first played by the woodwinds and then tossed back and forth around the orchestra. The Fate dirge later returns with some crashing chords worthy of Beethoven. Your interpretation may be quite unlike mine, but that's unimportant; you have begun to listen!

Tchaikovsky's orchestration with its dark coloring, yet brilliant sound, elicits admiring comment to this day. Nobody takes a backseat to him in the utter beauty and fluidity of his themes. This symphony is in a minor key, as is Beethoven's Fifth.

The proverb, "One picture is worth ten thousand words," comes to mind since these few minutes of listening will demonstrate the feeling that a minor key evokes better than any exposition. Now, listen to your sample of Beethoven's Fifth and compare it to Tchaikovsky's Fifth, paying particular attention to how the orchestra is used in each.

As you heard in Beethoven's Fifth Symphony, the entire first movement is developed by building upon the "destiny knocking" motif and its bucolic theme. This results in a flawless entity from the listener's viewpoint. The ability of a composer to take relatively simple building blocks like these and seamlessly meld them is what the musicologist means when referring to a composer as a great "symphonist." Tchaikovsky does not get that accolade because the music just flowed out of him without the technical attributes demanded by the professionals. Is he a lesser symphonist to you and me? A resounding NO is my answer, but understanding the argument will start you on the way to your own analyses. Music is no different from any other field, be it basketball or surgery. The more you know of the fine points, the more you appreciate the skills involved.

If you decide to purchase a recording of the entire symphony, spend some extra time with the third movement. It was stated earlier that the third symphonic movement is often in dance rhythm. This holds true in this symphony; it is indeed a waltz, but at its end you will again hear a repetition of the somber "Fate" theme you originally heard in our sample of the first movement.

You will now be introduced to Tchaikovsky's First Piano Concerto, Sixth Symphony, and music from *The Nutcracker* ballet. The Fourth Symphony, the ballets *Swan Lake* and *Sleeping Beauty*, the Violin Concerto in D, and the *Romeo and Juliet Overture* are absolute "musts" for your collection. If you like these as much as I do, on your next visit to the shop get *Francesca da Rimini*, the *Capriccio Italien*, the Serenade for Strings, and the *Hamlet Overture-Fantasy*. You might also explore the Piano Trio in A Minor and the three String Quartets. Among his most popular concert "fillers" are the *1812 Overture* and the *Marche Slave*.

Disc Two, Track 2—Concerto No. 1 in B-flat Minor for Piano and Orchestra, Op. 23

A concerto can be thought of as a symphony with a featured solo instrument (piano, violin, flute, horn, etc.). The concerto form is likened to an aria in an Italian opera, where the singer steps forward and belts out a song, either solo or with orchestral accompaniment. Occasionally, there are two different solo instruments, giving rise to the term "double concerto." Historically, there are concertos where the featured entity is a particular instrumental group of the orchestra (concerto grosso, grosso = fat or "plumped up" in Italian) rather than a solo instrument, but more on that later.

Tchaikovsky wrote three piano concertos, but this first one is the star of them all—amid some pretty stiff competition—in terms of frequency of performance and recognition by the public. One of the most often told stories of musical lore still bears repeating: Christmas Eve, 1874. The musical composition was completed, but not yet orchestrated. Tchaikovsky wrote the concerto with his close friend in mind, the piano virtuoso Nicolai Rubinstein, as the premiere performer. Tchaikovsky planned to dedicate it to Rubinstein, and also hoped for some practical suggestions about the piano technique. Rubinstein's reaction was vitriolic, stating that the music was worthless and unplayable—but in stronger terms than that. The friendship was ruptured, and the dedication shifted to the great pianist-conductor of the day, Hans von Bülow (a relative of the well-known Claus von Bülow who was tried twice and acquitted for attempting to kill his heiress wife.) Later, Rubinstein apologized, the friendship resumed, and Rubinstein played the great work through the concert halls of Europe. Subsequently, Tchaikovsky dedicated his second piano concerto to Rubinstein.

You may already be familiar with this startlingly beautiful opening theme because it was popularized many years ago in the song, "Tonight We Love." Surprisingly, it is never heard in this work again. How Tchaikovsky could have resisted repeating it we shall never know. Time constraints prevent us from hearing more of the concerto than the opening minutes. Beg, borrow, steal, buy a recording, or go to a complete performance!

The concerto premiered in Boston on October 25, 1875, conducted by von Bülow. Turnabout is fair play. Van Cliburn, a relatively unknown American pianist, was catapulted to world fame by winning the 1958 Tchaikovsky Competition in Moscow; you can guess what he played!

Unfortunately, Tchaikovsky's Violin Concerto did not make it into this book, but its early history is interesting. As in this piano concerto, it starts with a magnificent early theme that is never repeated. The premiere took place in Vienna on December 4, 1881. Viennese audiences were conservative; perhaps the orchestra hadn't rehearsed enough. Maybe new techniques were introduced that were liked by some, but hated by others. The following review, written by the powerful critic, Eduard Hanslick (1825–1904), must be one of the nastiest on record:

The Russian composer Tchaikovsky is surely not an ordinary talent, but rather an inflated one, with a genius-obsession without discrimination or taste, such is also his latest, long, and pretentious Violin Concerto. For a while it moves soberly, musically, and not without spirit. But soon vulgarity gains the upper hand and asserts itself to the end of the first movement. The violin is no longer played; it is pulled, torn, drubbed. The adagio is again on its best behavior, to pacify and win us. But it soon breaks off to make way for a finale that transfers us to a brutal and wretched jollity of a Russian holiday. We see plainly the savage vulgar faces, we hear curses, we smell vodka. Friedrich Vischer once observed, speaking of obscene pictures, that they stink to the eye. Tchaikovsky's Violin Concerto gives us for the first time the hideous notion that there can be music that stinks to the ear.

Uncharitable, to say the least! While you are buying the piano concerto, you had better buy the violin concerto as well. Tchaikovsky wrote only one and, in my opinion, Hanslick was wrong. Incidentally, Hanslick was pilloried by Wagner, who portrayed him as the thoroughly unlikable character of Beckmesser in his opera *Die Meistersinger von Nürnburg*.

You have only a couple minutes of the twenty-minute first movement of this bestselling classical work. Sales were helped along by Van Cliburn's triumph, and America's pride in the midst of the Cold War. It is difficult to conceive that Tchaikovsky was not a pianist. The opening horn call accompanied by the sweeping strings is as fine an introduction to the piano part that immediately follows as any you will ever hear. I am always amazed that in a large concert hall a piano can hold its own when it comes on after the whole orchestra, but for the next two minutes it does very well, sometimes in tandem with the orchestra, but more often as a solo instrument. The orchestra eventually takes over, yet the piano dishes out some mighty crashing chords, with the melody already familiar to you. I apologize for truncating the music, but it leaves you with no reasonable alternative other than to acquire the complete concerto.

Recommended Listening
Symphony No. 6 in B Minor, "Pathétique"

In the previous chapter, you were introduced to the Russian "Five," whose stated goal was to develop a distinct genre of Russian music. Tchaikovsky had no such pretensions, and the inevitable comparison of his work to theirs produced friction. You have listened enough to judge for yourself. The following is Tchaikovsky's opinion:

Borodin is a fifty-year-old professor of chemistry at the Academy of Medicine. Again, a talent—and even an impressive one—but lost because of a lack of knowledge, because blind fate led him to a chair of chemistry instead of to an active musical career. However, he has less taste than Cui, and his technique is so weak he cannot write a line without outside help. Musorgsky you very rightly call a has-been. In talent he perhaps exceeds all the others; but he has a narrow nature and lacks the need for self-perfection, blindly believing in the ridiculous theories of his circle and in his own genius. Besides, there is something low about him that loves coarseness, lack of polish, roughness.

This then, is my honest opinion of these gentlemen. What a sad thing! With the exception of Korsakov, how many talents from whom it is hard to await anything serious! And isn't this generally the way with us in Russia? Tremendous powers fatally hindered…from taking the open field and joining battle, as they should. Nevertheless, these powers exist. Even a Musorgsky, by his very lack of discipline, speaks a new language. It is ugly, but it is fresh. And that is why one may expect that Russia will one day produce a whole galaxy of great talents, who will point out new paths for art. Our ugliness is at any rate better than the sorry feebleness (disguised as serious creative work) of Brahms and the other Germans. They are hopelessly played out.

If he can dish it out like this, he must take it as well. Recall the scathing criticism of Tchaikovsky by Eduard Hanslick. At the time I quoted that review, I felt sorry for Tchaikovsky, but not any longer!

Tchaikovsky wrote six symphonies, or seven if you count his symphonic poem, *Manfred* Op. 58, subtitled "Symphony in Four Pictures after Byron's Dramatic Poem." Of the "Pathétique," he wrote to his beloved nephew on August 3, 1893: "I certainly regard it as the best—and especially the 'most sincere'—of all my works. I love it as I have never loved any one of my musical offspring before." Tchaikovsky conducted the premiere performance of the symphony on October 16th, and died on October 25th.

Was his death caused by an unlucky drink of water (cholera), suicide, or a death sentence imposed by a royal tribunal for a relationship with a male member of the royal family? It is unlikely that the question will ever be answered. Nevertheless, after listening to this piece from the funereal opening section to the end, the conclusion seems inescapable to me that this was Tchaikovsky's last testament, and he knew it!

The third movement, sometimes said to be the greatest single movement in all symphonic literature, was selected because it nears perfection in the development of a single theme. You initially hear its embryonic heartbeat, which will escalate to volcanic eruptions by the finale. I mentioned earlier that third symphonic movements were intended for the "body." This derived from the Classical period when the third movement was in dance form (originally a minuet.) As you listen to this movement of the "Pathétique," it, too, is for the body, but for the body of a sumo wrestler. It is wondrous to watch the evolution; dulcet interludes that relax briefly, but the momentum is always there. Alert yourself for a cannon barrage with a victory march immediately following that leads to the thunderous end.

What you will hear is a remarkable accomplishment. We have listened to a number of electrifying works, but none arising from a single theme!

Disc Two, Track 3—*The Nutcracker* (excerpts)

This is our first ballet music. Social dancing goes back to antiquity, and we have already seen dance forms, such as the minuet, incorporated into symphonic music. The art of ballet as an adjunct to musical theater goes back to the Italian Renaissance. Lully incorporated elaborate dances into his operas, but it is his monarch, Louis XIV, "The Sun King," an enthusiastic dancer himself, who is credited with establishing the first formal School of Dance. In the early eighteenth century, the so-called *ballet d'action* took form. It consisted of music, dance, and mime with no voices to distract attention from the spectacle. It was in this period that the first "pointe" shoes made their appearance, allowing the dancer to balance on extreme tiptoe. However, the Russians deserve the credit for combining a formal academic dance technique—the *danse d'écol*—with other artistic elements into the classical ballet, as we know it today. The ballerina is idealized as she floats on air almost escaping gravitational pull. The great "Pas de Deux" in *The Nutcracker* and the "Rose Adagio" in *Sleeping Beauty* lead me to think that

Tchaikovsky and the ballerina were soul mates even though he was not responsible for the choreography.

Tchaikovsky wrote the music for the early blockbuster ballets, *Swan Lake* (1877) and *The Sleeping Beauty* (1890). Both have maintained their popularity to the present day. *The Nutcracker* (1892), considering its many performances each Christmas season, must be the world's most frequently performed ballet. Having to choose a snippet from these three ballets brings to mind a fat man at a sumptuous buffet table. I've chosen *The Nutcracker* because of its popularity, and also because I want you to hear the celesta.

Tchaikovsky began composing *The Nutcracker* while visiting New York City in May 1891 to take part in the inaugural concerts of Carnegie Hall. On his journey, he wrote of "the absolute impossibility of depicting the Sugar Plum Fairy in music." At a Paris stop, he heard the newly invented celesta for the first time. The "impossibility" became a possibility, and the celesta benefited with lasting fame. The celesta looks much like a small upright piano except that the hammers strike vertical steel rods instead of strings.

Celebrated waltzes are found in each of the Tchaikovsky ballets, the Serenade for Strings, the opera *Eugene Onegin*, and in his Fifth Symphony.

In this selection, you will hear two excerpts, first the "Waltz of the Flowers," and then the variation of the "Dance of the Sugar Plum Fairy" that features the celesta. After opening chords as lush and smooth as hot fudge, the harps take over and you can visualize the ballerina en pointe (on the tips of her toes) making her entrance in tiny rapid steps, carrying her to center stage where she does a few pirouettes. The Waltz then commences, and goes on with some minor breaks for stage action until the opening chords, now louder and harsher, return. Compare this waltz with those of Johann Strauss, both father and son. The beat is the same, but you will find the music as unlike theirs as a surgeon is from an internist; I leave it to you to decide which you prefer.

Now comes the Sugar Plum Fairy in the guise of the celesta, for which you have been waiting. If you would like to explore the celesta further, pick up a recording of Bela Bartok's *Music for Strings, Percussion, and Celesta*.

I urge you to watch a ballet performance (many versions are available). The spectacle of the ballet enhances the music tremendously, and you will discover why the music veers this way or that. Composing music for a ballet is a give-and-take affair between the composer and the choreographer. Sometimes the composer is given the story line and then writes the music, with necessary modifications as the dances are worked out on stage. At other times, the music is written first without the conception of adaptation to a ballet; the story line and dances must then be fitted within its boundaries. Orff's *Carmina Burana* is a good example of the latter.

CHAPTER
TWENTY-TWO

Dvořák, Antonín (1841–1904)

"Mozart is sweet sunshine."

disc two
tracks 4–5

Smetana was the founder of Czech national music, but it was Dvořák (pronounced *De-vor-jak*) who popularized it. The great conductor, Hans von Bülow, said that Dvořák was, "next to Brahms, the most God-gifted composer of the present day." Dvořák's motto was "God, love, and motherland." He was not well read, but periodically he would try to correct this by reading a primer on this or that. Trains were his great passion. Whenever his students returned from a trip, he would closely question them about the locomotives that pulled their trains. He was never happier than when he was visiting the train station in Prague, where he would befriend the engineers. This simplicity, and his lack of revolutionary zeal in adhering to classical forms, have led people to underestimate him. Nevertheless, his music has sustained its popularity with concert audiences where the inventors of new music hardly appear. He was at his very best when creating the national music of Bohemia, and yet, ironically, the "New World" is his best-known piece.

Dvořák, a Czech, was the son of a zither-playing butcher. He received his early musical education from a schoolmaster, who encouraged him to play the violin, while his father apprenticed him to an uncle who was a butcher. In the end, music won out, and Dvořák trained at the Organ School in Prague. After graduation, he spent nine years playing the viola in a dance band. His compositions eventually met with resounding success, including a state stipend and a position as a church organist. The *Slavonic Dances* (1878) and *Moravian Duets* (1879) brought international recognition, in addition to conducting engagements in London.

In 1892, Dvořák left Prague to become director of the National Conservatory of Music in New York City. The three years he spent in the United States account for the influence of Native American and black spiritual song that is clearly present in the "New World."

For those of you who know New York, the "New World" Symphony was composed in a five-room apartment at 327 East 17th Street. Although he was homesick, Dvořák gave up returning to Czechoslovakia for vacation in favor of spending that summer in Spillville, Iowa (not as unlikely a place as it sounds since it was settled by Czechs), where he orchestrated the symphony and also composed some chamber music. (Spillville now has an annual Dvořák Festival.)

There were those who wanted to derive from this symphony the beginning of a new American national music, but Dvořák got fed up with this discussion, and declared that his composition was "genuine Bohemian music," a difficult contention to accept since "Swing Low, Sweet Chariot" and "Going Home" are easily recognizable in the first movement. Judge for yourself since this is a "must" for your collection! Whether American or Bohemian, the "New World" remains one of the most-played symphonies by any composer of any nationality.

Disc Two, Track 5—Symphony No. 9 in E Minor, Op. 95 *From the New World*

This is an excerpt at the beginning of the fourth movement of Dvořák's "New World" Symphony (note that the proper name is *From the New World*). Two thunderous chords immediately capture your attention. From these, a single theme develops that is interspersed throughout with bombastic chords. A sweet, understated melody ensues, but soon the thunderous orchestra returns with all its fury. When the fury is spent, no analytical effort is needed to enjoy the haunting music. Little imagination is required to envision Indians frenetically dancing around a campfire. Apparently, the wedding feast in Longfellow's *Hiawatha* suggested this passage.

Later in the movement, not played here but for you to discover, an Indian party going on the warpath is evoked more vividly than any music I've heard in a Cowboys-and-Indians Western.

While you're shopping, pick up the Carnival Overture (Op. 92), and the concertos for cello (Op. 104) and for violin (Op. 53), along with the complete *Slavonic Dances* (Op. 49 and 72). The String Quartet No. 12 (Op. 96 with the nickname "American") has my guaranteed recommendation as well. Other worthy additions to your Dvořák collection include the Concerto in B Minor for Cello and Orchestra, thought by many to be the Goliath of cello concertos, and the Concerto in A Minor for Violin and Orchestra, a parade of beautiful themes as well as a personal favorite.

I guarantee you will relish the Serenades, one for strings (Op. 22) and the other for winds (Op. 44). The Trio No. 4 in E Minor for Piano, Violin, and Cello is as sad as music comes and a perfect companion when you feel depressed. It has the memorable nickname of *Dumky,* which is often erroneously defined as a Czech dance, but is really the plural of the Russian word, *dumka,* denoting sadness. Many feel that Symphony No. 7 in D Minor is even greater than our selection, Symphony No. 9 (*From the New World*). I have particularly enjoyed the paired recording of the Quintet for Piano and Strings (Op. 81) and the String Quartet No. 12 (Op. 12), known as the "American" Quartet. If someone wants to give you a present, a boxed set of Dvořák's nine symphonies will give you and your CD player a fine workout.

CHAPTER TWENTY-THREE

Grieg, Edvard (1843–1907)

"Artists like Bach and Beethoven erected churches and
temples on the heights. I only wanted…to build dwellings
for men in which they might feel happy and at home."

disc two
tracks 6–8

Edvard Grieg, a true national hero in Norway and our first Norwegian composer, was an avowed champion of his nation's music. He was a founder of the Euterpe Society devoted to the discussion and performance of only Norwegian music. His dedication may be described as nationalistic, not tribalistic, because his great-grandfather came to Norway from Scotland and changed his name from Gre*ig* to Gr*ieg.*

The immigration bureaucrats on Ellis Island were infamous for pinning names on hapless immigrants with whom they communicated poorly early in the twentieth century. There is a classic story of a Jewish man with an accent so thick it could be cut with a scalpel, whose name was Sean (pronounced Shawn) Ferguson. When asked about his dubious Gaelic origin, he recounted that when he was asked what name he wished to use in America, he replied *"Schon, fergesen!"* meaning, "Already, I forgot!"

Edvard was originally given his mother's family name, Hagerup, as his first name, and eventually married a cousin with that as a last name. He founded a nationalist school just as Smetana and Bartók did in their countries. This rise of nationalism in music is a characteristic of the Romantic era.

He trained at the Leipzig Conservatory, a city that crops up over and over again in the course of this book. He was not happy in Leipzig, and spent the rest of his musical career trying to expunge the German influence (Mendelssohn and Schumann) from Norwegian music. He was a man who adhered to his principles. While in Copenhagen in 1867, he composed the Symphony in C Minor that he felt was too German (Leipzig training). After its premiere, he forbade further performances of it, a ban that was to last until 1981, when it was finally performed again.

Clearly, this piece suggests resonances of Schumann and Mendelssohn. Get it and see what you think!

The man with perhaps the greatest influence on his musical career was Rikard Nordraak (1842–1866), a Norwegian composer a year older than Grieg, who introduced Grieg to Norwegian folk music. On the day following Nordraak's untimely death at the age of twenty-three, Grieg composed a piano piece appropriately entitled *Funeral March in Memory of Rikard Nordraak*, which he later scored for a military band.

Liszt, that endearing scoundrel, was one of Grieg's mentors, and avidly promoted his Piano Concerto. To Liszt's everlasting credit, he provided both financial and emotional support to a great many of the young composers of Europe who eventually rose to stardom.

Disc Two, Track 7—Concerto for Piano in A Minor, Op. 16

You have an excerpt from the first movement of Grieg's Piano Concerto, one of the most popular piano concertos in the repertoire. Its "Norwegianess" does not pop out at me; see if you recognize it. What is apparent, however, is the influence of Liszt. Listen to your sample of Grieg, wait a day, and review the Liszt, and see whether you could mix up the two.

After the initial crashing chord and a piano introduction, the two main themes are presented by the orchestra, with the piano replaying each after its orchestral introduction. This give-and-take between the orchestra and the piano seems ideal for the entire length of the first half of this movement. The Aristotelian concept of the "Golden Mean" (not too much and not too little) is a prime goal of life that is difficult to achieve. With this in mind, you will certainly be anxious to see how the remainder of this movement, and the concerto as a whole, deals with the division of labor.

Grieg was basically a miniaturist. His Piano Concerto is his only "large" composition. You will hear the other side of Grieg next.

Disc Two, Track 8—*Peer Gynt:* Suites No. 1 and No. 2, Op. 46 and Op. 55

Like Grieg, the playwright Henrik Ibsen (1828–1906) was a Norwegian. His most famous plays are still enjoyed by audiences worldwide. They include *A Doll's House*, *Ghosts*, and *Hedda Gabler*. Ibsen led a turbulent life. He spent more time out of Norway than in. There was an illegitimate child, an eighteen-year-old mistress whom he described as his "May sun in a September life," and numerous peccadilloes—"small sins"—worthy of Liszt. This lifestyle is of particular note in that it pertains to what George Bernard Shaw dubbed "Ibsenism," meant as a critique of contemporary morality in dramatic form. Ibsen secured Grieg's services to write incidental music to accompany his play *Peer Gynt*. Ibsen was desperately unmusical, and never appreciated the magnificence of the music. I'm quite sure you will outshine Ibsen in this respect!

Despite the popularity of his Piano Concerto, the *Peer Gynt* suites are Grieg's best-known music. They were first performed along with Ibsen's strange fairy-tale play. They are nothing like his usual genre, and make no pretense of being operatic. The theater orchestra was anemic as compared to the capabilities of a full symphony orchestra. Grieg later rearranged the music into its present form, which the concert-going public immediately accepted. His wife had this to say of its composition:

> For several days he went about in a nervous, restless state, in great doubt and anxiety as to the heavy task. The more he saturated his mind with the powerful poem, the more clearly he saw that he was the right man for a work of such wild witchery and so permeated with the Norwegian spirit. In the suburb of Sandviken, outside Bergen, he found a pavilion, with windows on every side, high up on a hill…with a magnificent view of the sea on one side and the mountains on the other. "Solveig's Song" was the first number to see the light. Then "Ase's Death." I shall never forget the bright summer evening on the mountains, as we sang and played "Solveig's Song."'

Grieg himself wrote this of his beloved *Peer Gynt*:

> Peer Gynt, the only son of poor peasants, is drawn by the poet as a character of a morbidly developed fancy and a prey to megalomania. In his youth he had many wild adventures—comes, for instance, to a peasants' wedding where he carries off the bride up to the mountain peaks. Here he leaves her to roam about with the wild cowherd girls. He then enters the kingdom of the mountain king, whose daughter falls in love with him and dances to him. But he laughs at the dance and

the droll music, whereupon the enraged mountain folk wish to kill him. But he succeeds in escaping and wanders to foreign countries, among others to Morocco, where he appears as a prophet and is greeted by Arab girls. After many wonderful guidings of Fate, he at last returns as an old man, after suffering shipwreck on his way to his home as poor as he left it. Here the sweetheart of his youth, Solveig, who has stayed true to him all these years, meets him, and his weary head at last finds rest in her lap.

The first work you will hear is from Grieg's *Peer Gynt* Suite No. 1. "In the Hall of the Mountain King" is frequently taught in seventh grade music appreciation classes. Grieg vouchsafed to Ibsen: "I have written something for the hall of the Troll king which smacks of so much cow manure, ultra-Norwegianism, and self-satisfaction that I literally cannot bear to hear it." Do you think he was simply being self-deprecating?

"Solveig's Song" is one of my favorite pieces. As I said before, superlatives get you in trouble in music. How can you make a comparison between "Solveig's Song" and the chorale of Beethoven's Ninth Symphony? Obviously you can't. Perhaps a classification is in order similar to the Academy Award presentations where prizes are given in a multitude of categories? I hope you will agree that "Solveig's Song" would have won an Oscar for rhapsodic gentleness.

If you would like to plumb Grieg beyond his Piano Concerto and *Peer Gynt* Suites, try the *Holberg* Suite and his Sonata in A for Cello and Piano.

CHAPTER TWENTY-FOUR

Rimsky-Korsakov, Nikolay (1844–1908)

"I was young and self-confident; my self-confidence was encouraged by others and I joined the Conservatory.... Thus having been undeservedly accepted at the Conservatory as a professor, I soon became one of its best and possibly its very best pupil, judging by the quantity and value of the information it gave me!"

disc two
tracks 9–10

ikolay Andreyevich Rimsky-Korsakov was born in Novgorod to a well-to-do family. As a young man, he served as a naval officer but had written his first symphony (revised twenty-three years later) by age seventeen, while still on duty. Musically, he was almost entirely self-taught, but by the age of twenty-three, on the basis of his tone poem *Sadko* (a sea tale), he became the professor of composition at the prestigious St. Petersburg Conservatory. He was aware of his inadequacies, but overcame them by hard work.

He is considered the foremost theorist among the "mighty handful" of Russian composers. His intense loyalty to this group impelled him to complete Musorgsky's unfinished *Boris Godunov* after his colleague's untimely death. Had he not performed this obligation of friendship, it is unlikely that Musorgsky would be held in his present esteem. Rimsky-Korsakov's strong nationalism, intense rhythmic sense, and magnificent ability with orchestral coloration have led to his being frequently compared to Berlioz, which is no small compliment. Rimsky-Korsakov was also the musical mentor of Igor Stravinsky, who would become the premier composer of the twentieth century.

Disc Two, Track 10—*Scheherazade*

This music is based on the fifteenth century Oriental storybook *The 1001 Arabian Nights*. Scheherazade teaches these tales to her sister, Dinarzade, to enable her to divert her husband, the Sultan Schahriah, from his ugly habit of following one night's connubial bliss with each wife with her execution if he suspected her of unfaithfulness.

Scheherazade is "a symphonic suite for orchestra" in four movements. It is the last large-scale orchestral work Rimsky-Korsakov wrote. The final twenty years of his life were devoted to opera and vocal music. Our section is from the opening of the work. It begins with the Sultan's brassy baleful theme followed by the sensuous seductive voice of Scheherazade, played by a solo violin. These themes are repeated with variations throughout the four movements. The four stories are titled: "The Sea and Sinbad's Ship," "The Story of the Kalandar Prince," "The Young Prince and the Young Princess," and "Festival at Baghdad—The Sea—Shipwreck."

A repetition of themes throughout a longer musical work is known as the "cyclical form." It serves as a comfortable base and reference for the listener. Go back and listen to *Pictures* in which the Promenade theme conveniently points out when we leave one picture and go on to the next. Wagner's *leitmotifs* are comforting to hear when the character or object you have met before comes on stage or is recalled in spirit. Technically, *Pictures* is more a "ritornel" (same theme marking or linking divisions in the musical structure), but you wouldn't be a reader/listener of this book if that made a difference to you.

César Franck (1822–1890), another composer whom you will have to discover on your own, was the progenitor of the cyclic form. It was also used a great deal by Bruckner, and earned invective because symphonies were supposed to be in sonata form. Expect criticism anytime you innovate in your own life even if it concerns something as benign as a new hairstyle. Your friends will compliment you on it, but later comment to each other that they really liked the old style better. Music critics are paid to do this!

The enduring popularity of *Scheherazade* is due to its memorable tunes, vivid orchestration, and sultry Oriental atmosphere.

CHAPTER TWENTY-FIVE

Elgar, Sir Edward (1857–1934)

"The Enigma I will not explain—its 'dark saying'
must be left unguessed."
—Elgar on the *Enigma Variations*

disc two
tracks 11–13

Now you are in for a real treat! The British Empire was conquered and administered to the strains of music like this. Elgar's music expresses the Edwardian age just as his mien represented it with his perfect tailoring, ramrod posture, and Colonel Blimp mustache. He rose from obscure beginnings and a long apprenticeship to become the most illustrious composer of his country in the first third of the twentieth century.

Edward Elgar is the first significant English composer since Henry Purcell (1659–1695). He was born in Broadheath, Worcestershire, in 1857 and, take it as a sign of British conservatism, died in Worcester (Worcester, like the steak sauce, the city in Massachusetts, and the porcelain factory, is pronounced *Wuster*) as well. He was the fourth child of a music shop keeper and his Catholic wife. As a child, he learned to play the piano, organ, and violin, but began work as a solicitor's clerk. Not surprisingly, given the trend we've seen in these pages, music triumphed over the law. Apart from his instrumental training, he had no formal musical education, teaching himself from books the details of counterpoint and orchestration. To support himself, he freelanced in local orchestras and taught the violin. He began to compose, but his career did not have the early meteoric rise that we have seen so often in others. At the age of thirty-two, he married the daughter of an Indian Army general. She was nine years his senior. She had faith in his ability, and they moved to London to further his career, but the music publishers did not respond. Undaunted, Elgar and his wife again relocated, this time to Malvern. All the while, he churned out a steady stream of compositions that awarded him only local recognition.

Elgar's breakthrough came in 1899, at the age of forty-two, when the great conductor Hans Richter (see chapter 16) became his champion, and conducted the *Enigma Variations* (*Variations on an Original Theme*) in London. These are a series of fourteen very short pieces depicting his friends and, in the fourteenth, himself. Each is rather uniquely titled with the friend's initials or first name. Other conductors followed Richter in recognition of Elgar. From that time on, success was his.

Over the next twenty years, Elgar produced one acclaimed composition after another. *The Dream of Gerontius (St. Jerome),* an oratorio, is considered his masterpiece. The concert-overture *Cockaigne* dates from 1901, and the *Pomp and Circumstance Marches* were composed over the next six years. His works include the full complement of arrows in the composer's quiver, from symphonies to short gems such as *Serenade Lyrique.* His Cello Concerto in E Minor ranks with Dvořák's as one of the greatest.

Cockaigne is the name of an imaginary country, perhaps more enjoyable than Utopia, that is the abode of luxury and idleness. It is also humorously applied to London as the land of Cockneys. The origin of the word is unknown, although one scholar suggests that it derives from "kuchen," the German for cake, "because the houses there were covered with cake."

The death of his wife in 1920 marked the end of Edward's productive composing career, although he still conducted his own works from time to time. In the remaining fourteen years of his life, Elgar felt that the world had passed him over. He became something of a recluse, and adopted the role of a country squire. He was a much more complex man than the surface veneer of British solidity indicated. He possessed deep angers about the periodic religious prejudices he had suffered, and even claimed that he had lost interest in music. A knighthood and other honors heaped upon him did not assuage his feelings of disillusionment. Such desuetude by the Elgars of this world works only to deprive posterity of the beautiful music they might have produced had their ability been allowed to mature.

Disc Two, Tracks 12 & 13—*Pomp and Circumstance Military Marches*, Op. 39, No. 1 and No. 4

My personal preference is for Elgar's shorter works. Rather than deprive you of listening to each of my three favorites, I have truncated them, to their detriment but to your benefit.

... is from *Pomp and Circumstance*, March No. 1. Generations of schoolve marched to this theme at their graduation ceremonies; very likely you f them. You may well insert the name of your school as you hum along. I

The second selection is March No. 4. Here, you will recognize the music that was played in London during the Blitz, and imagine the indomitable ships of the Royal Navy steaming in formation to do battle.

Check out some further Elgar; he's worth knowing better. You have heard the gift for melody that pervades his entire output. He was no slouch at orchestration either.

You have now listened to enough composers from different countries to appreciate that, to a great degree, the country molds the composer. The English, the Germans and Austrians, the Russians, the Slovaks, the Scandinavians, and the French all have their singular characteristics that are often as different as day and night. Why this should be is a mystery. They had all heard each other's work, often studied at the same institutions, lived in each other's cities, and knew the works of their forebears from the other countries. Keep this national distinctiveness in mind and see if it holds true as you come to know new composers and their compositions.

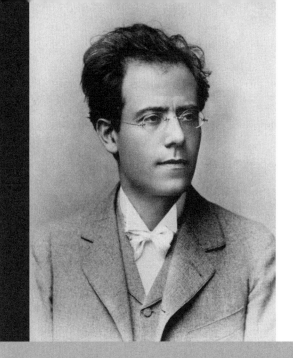

CHAPTER TWENTY-SIX

Mahler, Gustav (1860–1911)

"A symphony must be a world.
It must embrace everything."

disc two
tracks 14–15

Mahler was an institution. Citizens walking the streets of Vienna called him "Der Mahler" when they saw him, although for fifty years following his death, Mahler's music was largely neglected. Currently, however, it is *de rigueur*. This revival of interest in, and appreciation of, his music was unquestionably the result of the championing performances by Leonard Bernstein (chapter 42), conductor of the New York Philharmonic from 1958 to 1969, and guest conductor literally around the world.

There is no debate that Mahler is one of the great symphonists of all time. The evolution of symphonic form can be traced from Haydn to Beethoven, from Beethoven to Bruckner, and from Bruckner to Mahler. His ten symphonies, four of which use the human voice to bring about an unequaled synthesis of song and symphonic form, coincide with the end of the dominant Austro-German influence on European music. Simultaneously, he brought the Romantic era to its culmination with the grand emotionalism of his gigantic works. Men such as Berg, Britten, Schoenberg, Shostakovich, and Webern consider him a forerunner of the revolutionary developments to come in the restructuring of music. Mahler was one of the finest conductors who ever lived, but he did not know how to lead without alienating those with whom he worked. This unfortunately explains his peregrinations.

Mahler was born in Kalischt, Bohemia (a part of the former Czechoslovakia but in the Austrian Empire of the time), the son of a Jewish-Austrian innkeeper. Thus, he was part of a German-speaking Austrian minority, and an outsider among the indigenous Czech people while, as a Jew, he was an outsider among his own Austrian minority. When he went to Germany, he was again an outsider as an Austrian from Bohemia and a Jew. Mahler phrased it more succinctly: "I am thrice homeless. As a Bohemian born in Austria. As an Austrian among Germans. As a Jew throughout the world." He was the second of fourteen children. Despite the obvious contradiction, his parents didn't get along. Mahler took his mother's side in their frequent spats, and developed a mother fixation so strong that in years to come he would, in times of stress, unknowingly ape her slight limp. With this sterling background, it is not unexpected that neurotic tensions and an infatuation with death would be associated with his constant quest for some deeper meaning in life, and his striving to express it in music. Not surprisingly, his fierce irony and skepticism did not endear him to others.

The common thread in these pages of musical precocity applies to Mahler. By age four, he began playing military and folk songs on the piano and accordion. These early songs, and the sounds of nature, were to be his dominant inspirations for musical creation. He began composing before he was old enough to enter the first grade, and made his concert debut on the piano at the age of ten. At fifteen, he matriculated to the Vienna Conservatory, and swept on to win prize after prize.

Conservatory—a public establishment for special instruction in music and declamation. The French form of the word (*conservatoire*) is commonly used in England. In the U.S. the anglicized form *conservatory* is bestowed. An alternate meaning is greenhouse, which I choose to think is how the word got to music; a greenhouse for music students instead of flora!

Mahler earned his degree and, failing to win the coveted Beethoven Prize for his first mature piece, *Das klagende Lied (The Song of Complaint)*, he decided financial security could be found in conducting opera. For the next seventeen years, he went from post to post in city after city (including Budapest and Hamburg) until at age thirty-seven, in 1897, he reached the very pinnacle of a career for a conductor, the Vienna Court Opera. Mahler is universally acknowledged as having raised its standards in a spectacular way, not only in the areas of vocal and orchestral performance, but also in acting, set design, and lighting.

With this immense background in opera, it is surprising that he wrote symphonies. His forty songs were never meant to be lieder but rather embryonic symphonic movements. His works have a large religious element in them. He was tortured by his spiritual explorations; his father was a freethinker and he was not raised as a Jew in a religious household. He had himself baptized before taking the Vienna position. Obviously for a Jew there was expediency in this, as was the case with Mendelssohn, but he was also desperately seeking new metaphysical values.

His symphonies are of a confessional nature, and at times so sentimental that they border on obsession. He was not confined by standard forms, and didn't hesitate to inject into his works such popular material as marches, fanfares, folk melodies, and waltzes. The epithet "incoherent" has been leveled at Mahler symphonies because they fail to give one the comfort of a Haydn or Mozart, in terms of knowing where one is during a performance. Mahler was a great innovator in orchestration. Each instrument seems to stand out from the others, to coin a phrase, "contrapuntality of instrumentation." Often, the sublime coexists with the naïve and vulgar. Length was not a consideration. A symphony may have twenty separate parts divided artificially into as many as six movements. In his later symphonies, atonality made its appearance, a harbinger of what was to come in the twentieth century.

You will like what you are about to hear. I must warn you that I chose them with considerable care in order to give you a gentle introduction to Mahler. Much of his music is heavy indeed. To give you a concrete illustration, just after the third movement is completed, the fourth movement opens with a startlingly loud passage that is said to have served the purpose of awakening the nappers in the audience (remember our discussion of the *Paukenschlag* in Haydn's "Surprise" Symphony in chapter 4). One elegantly dressed woman is described as leaping up from her lethargy to spill the contents of her lap and purse on the floor. In Jonathan D. Kramer's excellent and often humorous book, *Listen To The Music,* he claims that his very pregnant wife felt her child suddenly wake up in the womb, jump violently, and visibly kick; such is the power of Mahler.

Disc Two, Track 15—Symphony No. 1

Mahler commenced to write his First Symphony when he was twenty-four years old. He actually wrote four symphonies prior to this one, all of which he destroyed. The work had its premiere performance five years later. Two selections from it are on your disc. The first is a funeral march from the second movement. I believe he lifted its propelling melody from another source. Listen a number of times to see what he has done with it. You will see that it is repeated twice, and then a typical Mahlerian orchestral mutation takes over, until the melody starts anew, but doesn't finish as a simple repeat.

The second fragment is from the third movement. The opening is somber, but I hear a theme from *Fiddler on the Roof*. Since *Fiddler* was written almost a century later, it is more accurate to say that it was probably aping Mahler, who subsequently heard it in a gypsy tavern when he was conducting in Budapest!

Recommended Listening
Das Lied von der Erde (The Song of the Earth)

In 1902, at the age of forty-two, Mahler married Alma Schindler, a composer herself and twenty years his junior. Hers is an enthralling story that entitles her to be classified as one of the greatest *femmes fatales* of history. In addition to Mahler, she married the architect Walter Gropius and the writer Franz Werfel, and had an affair with the painter, Oscar Kokoschka. Alban Berg dedicated his opera *Wozzeck* to her, and his Violin Concerto to the memory of her daughter, Manon. Others who came under her sway included the composer Hans Pfitzner and two painters of international repute, Gustav Klimt and Egon Schiele. All this and much more, including the intellectual life of Vienna during the charmed era that culminated ignobly in the rise of Hitler, is detailed in a worthwhile book by Françoise Giroud, *Alma Mahler, or the Art of Being Loved* (Oxford University Press, New York, 1991).

> **"Erde"** in German means earth or land. In English it is an obsolete word for earth.

In what amounted to a prenuptial agreement, Mahler insisted that Alma completely give up her composing and, to quote from his twenty-page letter: "You have only one profession from now on: to make me happy!—You must give yourself to me unconditionally, shape your future life, in every detail, entirely in accordance with my needs and desire nothing in return save my love!" Tyranny of this sort is laughable today, and must have been a bit much even then.

A friend gave me a clipping by Nancy Caldwell Sorel from the Sunday Supplement of the British newspaper, the *Independent*. I quote in full:

They were Jews by birth (unreligious, but puritanical) and Viennese by adoption. Freud had been a medical student in Vienna when Mahler was at the Conservatory. Later Mahler served as conductor of the Vienna Court Opera. Opera was one of Freud's few diversions. But they had not met until Freud was fifty-four and Mahler, at fifty, had less than a year to live. The encounter was occasioned by the composer's marital problems with the young and beautiful Alma. Engrossed in his Tenth Symphony, Mahler suddenly found himself the object of domestic rebellion. Alma had, she said, submitted to his tyranny and neglect long enough; she felt used, drained by his self-absorption. The truth of her accusations, together with a case of impotence, produced in Mahler both guilt and panic—panic was not eased by the appearance of another man (Walter Gropius) on the scene. Immediate action was called for.

Freud, holidaying in Leyden, Holland, that summer of 1910, received a telegram asking for an appointment. The following day came another telegram, cancelling.

Mahler's vacillation was repeated twice more before he managed to conquer his resistance. He and Freud met in a Leyden hotel and spent the next four hours strolling about the town—the stocky, confident doctor and the thin, intense composer—smoking the cigars both adored. Freud conducted a sort of mini-analysis. A mother fixation was diagnosed: Mahler was attracted by his wife's youthful beauty but resented the fact that she was not old and careworn like his mother. Alma, to even things out, had a father complex and found her husband's age appealing. Mahler was reassured.

The two men parted friends. Mahler's potency returned, and psychoanalysis got the credit. Alma said later that Freud had reproached her husband for marrying one so young, but his attitude was closer to sympathy than to censure. A good wife—in Freud's view as in Mahler's—was but a ministering angel put on earth for the comfort and support of her husband.

Alma bore Mahler two daughters, one in 1902 and the second in 1904. Through Alma, he encouraged the Sezession movement, and so became the focal point around which rallied a generation of younger composers, including Schoenberg, Berg, and Webern.

From 1894 to 1907, Mahler composed his fourth through eighth symphonies and *Das Lied von der Erde*. This was intended as his Ninth Symphony, but superstition interfered, inasmuch as the ninth symphony had been the last for both Beethoven and Bruckner, and he changed it to a "Song." He got up his nerve later, and composed a ninth and even a tenth symphony, which remained incomplete. Thus, if you are willing to count the "Song," Mahler composed a total of eleven symphonies.

The Sezessionists were a group of painters who rebelled against academic discipline and developed their own decorative and highly stylized art form that came to be known as Art Nouveau.

Nineteen hundred seven was a terrible year for the Mahlers. His three-year-old daughter died of scarlet fever, he was diagnosed as having a heart valve lesion (rheumatic fever) with a terrible prognosis, and an anti-Semitic clique forced his resignation from the Vienna Court Opera. He fled Europe for New York to conduct the Metropolitan Opera from 1908 to 1910, departing when Arturo Toscanini arrived. He never heard the performances of the Ninth, the uncompleted Tenth, or the "Song," but in 1910 in Munich he conducted his most monumental work, the

Eighth Symphony, named the *Symphony of a Thousand* for the number of performers used in its first performance. It was the crowning achievement of his life. He returned to New York to conduct the 1910–1911 season of the New York Philharmonic Orchestra, but became ill in February 1911. Expressing his wish to return to his precious Vienna, he died there in a clinic, having packed an incredibly full and productive life into his chronologically short fifty-one years.

Das Lied von der Erde began as a song cycle of Chinese poems in German, and grew to become "A Symphony for Tenor, Baritone (or Contralto) and Orchestra." It is a six-movement "song cycle symphony" reflecting upon the evanescence of life until it finds fulfillment in the beauty of the Earth that endures long after the players are gone.

You might enjoy reading the text in German with its translation from the song "Von der Jugend" (Youth):

Mitten in dem kleinen Teiche	In the middle of the little pool
Sicht ein Pavillon aus grünem	stands a pavilion of green
Und aus weissen Porzellan.	and white porcelain.
Wie der Rücken eines Tigers	Like a tiger's back,
Wölbt die Brücke sich aus Jade	the jade bridge arches itself
Zu dem Pavillon hinüber	over to the pavilion
In dem Häuschen sitzen Freunde,	In the little house friends are sitting
Schön gekleidet, trinken, plaudern:	prettily dressed, drinking and chattering:
Manche schreiben Verse nieder.	some are writing down verses.
Ihre seidnen Ärmel gleiten	Their silk leaves fall
Rückwärts, ihre seidnen Mützen	backwards; their silk caps perch
Hocken lustig tief im Nacken.	roguishly back on their heads.
Auf des kleinen Teiches stiller	On the still surface of the little pool
Wasser fläche zeigt sich alles	everything is reflected
Wunderlich im Spiegelbilde:	wonderfully as in a mirror:
Alles auf dem Kopfe stehend	Everything is standing on its head
In de Pavillon aus grünem	in the pavilion of green
Und aus weissen Porzellan.	and white porcelain.
Wie ein Halbmond steht die Brücke	The bridge stands like a half-moon
Umgekehrt der Bogen, Freunde.	with its arch upside-down. Friends
Schön gekleidet, trinken, plaudern.	prettily dressed are drinking and chattering.

This is a fine example of how the qualities of language affect the music. Had this been written in Italian or French with these respective language's rich vowels and elisions, the music itself would perforce be unrecognizable.

CHAPTER TWENTY-SEVEN

Debussy, Claude (1862–1918)

"I am more and more convinced that music is not,
in essence, a thing which can be cast
into a traditional and fixed form.
It is made up of colors and rhythms."

disc two
tracks 16–18

The French word "timbre" is known in English as "tone color." Timbre is analogous to color in painting. A man with a deep bass voice and a woman with a high-pitched soprano voice can sing exactly the same words, but the two sources are differentiated by their distinctive timbre (tone colors). Just as easily, one can separate the clarinet from the violin. Claude Debussy is credited as being one of the most influential of twentieth century composers inasmuch as his compositions demonstrate that timbre is quite as basic to musical response as rhythm, melody, and harmony. He was labeled an "impressionist," like the artistic movement, because of the pictorial images and delicate colorations his music conveys. Further, Debussy attempted to liberate musical composition from the shackles of conventional forms. No symphonies or concertos for him; when he wrote compositions with multiple parts he refused to use the word "movement," substituting the term "section" instead, although he lapsed once and wrote a single String Quartet in four *movements*. It is interesting to note that he gave it an opus number of ten, though it was certainly not his tenth work, and he never assigned opus numbers to any other compositions. Take a listen; the opening theme is particularly gripping, and thematic transfer appears in each movement (cyclic form).

Debussy was a native Parisian. His father, Manuel, was a ne'er-do-well who steered Achille-Claude (Claude's true name) toward being a sailor. Manuel was jailed during the Commune of 1871. Fortunately for those of us who like music, an aunt saw to it that Claude took piano lessons. Music won out over the sea! After these lessons, she switched his instruction to a Mme. Mauté de Fleurville who had studied with Chopin, and was the mother-in-law of the poet Verlaine. Verlaine had a great influence on Debussy in later life, and wrote the poem *Claire de lune,* upon which Debussy based his piece. There is no record that Debussy received any formal education until he entered the venerable, and ironically form-bound, Paris Conservatory at the age of eleven. Anecdotes are plentiful about his studies at the Conservatory. The one I like best concerns César Franck, who was conducting a class in piano improvisation.

Frustrated by Debussy's unwillingness to vary a passage, Franck shouted "Modulate! Modulate!" and received the unruffled reply, "Why? I'm perfectly happy where I am."

Debussy was recognized as an original, and spent a decade at the conservatory rebelling against the formalities of music, while continuing to take the requisite courses that taught them. During his teens, he spent three summers in the household of the wealthy Russian widow, Nadezhda von Meck, playing piano duets with the widow and giving piano lessons to her daughters. If you'll recall, von Meck was the lady who bailed Tchaikovsky out of his unhappy marriage, and supported him for sixteen years thereafter (see chapter 21). To have had Tchaikovsky and Debussy in your stable almost rivals Alma Mahler with her Gropius and Werfel. During these summers in Russia, and while touring Europe, Debussy absorbed a good deal of Borodin, Musorgsky in particular, but precious little Tchaikovsky.

By 1884 at age twenty-two, Debussy had won the coveted Prix de Rome. He won it on his third attempt, but during the five years he was studying and working toward this goal, he found the time to fall madly in love with his student, Madame Vasnier. As the college students of past generations said, we don't know whether she "went all the way." Nevertheless, we owe to her some wondrous love songs that Debussy wrote from 1880 to 1882. He ended up hating Rome, but while there had the opportunity to become immersed in Wagnerian opera, and begin developing his own pathfinding style.

One of the responsibilities of winning the Prix was to send back to Paris original compositions. The first of these, entitled *Zuleima*, was judged by the conservatory as "bizarre, incomprehensible, and impossible to play." He then sent the judges, supposedly from Rome, his *La Demoiselle élue* (*The Blessed Maiden*). Debussy left Rome short of his required three years, and returned to Paris.

He settled in Montmartre, the artists' quarter of Paris, in what may be described as fashionable poverty. The fires of passion had apparently dimmed between himself and Mme. Vasnier, for he landed a mistress, Gabrielle Dupont, who stayed with him for a decade. He called her "Gaby of the green eyes." With his flowing capes and swarthy complexion and hair cut in bangs, he rapidly became a Montmartre landmark. He began to attend the weekly meetings of the Symbolist Poets of such note as Baudelaire, Verlaine, Rimbaud, and Mallarmé. In essence, Debussy was a Symbolist tone poet composer. This was the period of painters, such as Monét and Renoir, who broke with tradition and took their canvasses outside to catch their impressions of light. Debussy, however, didn't like being compared to the Impressionists.

At the Paris Exposition of 1889, he encountered a Javanese assemblage of musical instruments known as the gamelan. Just as the Impressionist artists were to change color patterns in response to the Japanese wood block prints of Hokusai and others, Debussy reacted to the gamelan with new tone colors, and became further convinced that the fugues and symphonic forms he had learned as a student were redundant to the composition of beautiful music. He visited Bayreuth twice, only to reject Wagner but never to escape elements of his style in the music he produced. It doesn't require a degree in music to feel the Wagnerian influence in his most famous opera, *Pelléas et Mélisande*.

By 1905, Debussy had been married twice. Gaby of the green eyes lost out to Rosalie Texier, a dressmaker of no particular distinction except for his nickname for her, "Lilly-Lilo." She soon received short shrift when he eloped with Emma Bardac, the wife of a wealthy banker, and formerly the mistress of another composer, Gabriel Fauré (1845–1924). This caused a real scandal, even by Parisian standards, when the distraught Rosalie shot herself. The wound, however, was not fatal.

Claude and Emma had a child, named Claude-Emma. He called her "Chouchou," which reminds me of a cabbage dish from Alsace, and dedicated a piano suite called *Children's Corner* to her. Financially wiped out by the nasty litigation that followed the elopement, Debussy turned to writing newspaper articles as a means of supporting himself and his family. As in the case of Berlioz, some of these were first rate. Claude later developed cancer and received radiation treatment. His health slowly continued to deteriorate, but he died in a German bombardment of Paris in 1918. In the midst of the war, his death was little noticed.

> **Bergamasca**—a term originally used to describe peasant songs and dances from the Bergamo district in northern Italy. Bergamo is associated with the *commedia dell'arte* and the clown figure of Harlequin. Fauré composed an orchestral suite entitled *Masques et bergamasques*.

Disc Two, Track 17—"Claire de lune" from *Suite Bergamasque*

A new musical style developed with his *Suite Bergamasque* and its "Claire de lune," our first selection. It received an instant and wildly enthusiastic public acceptance, giving rise to the cult of "debussysm."

> This **"faune"** is not a cute little Bambi, but rather a man with goat's legs and the lustful behavior equated with satyrs.

Pay particular attention to "Claire de lune." As you listen to it now, a century later, you will have difficulty realizing what a radical departure it was from the musical norms of Debussy's time. Today it would be considered suitable for background music during tea at a fine London hotel.

Disc Two, Track 18—*Prelude à l'après-midi d'un Faune* *(Afternoon of a Faun)*

Prelude à l'après-midi d'un Faune starts with its entrancing flute passage worthy of an Indian *fakir* hypnotizing his cobra. Focus on the beautiful orchestral colorations that follow. To me, they don't evoke satyrs gamboling in the woods (or doing what satyrs do), but I can conjure up some ethereal nymphs.

The cult of "debussysm" was securely cemented in place by *Prelude à l'après-midi d'un Faune.*

CHAPTER TWENTY-EIGHT

Strauss, Richard (1864–1949)

"I may not be a first-class composer,
but I am a first-class second-rate composer."

disc two
tracks 19–20

Richard Strauss was yet another of those child prodigies who began studying the piano at the age of four. At six, he took up the violin and composed his first song. By the age of eleven, musical theory and composition had been introduced into his curriculum. He was born in Munich, the son of Germany's most celebrated French horn player. His mother was the daughter of a wealthy brewing family. In childhood, Richard played the violin in a semiprofessional orchestra conducted by his father, with the attendant dividends of sheltered discipline and experience.

This pattern of early exposure to a talented musician-parent combined with the wherewithal to obtain a musical education is a model we have seen repeatedly among the great composers. Mendelssohn was a paradigm. One might reasonably ponder upon the question: how many children are born with the spark of musical genius but without the kindling necessary for a flame?

During a visit to the People's Republic of China in 1978, my wife and I found that an obligatory part of the tour in each city was the Children's Palace. These were community centers in which multiple cultural activities were thrust upon the children, talented or not. I will never forget the horrific din of a violin class for three- to six-year-olds when some forty children were sawing away simultaneously. Only a festival in Scotland bested it with a thousand bagpipers!

A meeting in 1882 with the conductor Hans von Bülow, a ubiquitous figure in these pages, led to Strauss's conducting his Serenade for 13 Wind Instruments, Op. 4, a work worth listening to and owning. He became von Bülow's assistant, without pay, in the court at Meiningen. When von Bülow departed for six months,

Strauss was *the* conductor at age eighteen, giving him a valuable early exposure to the musical repertoire of the period. Following this, he returned to Munich as the third conductor of its major orchestra.

His musical mentors were Brahms, Liszt, and Wagner (the avant-garde of that time.) His respect for Wagner earned his father's stern disapproval. Von Bülow called Strauss "Richard the Second," because of the way he expanded some of Wagner's operatic concepts, an extraordinary complement from so distinguished a conductor. In 1889, Strauss became an assistant at the Bayreuth Festival. Wagner had died in 1883 leaving his wife, Cosima, to rule. She had plans for Strauss both as a member of her senior staff and as a son-in-law, but he was already enamored (after a torrid love affair with a divorcée named Dora) with Pauline, a Prussian general's daughter. She was a fine soprano, whom he eventually married. (Strauss wrote the *Symphonie Domestica*, musically describing the chores of home life, including both feeding and making a baby.) Pauline ruled him with an iron hand that she must have acquired from her father, the general. Had Strauss married a Wagner, Bayreuth might today have a dual annual festival. Be that as it may, Strauss's fame burst upon the musical scene when his passionate (passion then engendered by Dora, not Pauline) tone poem *Don Juan*, Op. 20, was given wild acclaim by the musical public.

Liszt is given credit for the invention of the tone poem, and Smetana refined it further. Tone poems up until Strauss depicted allegories, but he converted them to dramas that told stories. There are fashions in music just as in men's neckties. In Strauss's time, the symphony was considered passé. The objection to the symphony was that the artificiality of its form prevented true emotion from emerging and telling a story. To be the diplomat and mute the controversy, I would suggest that the tone poem could be properly labeled a symphonic poem. The symphony has survived and remains robust.

By age thirty, Strauss had gone on to lead the prestigious orchestras of both Berlin and Munich. Between the ages of twenty-four and thirty-four, he composed the tone poems that are a strong pillar of his reputation. These include *Don Juan, Death and Transfiguration, Thus Spake Zarathustra*—based on Nietzsche's masterpiece—*Don Quixote, Ein Heldenleben* (*A Hero's Life*), and our present selection, *Till Eulenspiegel's*

Merry Pranks. I commend each of them to you in their entirety, but don't acquire them all at once. Strauss had a miraculous creative energy that some find too florid.

Disc Two, Track 20—*Till Eulenspiegel's Merry Pranks*, Op. 28

You get to hear an excerpt from the first half of *Till Eulenspiegel's Merry Pranks.* It is in rondo form, which means that Till's theme is periodically introduced to label the different chapters of a story based on the life of Till Eulenspiegel, who lived in Germany during the first half of the fourteenth century. Till was a peasant who had no regard for class boundaries. He liked practical jokes that got him in trouble, but he usually survived by humor, quick wit, or trickery, with one major exception: he was eventually hanged! Strauss makes a point in his writings that it is best not to tell the plot to the audience, but better for them to make their own interpretations. For *Till* he relented. There is Till hidden in a mouse hole, Till dressed as an unctuous priest, Till meeting with the pedagogues, Till seducing beautiful girls, and Till going to the gallows. You will like Till, and by including only a piece of the first half, I have spared you his death!

Following the era of the tone poem, Strauss went on to write opera and lieder. There is *Der Rosenkavalier,* which seems entirely out of place in his oeuvre since it is a Mozart-like comic opera. More representative of the Strauss of the tone poems is the Biblical opera *Salomé,* with its title character who kisses the severed head of John the Baptist when it is served up on a plate, or the Greek myth-inspired *Elektra,* with its plot of murder and revenge.

Strauss lived to a ripe old age, clouded (again reminiscent of Wagner) by his embrace of Nazism. He accepted a high title and has been accused of collaborating in the purge of various "unholy" elements from music. I am dubious of this because when it embroiled his Jewish librettist, Stefan Zweig, he drew the line and escaped to Switzerland. He was tried as a collaborator after the war by an Allied tribunal, but was let off. Again, you will have to make your own decision as to whether a man can be separated from his music.

Stefan Zweig (1881–1942) was a German-Jewish writer exiled in 1934 by the Nazis. In 1942, he and his second wife committed suicide in Brazil.

CHAPTER TWENTY-NINE

Sibelius, Jean (1865–1957)

"The violin occupied my mind completely.
Henceforth, it was for ten years my ardent wish,
the proudest goal of my ambition
to become a great violin virtuoso."

disc two
tracks 21–23

Jean Sibelius was the greatest composer to come out of Finland and the premier symphonist ever produced by the Scandinavians, Grieg included. He was born in a Russian garrison town in Finland to Swedish-speaking parents. He studied at the first Finnish-speaking grammar school in what was then Russian-held Finland, and was exposed from childhood to the rich Finnish mythology.

He demonstrated an aptitude for music as a teenager, but began law studies in Helsinki. Again, music eventually triumphed, to the benefit of us all. Sibelius was a master of tonal coloration, but his life was colorless. He married and settled in a rustic home nestled in the woods, and never left it for long. His musical ability prompted a lifelong government stipend that relieved him of monetary cares. Alas, I have no juicy morsels to trot out for you. The best I can do is tell you that he changed his name to Jean Sibelius from Johann Julius Christian Sibelius. He gained the world's attention and glory early in his career, and was content to bask in this glory, with no further output, for the last twenty-nine of his ninety-two years. He required surgery for a throat cancer in his early forties and was forced to give up the cigars and wine on which he depended for stimulation. There may be a clue here to longevity.

Sibelius's reputation is founded on four or five of his seven symphonies, a violin concerto, and a half-dozen tone poems. He wrote more than a hundred songs, a third more piano pieces, fifty works for solo violin and piano, and many choruses. In 1894, he began work on an opera. To that end, he traveled to Bayreuth and Munich to hear some Wagnerian opera. This experience crushed his aspirations as an operatic composer. He transferred the ruins of his opera into *Lemminkainen, four legends from the Kalevala*. Interestingly, after initial criticism, he withdrew two of its movements from performance. These were not restored until a celebration of the one hundreth anniversary of the *Kalevala* in 1935.

Unquestionably, Sibelius brought a new idiom to the classical musical scene. It consisted of grumbling brass peaks, unmixed instrumental colorations in low registers,

Kalevala means "land of heroes." Its leader, a powerful seer of supernatural origin, was a master of the *kantele*, the harp-like stringed instrument of Finland. Ilmarinen was a blacksmith who forged the "lids of heaven" when the world was created; Tuonela was the Kingdom of Death surrounded by swirling black waters in which the swan glided and sang; Lemminkaïnen, an adventurer and warrior who charmed women; Pohjola, a powerful land in the north; Kullervo, the tragic hero who is forced to be a slave from childhood. Sibelius's first major orchestral work, the *Kullervo* Symphony (1892), brought immediate fame.

sussurating strings that at times require a cupping of the ear to hear, and a recreation of the sounds of nature. He said, "I love the mysterious sounds of the fields and forests, waters and mountains." His melodies are folk-like but entirely original.

The source for his tone poems—with wonderful names like *Pohjola's Daughter, Tapiola, Swan of Tuonela, Lemminkaïnen and the Maidens, and Karelia Suite*—was the *Kalevala*, the Finnish national epic. The *Kalevala* is a compilation of old Finnish ballads, incantations, and lyrical songs that were part of the oral Finnish tradition assembled by Elias Lönnrot. It is the Finnish mythical equivalent of Olympus or Valhalla.

Sibelius is considered the conservative among the twentieth century composers; no jangling dissonance for him. And yet he eschewed Romanticism. To me, his music is cold, and yet the listener is entranced in his or her hypothermia. As you listen to more and more of it, you may become aware that the building blocks of theme, rhythm, and harmony are almost begrudgingly doled out in small packets to be savored, and then later combined for your recognition and delight.

Disc Two, Track 22—*Finlandia*

Now for a bit of history. Finland was annexed loosely to Sweden in the twelfth century and became fully incorporated into that country in 1634. As Sweden lost its power, Finland was officially ceded to Russia in 1809. Throughout, Finland retained a strong feeling of national identity.

In 1899, the last vestiges of this independence were swept away by the withdrawal of freedom of speech. In response, a series of public meetings was held, ostensibly to help the Press Pension Fund, but really to whip up Finnish patriotism. As a culmination of these events, a theatrical evening was held at the Swedish Theater. Sibelius contributed music to accompany six stirring episodes of Finnish history. The last of these was entitled "Finland Awakes." It was reworked slightly, separated from its companions, and given its present title *Finlandia*. The story that the Russians frowned on its being played has no documentation; it is suggested that Sibelius planted this tale. Whatever the truth, there is no doubt that the music became almost a national anthem without words, and that Sibelius thereafter was considered *the* Finnish composer.

The Russian defeat by the Japanese in 1905, World War I, and the Russian Revolution led to Finnish independence in 1917. When Finland refused to cede some disputed territory in 1939, the Russians invaded and Finland capitulated after a brief, but valiant, war in 1940. Fighting continued, however, and was finally stopped in 1944, with the territorial lines drawn as of 1940. The Finns paid huge reparations. Despite this, the country has prospered. A recent newspaper article lists Finland as the most expensive country in the world in which to travel.

While *Finlandia* is no match for the *Marseillaise,* it is easy to understand why the Russians didn't want it played while they were subjugating Finland just before the turn of the century. It is full of throbbing tunes and thundering brass. You will like it immediately.

The swelling chords in the introduction are unequaled. Tension is released by an innocuous interlude with an unmemorable melody. Force returns gradually until the really patriotic fervor arrives with the timpani and brass having a field day. The tremendous tension is released momentarily by a pleasant tune suggesting the countryside. This gradually swells until the mighty chords return. From then on, Sibelius demonstrates all he can do with the full orchestra, which is quite a lot.

At your leisure, go back and review the "March to the Gallows" from the *Symphonie fantastique*. I don't think Sibelius has much to teach Berlioz. Would *Finlandia* have benefited from the use of the ophicleides?

Disc Two, Track 23—Symphony No. 2 in D, Op. 43

Your sample in this section is a snippet from the first movement of the Second Symphony, the most popular of Sibelius's symphonies. I suspect you will find it as complex as I do. Trying to fathom what a composer is saying is the challenge of music. Sometimes the composer makes it easy by giving you a story, but more often it is undistilled feeling that doesn't require language as an intermediary.

I believe Sibelius has taken diverse motifs from his beloved *Kalevala* and created a structure to exhibit them quite like a building has an architectural façade. To continue with the analogy, the remaining movements serve to fill in the interior details of the building.

The sussurating chords and melody of the first minute are happy, carefree, and seem to represent a peasant dance. The second theme possesses a brooding and majestic quality foretelling trouble ahead, heralded by the sounds of running feet with a veritable catastrophe looming. A breath of the first melody, with its unforgettable sussuration, indicates that the peasants sense the problem. They are lulled into complacency, until the unease returns and the evil force (possibly a storm) is upon them. This builds slowly and ends with less fury than expected. Happiness returns but, unexpectedly, the problem makes another brief appearance until tranquillity is once again restored, and the initial lighthearted dance resumes.

Study the music in detail and carry out your own analysis. You will find it pleasurable. You will have listened as never before which, after all, is what you are trying to accomplish. I wondered, as I went through the analysis, whether the inspiration for the unusual rhythm of the initial chords was the chattering of Sibelius's teeth during a Finnish winter!

Every decade or so the critics shift Sibelius in the rating spectrum of composers, sometimes for the better and often for the worse. Lovely pieces of his popular music are often decried, or ignored, by the musicologists. Explore some of them, particularly *Valse Triste* and *Valse Lyrique.*

CHAPTER THIRTY

Vaughan Williams, Ralph
(1872–1958)

"Wagner used to read the libretti of his operas to
his friends; I am glad I was not there."

disc two
tracks 24–25

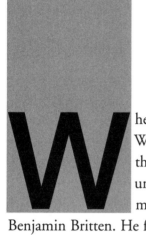hen you visit a music store for the music of Ralph Vaughan Williams, look him up under "V" and not the "W," even though the name is not hyphenated and logic suggests otherwise. He is unarguably the dominant composer in the renaissance of British musical life that began with Edward Elgar and continued with Benjamin Britten. He founded the nationalist movement in English music, breaking ties with continental European music that for several hundred years, through Handel and Mendelssohn, had made Britain a virtual satrapy of Germany.

Ralph Vaughan Williams (pronounced "Rafe") was the son of a well-to-do clergyman descended from the Wedgwoods (pottery) and Darwins (natural selection). He had a conventional upper-class education at Trinity College, Cambridge, and the Royal College of Music in London. Following this, he went to the continent and studied with Max Bruch. Early on, he worked as a church organist, but then devoted his life to composition. He composed that seemingly magic number of nine symphonies, and died soon after completing the ninth, upholding the tradition of Beethoven and Schubert, but at eighty-seven years of age. Like Bruckner and Mahler, Vaughan Williams is considered one of the world's great symphonists. The Second (the "London") and the Fourth symphonies are worth your purchasing immediately. He also wrote a great deal of nonsymphonic instrumental and choral music. These include concertos not only for piano and violin but also for oboe, tuba and—wonder of all wonders—a romance for the harmonica. I have not heard either the tuba concerto or the harmonica, but plan to get them for sheer novelty and, considering the source, for some very fine music as well.

In 1906, Vaughan Williams edited the *English Hymnala*, a new hymnbook. Because he felt he was getting "stodgy," for three months in 1908 he studied with Ravel, whose influence can be seen in his works. His *A Sea Symphony* was composed in 1910, and *A London Symphony* in 1914; I recommend both for your purchase. A measure of the man is that he enlisted in the army in 1914, even though he was forty-two years old, and spent most of the next four years in France. In 1919, he joined the staff of the Royal College of Music, and two years later became the conductor of the Bach Choir. Among his best-known nonsymphonic works are your two selections, along with the *Lark Ascending* for Violin and Orchestra (1914) and *Flos Campi* (1925) a suite for viola, small chorus, and small orchestra. For the opening of the New York World's Fair of 1939, he composed *Five Variants of "Dives and Lazarus."* (This Lazarus is not the one raised from the dead by Jesus. The Lazarus here figures in the parable about the rich man and the poor man (Luke 16:20–25). "Dives" is Latin for "rich man." I do not know what impelled Vaughan Williams to pick this for the opening of a World's Fair, but I suspect that it was the beauty of the song, and had nothing to do with the story.) Occasionally he succumbed to the modern fad for dissonance, but critics use words and phrases such as "noble in tone," "melodic but reserved," "strong," and "honest" to describe his work.

Disc Two, Track 25—*Fantasia on a Theme by Thomas Tallis*

The *Fantasia on a Theme by Thomas Tallis* is his best-known work. Your disc contains a portion from its first half. As mentioned in the chapter on Chopin, a fantasy is a musical work without a predefined form.

Thomas Tallis (1505–1585) was an English composer and organist. He was in the royal service most of his life. Queen Mary was a great support to him. A good many of his works were in Latin. On the accession of Elizabeth I, his music remained in Latin but became more restrained. He made the reference books on the basis of his own accomplishments, but one wonders if he would have remained in them had Vaughan Williams not resurrected one of the themes originally contributed by Tallis to Archbishop Parker's Metrical Psalter of 1576.

The theme, combined with the striking orchestration for string instruments only, is haunting and grand. Turn up the volume on this one; there are very quiet passages that you will otherwise completely miss. Toward the end of your sample, there is a cello passage that demonstrates the beauty of that instrument as a solo performer of unmatched emotion.

The entire work should be in your collection. Inasmuch as it is a short work, spend a few minutes with OPUS to find what other pieces you can get as dividends. We shall be exposed to the folk song aspect of Vaughan Williams in the next selection.

Recommended Listening
Fantasia on Greensleeves

The earliest reference to *Greensleeves* occurs in the Registers of the Stationers' Company in 1580, where it was called "a new Northern Dittye." At times the tune has been diverted to religious accompaniments. In *The Merry Wives of Windsor*, Shakespeare refers to Falstaff's disparity between words and deeds with "they do no more adhere and keep pace together, than the Hundredth Psalm to the tune of Green Sleeves!" In the same play, Falstaff says, "Let the skye raine potatoes; let it thunder to the tune of Green Sleeves."

Gustav Holst (1874–1934), a lifelong friend of Vaughan Williams, uses it in the finale of the *St. Paul's Suite*, as does Vaughan Williams again in his opera *Sir John in Love*.

Like Smetana and Janaček in Czechoslovakia, Bartok in Hungary, and Sibelius in Finland, Ralph Vaughan Williams collected the folk songs of his country and incorporated them into his compositions. He did not often use the actual melodies themselves, as he did with *Greensleeves* in 1934, but developed a uniquely English idiom of his own based on their modes, harmonies, rhythms, and colorations. His explorations were largely based on music of the Tudor times. The results are distinctive. For a French equivalent, get the *Songs of the Auvergne*, which were collected and arranged by Joseph Canteloube (1879–1957). You will find them as French as the chanteuse Edith Piaf belting out her wonderful and idiosyncratic nightclub songs.

When you listen, pay heed to the harp and flute introduction that sets the mood for the first playing of this well-known theme. I find the variations between its completion and the start of *Greensleeves'* final presentation intricate and particularly beautiful.

CHAPTER THIRTY-ONE

Schoenberg, Arnold (1874–1951)

"I am quite conscious of the fact that a full understanding
of my music cannot be expected before some decades…
I have personally renounced my early success,
and I know that—success or not—it is my historic duty
to write what my destiny orders me to write."

disc two
tracks 26–28

A little background is required before tackling Schoenberg because he literally turned Western music on its ear. Asian music sounds strange to us because its basic ingredients are entirely out of keeping with what our ears are accustomed to hearing. Western music, as we have been listening to it, has been based on a scale of eight notes—*do, re, me, fa, so, la, te, do* (these syllables are used in a method of teaching scales and intervals called *solmisation*)—known as the *diatonic scale* which, as far as we know, was first used in ancient Greece. Between these eight notes lie gaps, some greater than others. They are sometimes a whole tone or a half tone apart. These distances are measurable and are based on frequency of vibrations; your singing teacher might have used a tuning fork to let you hear the note at which to begin. When the distance between notes is a whole tone, there is room for a half tone in between. Thus the *do* we sing is called the note of C. (The use of "note" and "tone" may cause confusion. *Note* refers to musical *notation* while *tone* refers to *pitch*.) If we choose to go only a halfnote higher, and on the piano keyboard striking a black key carries this out, that note is called C-sharp (C#). If we started at *re* and go down a halfnote, the same black key would be struck, but now the note is called D-flat (D♭). From *do* to *do* there are twelve halfnote intervals. A scale built on these halfnotes is called a "twelve-tone" or "chromatic" scale. The term "twelve-tone," however, refers to a basic arrangement of the pitches (a "row") for a composition written in twelve-tone technique. The "row" uses all twelve tones, but never in absolute chromatic sequence. More of this and how Schoenberg figures in comes later.

A science called harmony has developed around these eight notes of the diatonic scale. Some sets of these notes sound fine when played simultaneously or sequentially. This is a consonant combination. If the set of notes played is jarring to the ear, they are called dissonant. Beethoven began to explore the use of dissonance in his late string quartets. This is the reason he is said to have anticipated modern music. To go a bit further, if the first note is *do,* it simply *feels* correct to end the piece on *do.* There are books of rules about combinations of notes and how they go together, and how to switch from a key that starts on one note, goes to ("modulates" is the jargon word) a key based on another note and come back again. When these rules are adhered to, the music is called *tonal*.

When you sing "Old MacDonald Had A Farm," you sing in the key of C Major. We can sing it in any of the other major keys—e.g., C, D, E, F, G, A, or B—plus a halfnote up or down when there is one. There is instinctive comfort from starting and ending the song on the same note because we are used to this Western scale of music. In Asia, people have grown up with other scales, so ours sounds peculiar to them, as their music does to us. One of the oddities of our time is how the Japanese have so embraced Western music. This is partially explained by the great preponderance of young people in their audiences.

When a composer ignores these rules and starts where he or she wants and ends somewhere else, the music is called *atonal* (music not based on a particular tonality). Wagner, in *Tristan und Isolde,* began to experiment with wandering tonalities. As we shall see, in the course of Schoenberg's musical development, he abandoned tonality for atonality, and deserves either the kudos or derision associated with such a major change, depending upon whether the specific piece of music was liked or disliked.

Arnold Franz Walter Schoenberg (1874–1951) is one of those seminal figures whose impact upon a discipline is so dramatic that it is recognizably changed by his or her influence. Einstein was such a force in physics; Newton's calculus produced a differentiation in mathematics, just as the Impressionists brought new light into pictures.

Schoenberg's parents moved to Vienna from what was then a town in Hungary, in 1918 became a part of Czechoslovakia, and is now esconced in Slovakia. They were Orthodox Jews, and not very musical; still, Arnold began to play the violin at the age of eight and soon began composing. As a teenager, he played in a musical ensemble, but there was no money to be had for musical training or attending concerts.

He eventually joined an amateur orchestra conducted by Alexander von Zemlinsky, who had attended the Vienna Conservatory. Schoenberg received his only formal musical instruction from Zemlinsky. The two became close friends, and in 1901, Arnold married Alexander's sister.

Alexander von Zemlinsky (1871–1942) became one of the leading conductors of Vienna. His best-known composition is the *Lyrical Symphony* which is a song symphony very reminiscent of **Mahler's** *Das Lied von der Erde*. He also has written some quite wonderful lieder.

Schoenberg's earliest published composition, *Verklärte Nacht* (*Transfigured Night*), was written in 1899, and was originally scored for a string sextet. (The version on your disc was made for string orchestra in 1917 and later revised in 1947.) Newly married in 1901, he moved to Berlin to conduct a cabaret orchestra. Here, he began work on his magnum opus, *Gurreleider,* a gigantic work for five solo voices, a narrator, three male choruses, and a large (eight-part) mixed chorus and orchestra. *Gurrelieder* was not played until 1913. Although not an opera, it has the grand sweep of Wagner's *Ring.* In Berlin, he met Richard Strauss, who was impressed enough by the parts of the *Gurrelieder* he heard to obtain for Arnold a scholarship and teaching position at a conservatory in Berlin. A year later, Schoenberg moved back to Vienna, where he was championed by none other than Gustav Mahler.

With the rise of the Nazis in 1933, Schoenberg lost his teaching post in Berlin, at about the same time he formally returned to Judaism (he had converted to Protestantism in his youth). Musically, he had earlier indicated this transition by writing the opera *Moses und Aron.* He immigrated to the United States and secured a teaching post at the University of California in Los Angeles, where he lived out the rest of his life. In this last period, his musical compositions returned to basic tonality.

Schoenberg's disciples, Alban Berg (1885–1935) and Anton Webern (1883–1945), are being left for your discovery. Neither of them is likely to capture you on first hearing, but the acquired taste that comes with effort will pay dividends. Berg's Violin Concerto is considered to be great. Webern wrote a series of miniatures lasting only a few minutes per piece with his entire life's output of music lasting only about four hours. Start with his song cycles, Op. No. 3 and No. 4, and then try *Six Pieces for Orchestra.*

You are likely to run across the term "Second Viennese School," which means Schoenberg, Berg, and Webern. The "First Viennese School" consisted of Haydn, Mozart, Beethoven, and Schubert. Terms like these are a delight when you know them, but may otherwise irritate! Schoenberg ceaselessly strove to explore new musical boundaries in his compositions. Perhaps the best way to impart this to you is to stop the biographical narrative, and have you listen to four short examples that illustrate his musical evolution.

Disc Two, Track *27—Verklärte Nacht* (*Transfigured Night*), Op. 4

To begin, listen to the opening minutes of the fourth section of *Verklärte Nacht* (1899). It is a tone poem that takes place on a winter night with two lovers walking in the woods. She confesses to him that the baby she is carrying was conceived before they met. He says that he doesn't care, and that they will make the child their own—all this as the moon comes up to light the forest. As you will hear, this music is fully rounded and wonderfully orchestrated for string orchestra in the best romantic tradition. It is consonant, and not jarring, because the standard rules of harmony are fully obeyed.

Recommended Listening
Five Pieces for Orchestra, Op. 16

Five Pieces for Orchestra was written in 1909. By this time, Schoenberg had thrown out the classic harmonic rules. He had discarded the key, chords, and explicitly the need for formal modulation from one place to another. He termed this "emancipation of the dissonance." You will find as a truism in "modern" music that as dissonance becomes increasingly important, rhythmic variation and pauses take on a new role of filling in between musical passages—more epigrammatically put as "it's the notes between the notes." You've lost your comfort level to a degree, but there is a new substance to the music that you might even like. Dissonant music requires much greater concentration than consonant.

The right and left sides of the brain have quite different functions, one side being the dominant side that controls speech. Neurophysiologists have begun to study the brain's reaction to music. These studies have made use of sophisticated brain scan technology that is able to show the area of the brain that is being stimulated at a particular time. Quite convincingly on these scans, tonal music lights up one side of the brain and atonal music the other.

Disc Two, Track 28—*Pierrot lunaire*, Op. 21

Pierrot lunaire (Moonstruck Pierre) (1912) represents another new frontier that Schoenberg grappled with—the actual melding of speech with pitch notation. He called this *Sprechgesang*. As you listen, you will hear a new entity in which the instruments (piano, flute and piccolo, clarinet and bass clarinet, violin and viola, and cello—five performers doubling on related instruments, two of them string) are speaking, along with the vocalist who, in turn, is half-singing and half-speaking. Such an effect is best accomplished in non-tonal music. The result is a completely new experience for the listener which, relish it or not, is unusual in this jaded world. For a greater appreciation of this style, I suggest that you get the entire work. The poet Albert Giraud wrote the text at the request of an actress who wanted to recite the poems of the same title. In the original performance, the five instrumentalists (including Schoenberg) were hidden behind a white sheet with the actress in front of it, half-singing and half-speaking (*sprechstimme*) her lines.

Babbitt, Milton (b. 1916) became the American leader of serial music (twelve-tone). Try listening to his *Relata II*, and I say, "try" advisedly. He was on the Princeton faculty and not dependent on public tastes. He wrote a 1958 article for *High Fidelity* magazine entitled "Who Cares If You Listen?"

Recommended Listening
Concerto for Piano, Op. 42

Following the completion of *Pierrot lunaire,* Schoenberg directed his innovative genius toward imposing order to atonality. He developed what is known as "serial music" or "serialism."

Schoenberg took the twelve-tone scale (chromatic scale) and established a series of rules for its use. (For those of you who like words, those compositions that use the twelve tones are referred to as dodecaphonic.) He set up rows of notes, consisting of the twelve notes of the chromatic scale in a chosen order, for each composition, known as a row. This could be played straightforward, inverted, backward, or inverted backward, or transposed to any of the other pitches. A total of forty-eight different results thereby are produced from a single row. Many other commutations and permutations were worked out. If you think about it, the mechanisms are quite analogous to the rules set up by earlier composers in writing fugues, in which the interaction of voices adhered to definite rules. Serial music is neither mathematical nor cerebral. It is simply Eastern based upon a set of rules that are foreign to our experience, just as the Asian is different from the Western.

The Concerto for Piano is an example of serial music. Obviously, listening to it once will only scratch the surface, akin to cuddling with your new pet, a porcupine.

CHAPTER THIRTY-TWO

Ives, Charles (1874–1954)

"Beauty in music is too often confused with something
that lets the ears lie back in an easy chair.
Many sounds that we are used to do not bother us,
and for that reason, we are inclined to call them beautiful."

disc two
tracks 29–30

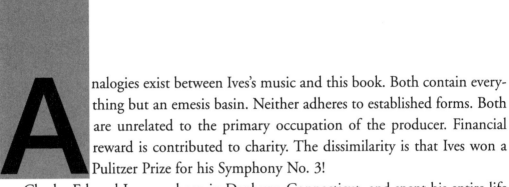

Analogies exist between Ives's music and this book. Both contain everything but an emesis basin. Neither adheres to established forms. Both are unrelated to the primary occupation of the producer. Financial reward is contributed to charity. The dissimilarity is that Ives won a Pulitzer Prize for his Symphony No. 3!

Charles Edward Ives was born in Danbury, Connecticut, and spent his entire life in its vicinity. The Ives were a respected commercial family, but Charles's father, George, taught music and directed bands. George urged his son to be a concert pianist, but painfully shy Charles preferred the anonymity of the organ, playing it with enough brilliance to become a professional church organist while still in his teens. In addition to teaching him the basic canons of musical technique, the father passed on to the son his love of musical experimentation. For example, Charlie took up the drum and practiced it on the piano keyboard with his fists; Eureka! the invention of the "tone cluster," simply a series of consecutive notes struck simultaneously. The first use of this hi-tech virtuosity is credited to Henry Cowell (1897–1965) in his *The Tides of Manaunaun* (1912). As a teenager, Charlie wrote the feisty *Variations on America* for the organ. You will enjoy its orchestral form arranged by William Schuman.

Ives matriculated to Yale (1894–1898) with a major in music. He was taught to think in symphonic terms, but had more fun writing fraternity shows and popular songs for local orchestras. He played intramural sports and held down the most prestigious church organ post in New Haven. In this milieu, he began experimenting with weaving popular songs into classical musical forms. This combination became his lifelong avocation. He was a poor student, and abandoned his thoughts of a musical career, most probably because of the life he saw his father leading with its lack of financial reward. He is quoted as saying, "Father felt that a man could keep his music interest stronger, cleaner, bigger, and freer if he didn't try to make a living out of it."

After graduation, he found a five-dollar-a-week clerk's job in an insurance firm in New York City. In the end, he parlayed this early experience into the formation of one of the largest insurance agencies in the country. His name is still known and respected in the insurance industry for pioneering estate planning. This was his full-time occupation for the rest of his life, and he never regretted it. He said, "My work in music helped my business, and my work in business helped my music." Sibelius, on the other hand, rarely entertained musicians. "They talk of nothing but money and jobs. Give me a businessman every time," he said. "They really *are* interested in music and art."

Ives devoted time to musical composition on free nights and weekends and on the commuter train to and from Danbury. There was simply no opportunity in this frenetically busy life to cross-fertilize ideas and experiences with the classical music *mise-en-scene* of his day. Keep in mind that this was before radio and records could convert the living room into a concert hall. His compositional output was prodigious, but he lacked time and discipline for organizing it and pushing for its performance.

Only in the mid-eighteenth century did the concert hall become a significant force in music. Europe's first concert hall, built in 1748, not surprisingly, was in a university town, Oxford. Still in use, the Holywell Music Room seats about 150 people. Prior to this, aristocratic patronage, the church, and the opera house were the main sources of income for the musician and composer.

Ives wrote a great many songs and much orchestral music that nobody would champion. He stopped playing the organ in churches in 1902, and essentially went underground for the next twenty years. He did have some compositions published privately, and slowly he came to be appreciated. Leonard Bernstein, always interested in "discovering" new music, conducted the premiere of Ives's Second Symphony in 1951, just as he had resurrected Mahler. Ives funneled all the income derived from his music to needy musicians and other worthy musical causes. Truly, he never made a penny from it! The Second Symphony was composed in 1902; the Third Symphony was written in 1911, and not performed until 1945. The Fourth Symphony was finished in 1916, and was not performed until 1965. There is something to be said for financial independence.

His zeal for experimentation never left him; there were constant revisions of his output, sometimes years apart for a specific work, and constant mutations from one form to another. He would convert a song to an orchestral work and then change it into a piece for a combination of instruments never tried before. The first movement of Ives's *A Symphony: New England Holidays* on my recording, has printed just under its title, "Washington's Birthday": "Fred Spector, Jew's Harp." This is the only work in the orchestral literature that calls for this instrument. He would then combine three or four such works into a symphony. All this was notated in a scrawl that was either difficult to read or illegible. His manuscripts eventually came to rest in an archive at Yale. By that time his works had gained appreciation, and their organization no doubt required considerable intake of Valium and antacids on the part of the scholars entrusted to bring order to chaos.

His innovations included orchestral works that were distinctly "Ivesian" in feel, but containing within them a potpourri of popular songs and tidbits lifted from other composers, ranging from Beethoven to Wagner. When I say lifted, I mean taken and transformed in such a way that one, if astute, might recognize only a glimmer of the original source. A case in point are those famous four notes that begin Beethoven's Fifth Symphony. They are to be found in the third movement of Ives's Second Symphony (worth owning and not difficult) but now hushed and mysterious. There is said to be some Brahms in there as well. Ives was awarded the Pulitzer Prize in 1947 for the Third Symphony, thirty-six years after its completion. He never attended performances of his own works, and once said, "I'm the only one, with the exception of Mrs. Ives (and one or two others, perhaps) who likes any of my music."

Ives's most celebrated innovation is shown in *The Unanswered Question.* Three separate groups of instruments, with completely different textures and moving at different tempi, play simultaneously, though any interaction between them comes purely by chance (no lessons in counterpoint to be learned here.) This piece also demonstrates the difficulty in making a coherent catalog of Ives's works. The original version was composed in 1906. Sometime between 1930 and 1935, he completely revised it. Both versions are recorded and played in the concert halls under the same name.

Disc Two, Track 30—"The Fourth of July" from *A Symphony: New England Holidays*

This selection is from *A Symphony: New England Holidays,* a work in four movements: "Washington's Birthday," "Decoration Day" (now called "Memorial Day"), "The Fourth of July," and "Thanksgiving and Forefathers' Day."

Ours is "The Fourth of July." Its benign beginning is deceptive. Listen for "The Battle Hymn of the Republic" and "Columbia the Gem of the Ocean," first intoned by a bugle, but heard multiple times thereafter. I once heard a fragment of "Yankee Doodle" but haven't been able to find it since. Can you identify others? There is some dissonance, but listening will not be onerous, except for the two explosions.

With someone as innovative as Ives, a single example should whet your appetite and not turn you away. I debated about putting him in the book because of this, but he is just too important for you not to have at least an introduction. His life was unlike any of the other composers we have come across, and so is his music.

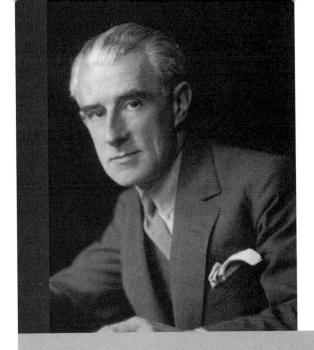

CHAPTER THIRTY-THREE

Ravel, Maurice (1875–1937)

"We should always remember that sensitiveness and emotion constitute the real content of a work of art."

disc two
tracks 31–32

**M**aurice Joseph Ravel was born in a French fishing village, Ciboure, near the Spanish frontier in the Basque region of France. His father was a Swiss engineer and his mother descended from a proud line of Basque inhabitants of this southwest corner of France. A fascination with all things Spanish was a lifelong influence, as you will see from titles such as *Alborada del gracioso* (1905) and *Rapsodie espagnole* (1907), which contains his famous "Habanera" and "Don Quixote à Dulcinée" (1934). *Pavane pour une infante défunte* (1899) translates to *A Dance for a Dead Princess;* "infante" being the term for a Spanish princess. Ravel had no such princess in mind when he composed the music; he simply gave it this title because the sound of it pleased his ear.

The Basque country is situated on both sides of the border (the Pyrenees Mountains) between Spain and France. The people in this region speak the Basque language in addition to either Spanish or French. The Basque language, most closely resembling Spanish, is the remnant of the language spoken before the region was Romanized. The region is politically turbulent because of an ongoing terrorist campaign conducted against the Spanish government by a Basque separatist movement. On the Spanish side, the so-called "Autonomous Basque Region" has a population of over two million people.

The family moved to Paris when Maurice was a child. He was the elder of two sons born to a father of singular charm and wide culture who recognized and nurtured Maurice's talent. He entered the Paris Conservatoire at the age of fourteen, and would remain in its classrooms for sixteen more years. A sure path to recognition in French music was the much-coveted Prix de Rome, awarded by the Académie des Beaux-Arts. You have heard the music of three winners already—Berlioz, Bizet, and Debussy.

Ravel entered this competition four times, though he failed to win. The first time he entered, he was already known for *Pavane pour une infante défunte*. By the last time, the scope of his talent was so widely recognized that a brouhaha resulted in the dismissal of the director of the Paris Conservatoire that conferred the award. A leading force behind this was the musicologist and novelist, Romaine Rolland, whose fictionalized biography of Beethoven, *Jean Christophe*, I have already highly recommended. He wrote to the Director of the Conservatoire: "I cannot understand why one should persist in keeping a school in Rome if it is to close its doors to those rare artists who have originality…to a man like Ravel." Another composer, Gabriel Fauré, a teacher and mentor of Ravel, replaced him. Ravel's disgust over the machinations of awarding the Prix de Rome remained with him into later life, when he twice refused the highest distinction that France can give, the Legion of Honor. Such a refusal was unheard of in 1920. Ravel's justification was a disdain for the state's right to judge its citizens. His friend and fellow composer, Eric Satie (1866–1925), quipped, "Ravel refuses the Légion d'Honneur but all his music accepts it."

In his student days, Ravel became a member of the "Apaches" who met in cafés and debated the merits of new works and new ideas long into the Parisian nights. A member later wrote of him, "Ravel shared our preference, weakness, or mania respectively for Chinese art, Mallarmé and Verlaine, Rimbaud, Cézanne, and Van Gogh, Rameau and Chopin, Whistler and Valéry, the Russians, and Debussy." Ravel spent his life in Paris, or at his villa living with his mother and his cats. Apparently, he went a bit overboard with the cats, allowing them to invade his worktable, speaking to them in cat language, playing with them ceaselessly, and filling letters to his friends with their details. Debussy also kept cats, but this commonality of interest was not enough to keep these men from the center of a heated Parisian controversy. Ravel, thirteen years younger, was accused of imitating Debussy's work.

Listen again to *Prelude à l'après-midi d'un Faune* and then to the next selection, *Pavane pour une infante défunte*. The melodies are different, but the styles are

Apache refers to the people of the Asthabascan Indians in New Mexico and Arizona. It came to be used for the street thugs infesting Paris. The George Orwell quote, "He wore side whiskers, which are the mark of an apache or an intellectual," reminds one of how often the type of hairdo is identified with social movements. Think of the "hippies" of yesterday and the "skinheads" of today. It is interesting how the definition of words can evolve. There is a new computer language named Apache, amusingly so because as it matured, so many program patches were added to it.

similar. The names and subjects of compositions buttress the dispute. If one is of a suspicious nature, Ravel's *Rapsodie espagnole* can't help but call to mind Debussy's *Ibéria*. Further, *Miroirs* and *Images*, two collections of piano pieces, respectively one by the older and the other by the younger, and *Jeux d'eau* and *Reflets dans l'eau* are two more in the same respective order of composition. Debussy is said to have felt that Ravel's String Quartet in F was awfully close to his own, but in the end told him not to change a note. There are many discs that pair the two quartets. See what you think of this "twofer." To me, they are quite different.

In the reverse direction, there are those who say Ravel's *Gaspard de la nuit*, a pathfinding piano work, had a clear influence on Debussy. So what? I would rather think of Ravel as a successor to Debussy rather than an imitator. And so history has judged him. Knowing about the dispute should sharpen your perceptions when listening to either of their works. Do not forget that it was Ravel, a true master of the orchestra, who converted Musorgsky's *Pictures from an Exhibition* from the piano to one of the staples of the symphonic repertoire, but this is not meant to imply that Debussy was the lesser of the two—not so!

Ravel avoided teaching, but gave friendly advice to a few, including Ralph Vaughan Williams. He was said to be a delightful personal companion, full of practical jokes, but preferred to stay at home with his mother and the cats. In 1928, when he was fifty-three years old, he had a wildly successful concert tour in the United States. He became enamored with jazz, identifying it as one of the most important developments in the music of the twentieth century. George Gershwin became a friend. These new influences are readily heard in the two piano concertos and the violin sonata he composed upon his return to France. The tempo direction of the Violin Sonata's second movement is "Blues: moderato."

I decided to look into the medical history concerning Ravel's mental deterioration and death. In some of the biographic accounts, much is made of a head injury incurred in a taxi accident in 1932. This suggested a blood clot between the brain and the skull (subdural hematoma) that should have been amenable to treatment. In actuality, in 1927 when he was forty-seven, signs of cerebral dysfunction began to appear. He would lose his place at the piano while performing, his precise handwriting became sloppy, and he would make obvious mistakes in erasure. Later, he would spend hours playing with mechanical toys, an entirely uncharacteristic pastime. He then suffered from an aphasia that kept him from committing his musical ideas to written form. Still later, he couldn't sign his name. He finally consented to a neurosurgical operation. It was performed on December 17, 1937, and he died eleven days later. An autopsy was not performed. On the basis of the surgical findings, and in the light of present knowledge, the diagnosis of Alzheimer's Disease is highly probable. (R. A. Henson, *British Medical Journal*, Volume 296, 1585–1588, June 4, 1988.)

Disc Two, Track 32—*Pavane pour une infante défunte* (Pavane for a Dead Princess)

Fauré gave Ravel a healthy dose of classicism in his education, and his direct influence is evident in the *Pavane pour une infante défunte*. The *Pavane* did for Ravel what winning the Prix de Rome might have done. The salons and drawing rooms of Paris lionized him, and the tune would have made number one had the Hit Parade existed.

It was originally written for the piano, and orchestrated years later. You have a sample from the orchestral version. While Ravel could pump up the decibels at times, this *pavane* is vintage Ravel. His compositions are most often like a large but flawless, perfectly cut diamond that glows so brilliantly from its shimmering facets that the woman wearing it can't possibly be accused of bad taste because of its size. Listen, see if you agree, and then go on to the *Boléro*.

> The **pavan** is a sixteenth and seventeenth century dance thought to have originated in Italy and named after the town of Padua. It is generally coupled with a faster dance, at times with thematic links. In Italy the accompanying dance was a saltarello, in France and in England a galliard.

Recommended Listening
Boléro

Undoubtedly his best-known work and the one that rocketed him to world acclaim is the *Boléro* (1928) composed for a solo dancer, Ida Rubinstein. This is a truly extraordinary work in both form and hypnotic power. Its simple theme is repeated over and over again, with each repetition just perceptibly more forceful than the last. In effect, the whole piece is a single crescendo. The variations in orchestration featuring solo instruments make the repetition palatable. Go back and listen to that 131-bar introduction to Wagner's *Das Rheingold*. Wagner's innovation in the "Prelude" of *Das Rheingold* was to make a crescendo of one note; Ravel did the same with a single theme and must have been aware of the similarity of approach.

I have three renditions of the *Boléro* in my compact disc collection. Two last fourteen-and-a-half minutes, one within two seconds of the other. The third goes on for over sixteen minutes. There is a performance conducted by Daniel Barenboim that lingers for seventeen-and-a-half minutes. A classic story concerns a 1929 performance in New York by Arturo Toscanini that came in at twelve minutes and seventeen seconds. Ravel angrily said to the great maestro, "Too fast, Signor, much too fast!" Toscanini, never one to have his opinions challenged, retorted, "You know nothing about your music!"

The basic structure is a single entity repeated over and over again with gradually increasing volume. When you come to the last part, an aural shock is felt because of the suddenly increased volume. At the very end, listen for the jazz touch.

Ravel is not considered an important figure in the evolution of the music of the twentieth century, yet his musical output remains one of the most beloved. Musicologists largely agree that the *Daphne and Chloé Suite* is his greatest single accomplishment. *Ma mère l'oye (Mother Goose Suite)* is worth owning. I am particularly fond of its third section where the Chinese influence comes to the fore.

Mother Goose first appeared in Charles Perrault's *Mother Goose Tales* (1697), a group of folk stories. She is illustrated as an old woman telling tales by firelight to children. This is a long way from Perrault's story, *Barbebleue,* in which Bluebeard kills his wives for looking into a forbidden room where the corpses of other disobedient wives are kept.

CHAPTER THIRTY-FOUR

Orff, Carl (1895–1982)

"Elementary music is never music alone,
it is connected with movement, dance, and language."

disc two
tracks 33–34

Orff was a German composer who had a great interest in teaching music to children. The most elemental aspect of music is rhythm; thus, as some people cannot talk without hand and arm movement, you will find it difficult to enjoy this music sitting still. This is the first cantata we have heard, which simply means a not-long piece of music composed for voices and orchestra, not necessarily on a religious theme. The cantata is a first and shorter cousin of the oratorio, which is almost always based on a theme of biblical origin. The oratorio has no costumes or action accompanying it, although the cantata may. Orff composed this music as a theatrical work, believing that the salvation of German music was to be found in a synthesis of dance, voice, costume, and action. Only in this way could the experience be complete.

Carmina burana gained extraordinary popularity, and in no small measure accounted for my generation's surge of interest in classical music, which appears to be waning and is the main impetus for the writing of this book. While *Carmina burana* certainly succeeded, there was a twenty-year hiatus from composition to wide popularity, which may well have been due in part to World War II, for the work was considered a German showpiece of what music should be in the Third Reich. For whatever reason, it had special appeal to the elemental barbarism inherent in the Nazi psyche. But no matter its genesis, no apology is necessary for its being appreciated as pure music outside of the theater. Sadly, after its highly successful premiere, Orff withdrew all his earlier works from circulation, and spent the remainder of his life composing works for the stage using a combination of the *Carmina burana* style with Greek theater trappings.

Disc Two, Track 34—*Carmina burana*

Without seeing the biographical dates, you might justifiably think this music predates that which we have heard before. Indeed, the composer does use themes from thirteenth century Latin, German, and French songs, but the year of composition is 1936. On stage, *Carmina burana* (*Song of Beuren*) is a collection of songs for runaway monks and wandering students doing what comes naturally!

Beuren gets its name from poems emananting from a thirteenth century manuscript that came from the Benedictine Abby of Benedict-beuren, situated a short distance from Munich. *Carmina burana* is based on these poems.

The entire piece lasts approximately an hour, while your sample lasts only minutes. The drumbeat and loud choral introduction are contained within twenty-five seconds, but in this short time you immediately know you are in for a momentous experience. The male chorus sings quietly, but with a relentlessly captivating beat. Suddenly, without change in the ruthless rhythm, the decibels get turned up to the point where you may have to turn the volume down as the full and mighty chorus sings out with tremendous force. Even though the melody is very simple, the dominant power is clearly the barbaric and primeval beat. The volume decreases for a while, but gradually becomes louder and ends with a full crescendo. This sequence is repeated again, and our unhappily short sample is over, but never to be forgotten.

You absolutely must listen to the entire work! Only then will you understand how a piece of classical music eclipsed the popular songs of its day. To me, the rhythms—probably a thousand years old—anticipated the rock music of today.

Perhaps Orff's most enduring legacy is the system he devised for teaching music to children. As you might predict, it uses much in the way of percussion instruments and body motion.

His music distills the essence of Bavaria. I commend you to listen to *Der Mond*, a sort of folk opera that is pleasant listening as compared to the much rawer and more brutal treatment given to the Greek myths in *Oedipus der Tyrann* and *Antigonae*.

CHAPTER THIRTY-FIVE

Bartók, Béla (1881–1945)

"I do not reject any influence whether its source be
Slovak, Rumanian, Arab, or some other;
provided this source be pure, fresh, and healthy."

disc two
tracks 35–36

Béla Bartók was the greatest composer produced by Hungary, although some may dispute this since Franz Liszt was Hungarian as well. He was intensely taken with his country's folk music, and collected and published some two thousand Hungarian and Romanian folk tunes. (He also had a reverence for Bach and Beethoven.) Bartók synthesized these elements in his compositions, resulting in a homogeneous style quite distinctly his own: part Classical, part Romantic, part Modern, and often featuring unfamiliar scales and rhythms, or none at all. To quote Bartók: "The excesses of the Romantic began to be unbearable to many," and, "It may sound odd, but I do not hesitate to say that the simpler the melody, the more complex and strange may be the harmonization and accompaniments that go well with it." In my opinion, the impact of the dissonance increases the pleasure in the consonance.

He wrote sonatas for violin and piano, string quartets, piano concertos, one opera, two major ballets, and a six-volume set of piano pieces provocatively titled, *Mikrokosmos* —but no symphonies. The present selection is his only concerto for orchestra. I had a difficult time deciding whether to give you a sample from this, or from what some consider his finest orchestral work, *Music for Strings, Percussion and Celesta*. I think I would have chosen the latter if I had the luxury of providing you with complete works on the accompanying discs.

Although he was born in the Hungary of his time, his actual birthplace is now in Romania. When he realized that music would be his future, he turned down a scholarship in Vienna to study in Budapest. This was a decisive moment for him because it was in Budapest that he heard the first true folk songs, as opposed to the gypsy melodies quoted by Liszt and Brahms. His productivity flourished in this environment. He achieved worldwide fame, but refused to have his works published in Nazi Germany. In 1940, he fled Europe for the United States.

Budapest is one of the world's most beautiful and striking cities. It is really two cities, Buda and Pest with the Danube in between. Pest is on the low bank facing Buda that is high up, with a medieval castle and many imposing buildings. I had the honor of speaking there at an institute bearing the name of Ignaz Phillip Semmelweis (1818–1865), see chapter 1.

In the midst of war and the turmoil of the time, Bartók was hardly recognized in the States, and almost became destitute. He wrote a friend in 1942: "My career as a composer is as much as finished." Serge Koussevitzky, a famous conductor, commissioned a work for one thousand dollars ($11,070 in the year 2002). Little did Koussevitzky or Bartók, for that matter, have an inkling of the success and renewal of recognition that the Concerto for Orchestra would bring to Bartók when it premiered two years later. Koussevitzky then took up the cudgel for Bartók by inviting Yehudi Menuhin, a truly great violinist of the day, to give the Boston premier performance of Bartók's Violin Concerto No. 2 in December 1945. Sadly, Bartók did not live to attend that concert.

Disc Two, Track 36—Concerto for Orchestra

Bartók's Concerto for Orchestra was first performed in 1944. In this work, I hear Times Square at evening rush hour with its din of traffic, teenagers cavorting, a Salvation Army contingent rattling the collection plate, and the tramp of a policeman. This image is unlike the descriptive, literal picture evoked by Smetana's tone poem, *The Moldau,* but instead, something arising from the subconscious that a psychoanalyst might be proud to dredge up. Bartók's music has a good deal of dissonance in it which makes it more difficult to listen to than that of many of the composers we've heard but, as the pushy waiter says, "Give it a try, you'll like it." It will become an acquired taste. Repetition does wonders for those synapses in the brain.

Rather than try to guide you directly through this aural thicket, some generalizations may help pave the way. Modern music is difficult, and requires more of an effort on the listener's part than much of what we have explored so far. Say goodbye to those long and lovely expanses of beautiful melody. Bartók's music, however, is much easier to take in than most of the so-called "moderns." Modern music is typified, in my mind, by rhythm assuming a greater role than melody. The sense of a "time center"—beginning, middle, and end—is often abandoned. The "tonal center," which gives the listener a sense of going back to the familiar, has largely been thrown out. You may be thinking, "Why bother to put yourself through this?" The answer is that Modern music can touch deep psychological areas that are inaccessible without it, just as a psychoanalyst probes more deeply than a conventional psychiatrist. Personally, I don't crave music that can evoke the primal scream, or that will nurture my soul when going a half-mile an hour in a bad traffic jam. On the other hand, I've never felt the need for calculus in my day-to-day existence, and yet I'm glad I was exposed to it.

Now to the piece at hand. When you listen to the complete piece, it begins with ten seconds of an innocuous tattoo on the drum before proceeding into several short but pleasant melodies lasting for about a minute, just long enough to perhaps make you wonder why all that prelude in the last paragraph. Then the melody is overpowered by a spiky beat that goes on and on with tantalizing fragments of unrelated melody peeking through. Pay particular attention at two minutes when a series of honking horns—reminiscent of a traffic jam—take over. These are known as "ostinatos" (an incessant repetition of a rhythmic figure or motif) and are often employed in modern music, although you've heard them used before. Soon after, a not unpleasant dirge emerges in a minor dissonant key. A minute later, we are rewarded by the reappearance of the respectable opening theme, only to have it lost in a host of strange rhythms suitable for an aborigine tribal dance, and ending in a few lone drum beats as we heard at the start. Repeat your listening enough times to gain familiarity; I think you may end up liking it.

CHAPTER THIRTY SIX

Stravinsky, Igor (1882–1971)

"Music to me is a power which justifies things."

disc two
tracks 37–38

That "classic" and "modern" are two irreconcilable styles of music is an entirely misleading idea. Its genesis is clearly rooted in the comfort that one feels listening to a Beethoven symphony as contrasted with the dis comfort elicited by a Schoenberg twelve-tone composition. Creative artists are a restless breed, not content to replicate their antecedents. The classic landscape painters had their day until the impressionists came along. These, of course, were roundly damned by the critics of their day who refused to exhibit their paintings in the official salons. In approaching "the new" in any field, what must be kept in mind is that a steep learning curve must be climbed to reach understanding and eventual enjoyment. This is not to say, by any means, that on the way you will not, or should not, deny the new form. Furthermore, the same artist may originate different styles, ones you like and ones you don't. Keep these thoughts in mind as you begin your exploration of modern music. Some composers are easy and some are difficult, but you will never know unless you listen.

Igor Fyodorovich Stravinsky (1882–1971) is considered by many to be the foremost composer of the twentieth century. When *The Rite of Spring* had its premiere in Paris at the Théâtre des Champs-Élysées on May 29, 1913, there was a near riot. Catcalls and boos broke out during the performance. There were even fistfights. The Princess de Portalès bellowed from her box (I am sure in royal fashion), "I am sixty years old, but this is the first time anyone has dared to make a fool of me!" A well-dressed lady in the audience spat in the face of a heckler. An elderly gentleman fixed a white handkerchief to his stick and raised it in surrender. Ravel shouted, "Genius, genius!" Debussy implored the audience for silence. Programs rained into the orchestra pit, but the conductor, Pierre Monteux, continued the performance as, Stravinsky recalled, "apparently impervious and as nerveless as a crocodile." (Reading the remainder of this section before listening will increase your enjoyment.)

Actual rioting had occurred during the first performance of J. M. Synge's comedy, *The Playboy of the Western World*, at the Abbey Theater in Dublin in 1907. The offense was in reference to an undergarment. How the world has changed!

Stravinsky was born at a summer resort near St. Petersburg where his father was a renowned singer at the famed imperial opera house, the Mariinsky. He commenced piano studies at the age of eight, and soon was taking lessons in counterpoint and harmony. One of his treasured memories of childhood was seeing Tchaikovsky, a few weeks before his death in 1893, at a fiftieth anniversary celebration of Glinka's opera, *Russlan and Ludmila*. It is variously stated as to whether his parents wished him to be a pianist or a lawyer, but it is definite that he spent eight terms in law school. (Our current students tell us as they near the uncertainties of college graduation, "Law is a good background for everything!") He was a poor student, but music was different. He showed some of his early piano pieces to a boyhood friend who was the son of the composer Nikolai Rimsky-Korsakov. Nikolai offered to instruct the boy himself, and advised him not to attend the conservatory for fear of stifling his originality. Igor's father died in 1892, and for the next six years, Nikolai became Stravinsky's tutor, largely in instrumentation, and a father figure as well.

Unconstrained by the rules, in 1906, Stravinsky married his first cousin, although such a union was forbidden by imperial law. He settled down to married life, built a house along a canal in St. Petersburg, and composed a work for the wedding of Rimsky-Korsakov's daughter. It was entitled *Feu d'artifice (Fireworks)*, and so impressed Sergei Diaghilev that he commissioned Stravinsky to write a work for a new ballet company. This led to his composing three

Sergei Diaghilev (1872–1929) was the seminal impresario who made Russian ballet the envy of the world. By founding the Ballet Russe in Paris (1909), he brought dance-theater to its present heights. He was one of those bigger-than-life people with a genius for recognizing talent in others and spurring them to new heights of productivity. Not only did he establish Stravinsky as an internationally-recognized composer, but involved such notables as Debussy, Ravel, Richard Strauss, Prokofiev, Poulenc, and Falla in the creation of music for the dance. Choreographers Michel Fokine (1880–1942) and George Balanchine (1904–1983), set and costume designer Léon Bakst (1866–1924), and dancers Vaslav Nijinsky (1890–1950) and Anna Pavlova (1881–1931)—each legendary in their own right—all worked with Diaghilev.

ballet scores in three years, resulting in a rapid rise to world fame. They were *L'oiseau de feu* (*The Firebird*), *Pétrouchka* (*Petrushka*), and *Le sacre du printemps* (*The Rite of Spring*—literally "sacred spring").

From 1910 on, Stravinsky spent more and more time in Paris overseeing the use of his ballet music in *The Firebird, Petrushka,* and *The Rite of Spring.* Never again was he to compose anything with the sheer audacity of *The Rite of Spring.* World War I saw him move to Switzerland where he continued, successfully, to search for new idioms. His next great masterpiece was a choral work, *Les Noces* (*The Wedding*), followed by *L'Histoire du soldat* (*The Soldier's Tale*). The war forced the Ballet Russe into decline. During the Russian Revolution, his property was seized and severe financial difficulties compelled him to augment his income by conducting and giving solo piano performances.

Stravinsky and his family returned to Paris in 1920. The irrepressible Diaghilev prevailed on him to adapt the music of an eighteenth-century composer, Pergolesi, for a ballet, *Pulcinella* (1920). He used the melodies, but converted the music to an entirely new genre. This approach to converting the classical for his own uses brought about works with a lucidity and restraint that has since become known as *neoclassicism.* Stravinsky's *Octet for Winds* (1923) is not happy music, but you should listen to it. Such evolutions are an integral part of creative development: Stravinsky's changes are compared to Picasso's with his periods of Blue, Pink, Cubism, and Surrealism.

Stravinsky wrote the music for the ballets *Oedipus Rex* in 1927 and *Appolon Musagète* (*Apollo, Leader of the Muses*) in 1926 for Diaghilev, but then accepted a commission from another ballet company. This treason did not go over well with Diaghilev, who died soon after. The rift was never healed. Stravinsky had great influence during the '20s on composers Darius Milhaud (1892–1974) and Francis Poulenc (1899–1963) and the famous woman teacher, Nadia Boulanger, who taught and inculcated neoclassicism to a young American composer, Aaron Copland, whom we shall meet soon.

A group of composers congregated around the great writer Jean Cocteau. A newspaper critic dubbed them "Les Six," and the name has stuck. They were: Darius Milhaud, Francis Poulenc, Georges Auric, Arthur Honegger, Louis Durey, and Germaine Tailleferre. While they followed the example of Cocteau, who could, it was said, turn what was chic into art, Stravinsky's neoclassicism and American jazz were influential. While you're at it, let me refresh you on some old Russian friends "The Five"—Balakirev, Borodin, Musorgsky, Rimsky-Korsakov (Stravinsky's mentor and father figure), and César Cui.

Stravinsky began to travel to America, and in 1930 the legendary conductor and his American champion, Serge Koussevitzky, commissioned him to write the *Symphony of Psalms*. In 1936, he wrote a score for the newly formed American Ballet Company, choreographed by the great Balanchine. It was presented in 1937 at the Metropolitan Opera House with Stravinsky conducting his *Jeu de cartes* (*The Card Party*). Although he had failed to consolidate his position as the most eminent composer in France, acclaim was his in the States, and other commissions followed.

In 1938, his oldest daughter succumbed to tuberculosis, and in 1939, both his wife and mother also died. The time was ripe for a permanent move to the States. The decision was made easy by an invitation to present the Charles Elliot Norton Lectures at Harvard during the 1939–1940 academic year. He delivered them in French to enthusiastic audiences. He remarried in 1940, and settled in Hollywood, where he and his new wife remained for the next twenty-five years. Arnold Schoenberg was living there as well, but they did not meet for ten years. In 1945, Stravinsky became an American citizen.

Living in Hollywood, Stravinsky was tantalized by the plums of writing film music, but never succumbed because of the poor remuneration. Nevertheless, in 1942, he couldn't resist the notoriety of Barnum and Bailey with his work *Circus Polka,* composed for the elephants to display their terpsichorean skills.

Terpischore was the Muse of dancing. The Muses were the nine daughters of the Greek gods Zeus and Mnemosyne (Memory).

During World War II, he composed two pieces of major importance, *Symphony in C Major* and *Symphony in Three Movements* (1942–1945). From 1948 to 1951, he worked on a full-length neoclassical opera in English, *The Rake's Progress* (W. H. Auden was one of the librettists). It had the accoutrement of classical opera that would have been recognized, and possibly enjoyed, by Mozart.

With these works he felt that he had exhausted his neoclassical style, and began to explore the serial music of Webern. His serial compositions have garnered as much honor in that genre as his earlier ballet and neoclassical works did in theirs, an astonishing accomplishment akin to the old dog's mastery of fresh hoaxes.

His eightieth birthday was celebrated at a White House dinner party hosted by the Kennedys. That same year, 1962, he returned to Russia, where his modern music had been considered unacceptable. At the end of his tour, he was received by Khrushchev, crowning his return to his origins, and one of the greatest events of his life.

Disc Two, Track 38—*Le sacre du printemps* (*The Rite of Spring*)

This tale is one of unrequited love (remember *Tristan and Isolde?*) in which the disappointed lover dances herself to death. A return to primitivism was roaring through the arts in France, most notably the "Fauves" (wild beasts) with their child-like drawings and flamboyant colors. Walt Disney used this music in *Fantasia* (1940) for a dance of his animated dinosaurs.

Now it's time to listen to Stravinsky's *The Rite of Spring*. The beautiful opening melody, played by a bassoon in a register so vaporous that it was difficult to identify the instrument, reminds you of Debussy's introductory melody in *Prelude à l'après-midi d'un faune*, before suddenly, music as you know it begins to change. There is a brief respite, then out of nowhere, you are assaulted with harsh drumming rhythms and jangling sounds never before heard. The rhythms are about as complex as any score ever written; it veritably bristles with changing rhythms and time signatures. A less jarring but more compelling repetition of the asymmetric hammering rhythms takes place, followed by another respite at the end of your sample.

Imagine that you were going to its premiere expecting more of the classical music you knew and loved. Might you not have booed a little too? An equivalent today would be going to hear an oratorio at your local church. For the first few minutes the choir sings traditionally, and suddenly switches to rock and roll.

Pick up *Petrouchka*, a more melodically accessible work, and *The Firebird*, which is likely to recall the spirit of Rimsky-Korsakov, Stravinsky's teacher. Another student of Rimsky-Korsakov (and Max Bruch) was the Italian, Ottorino Respighi (1879-1936) whose two best-known works, *The Pines of Rome* and *The Fountains of Rome*, will beguile you on first listen. While at it, Respighi's *Suites 1, 2, and 3 on Ancient Dances* and *Airs for Lute* distill centuries of old melodies and rhythms that you will find a pure joy from first to last.

Recommended Listening
Symphony in Three Movements

The slow movement of the *Symphony in Three Movements* was originally written for the "Apparition of the Virgin" scene in a 1942 film called *The Song of Bernadette,* starring Jennifer Jones. Stravinsky changed his mind and used the music for this symphony. I find no programmatic content at all that suggests seeing an apparition.

Rhythm dominates over melody and a few beats reminded me of *Le sacre du printemps* but without the violence. Listen for the strings and harp playing together. It is complex but not difficult music, from which you will derive something new with each listen. To me, each movement is an entirely separate entity, although there must be bridges in between that will require more listening. On this one, it's up to you in regard to securing it for your collection. It doesn't sound foreign to the ear, but is quite unlike other symphonic movements you've heard, which I suppose is the simplest way of defining neoclassicism!

CHAPTER THIRTY-SEVEN

Prokofiev, Sergey (1891–1953)

"I strive for greater simplicity and more melody....
Music, in other words, has definitely reached and passed
the greatest degree of discord and of complexity
that is practicable to attain."

disc two
tracks 39–41

Prokofiev is another colossus. Sergey Sergeyevich Prokofiev was born in the Ukraine to a well-educated and well-off family. His father was an agricultural engineer, and his mother a respect-able pianist who was devoted to Beethoven, Chopin, and Nicolay Rubinstein, the brother of Anton. Sergey wrote his first piano composition at the age of five, could play a Beethoven sonata by nine, and had composed two operas by the age of eleven when Glière traveled to the Ukraine to tutor the boy.

Reinhold Glière (1875–1956) was schooled at the Moscow Conservatory. You would do well to acquire his Harp Concerto and Third Symphony. His *Red Poppy* is in the standard ballet repertoire.

Nicolay Rubinstein (1835–1881) was a founder of the St. Petersburg conserva-tory, and its director until his death. He was a close friend of Tchaikovsky and is remembered for making one of the great gaffes in musical history, namely, labeling his friend's first piano concerto as "worthless and unplayable." He goes down wonderfully in my memory as the man who consumed a dozen oysters on his deathbed in Paris. His younger brother, Anton Rubinstein (1829–1894), a piano prodigy and lesser composer, was roundly condemned in anti-Semitic terms by "The Five." Balakirev despised Rubinstein's German-Jewish origins and refused to attend a major celebration in honor of Anton's sixtieth birthday; instead he wrote a letter to the authorities castigating his effect on Russian music.

Don't confuse Anton with Artur (1887–1982), one of the finest American piano virtuosos of the twentieth century who was very helpful to Brazilian com-poser Villa-Lobos. There is a historic laser videodisc recording of a benefit con-cert for Israel given by Artur in 1975. At a concluding ceremony, the announcement was made that the piano was to have a brass plaque affixed to it labeled "The Rubinstein Piano." Artur humorously requested that his first name be added because for the first forty years of his life he was constantly asked, "Are you related to the great pianist, Anton?"

Prokofiev continued to compose short piano pieces at a prodigious rate. He entered the St. Petersburg Conservatory at thirteen and spent the next ten years there. Those were tempestuous times in Russia and at the Conservatory. The first rumblings of the Russian Revolution occurred on the "Bloody Sunday" of 1905. Rimsky-Korsakov was temporarily dismissed for manifesting sympathy for the aborted revolution.

He was an arrogant and indifferent student, but he carried the seeds of greatness. He gave his first public concert in 1911. This was financially important because his father had died, the estate had been lost, and his mother had come to St. Petersburg to support her son.

Sergey continued to produce unconventional music, and became something of an *enfant terrible* with the advent of his First and Second Piano Concertos (1911–1913) and the Violin Concerto No. 1 (1916). In the strongest terms, I commend all three to you. Nevertheless, he produced nothing as iconoclastic as Stravinsky's *Le sacre du printemps.* Diaghilev took note of his talent and commissioned a ballet that resulted in the *Scythian Suite,* aping Stravinsky but original in its own way. It was never produced, but the bond that was formed led to successful collaborations later.

In 1918, twenty-seven-year-old Prokofiev immigrated to the United States, and ended up in New York after a four-month trip by way of Vladivostok, Tokyo, and San Francisco. Aboard ship, he began to sketch out a new opera *Lyubov tryom apelsinam* (*Love for Three Oranges*). In New York, his piano performances of his own works were enthusiastically received. He was immediately engaged to do a recording for the Steinway-Duo-art player piano company. This is the earliest reference I've come across to a recording by one of our composers. (It was done on a roll of paper with holes punched in it.) Unhappily, his success rapidly waned since, with his fame in Russia having preceded him and the Bolshevik revolution on everyone's mind, the public had expected a Rachmaninoff at the keyboard, and music that would outdo Stravinsky in abandon.

He went to France in 1920 and renewed his contacts with Diaghilev and Stravinsky. In Paris, his ballet, *Chout* (*The Tale of the Buffoon*), won acclaim. At the behest of the conductor, Serge Koussevitzky, he briefly returned to the States in December 1921 to attend the opening of the *Love for Three Oranges*. This and *War and Peace* are the only two of his ten operas to win lasting success. His Third Piano Concerto was also premiered, with Prokofiev serving as the solo pianist. He returned to Paris once again in 1922, and thereby made it his home base. In 1923, he married a Spanish soprano (whom he later left for a poetess). In this same year, he was invited, but declined, to return to Russia where his works had now become popular. He subsequently wrote the ballet, *Prodigal Son* (1928), for Diaghilev.

As previously mentioned, despite material success and international acclaim, Prokofiev missed the homeland that he had visited in 1927, 1929, and 1932. He finally succumbed, and returned to live in Russia in 1933. In the twenty years that remained of his life, he became a leading figure of the Soviet cultural scene.

To be in the top echelon of the cultural establishment meant much more to a Soviet artist than to a counterpart in the West. While the "bread and circuses" approach to pacifying an underserved population is credited to ancient Rome, the USSR carried it to new heights in the diversity and quality of its offerings, from symphony orchestras and ballet companies to actual circuses. The average Soviet citizen ended up more interested in "culture" than his counterpart in the West, and the "heroes" of this regard were the artists whose fringe benefits, such as *dachas*, access to stores dealing in Western goods, and chauffeur-driven limousines, were more luxurious even than those of the top politicos.

In the 1980s, my wife and I attended a surgical congress in Moscow as guests of the leading surgical administrator and former minister of health. One morning, a ninety-minute music and dance recital was scheduled. My wife, who was then president of a leading cultural institution in New York City, was reluctant to attend because she expected that the presentations would be second rate. Not at all! As I recall, there were eight "acts" which included performers of the Bolshoi ballet, the Moyseiev dancers, and several famous artists including Vladimir Feltsman, the great pianist whom my wife's institution had been trying to bring to New York. She later observed that it would have been almost impossible to bring together such a diversity of talent in New York. In Moscow, it was easy! The surgical administrator called up the minister of culture, who in turn simply sent out notices to the performers who, in spite of their fame, were, in effect, civil service employees!

In the years before World War II, Prokofiev composed his Violin Concerto No. 2 (1935), the *Romeo and Juliet* ballet (1936), *Peter and the Wolf* (1936), and the music for Sergei Eisenstein's epic film, *Alexander Nevsky* (1938).

As they say, "there is no free lunch." In 1937, he created, based on texts by Lenin, the music for an imposing work with an even more imposing name, *The Cantata for the 20th Anniversary of the October Revolution (1937)*. He became a real toady in 1939 by writing *Toast to Stalin*. On the eve of World War II, he left his first family to marry the poet Mira Mendelssohn. He continued to compose assiduously during the war and was one of those evacuated from Moscow in 1941. His major work during this period was an operatic adaptation of Tolstoy's *War and Peace*. The very majestic and somber Symphony No. 5 dates from the end of the war. Compare it to the Symphony No. 6, which is light and lyrical. The three piano concertos and two violin concertos will also give you pleasure.

By 1948, Stalin's thought control was in and atonality out. Prokofiev did not escape the whip even though he, along with Shostakovich, was a leading Russian composer. He groveled, and in an infamous apology wrote,

> The Resolution of the Central Committee has separated decayed tissue in our composers' creative production from the healthy part. No matter how painful it may be for many composers, myself included, I welcome the Resolution.... Apparently the infection was caught from contact with some Western ideas...I must admit that I, too, have indulged in atonality...I should like to express my gratitude to our Party for the precise directives of the Resolution, which will help me in my search for a musical language accessible and natural to our people and of our great country.

You or I may have been offended by the Mapplethorpe exhibit that provoked such controversy in 1991 between Congress and the National Endowment for the Arts, but a government bureaucracy must never become the arbiter of artistic taste.

Disc Two, Track 40—Symphony No. 1 in D, Op. 25, "Classical"

The Russian Revolution of 1917 seemed to have little effect on the musical establishment in St. Petersburg. Sergey's teacher of conducting at that time was the conductor and composer Nicolas Tcherepnin (1873–1945), who was grounding Prokofiev in the symphonic history that began with "Papa" Haydn.

Tcherepnin was a prominent conductor in St. Petersburg and Paris, where he was associated with Diaghilev's Ballet Russe. In 1918, he became director of the Tiflis Conservatory in Georgia, the birthplace of Joseph Stalin who died in 1953. I visited Tiblisi (the new name for Tiflis) in 1964. The only picture that I saw of Stalin during an extensive trip through the USSR was in a back room of a restaurant there.

Prokofiev decided to write a symphony in the old idiom but in the light of his more modern knowledge, hence the name "Classical" Symphony. It is in four movements, excerpts of the last two are on your disc. When you start to listen, the music will sound as though it could have been written in the eighteenth century, but then little dissonances creep in and the orchestration doesn't ring true. Do you hear the Lone Ranger on Silver pursuing the villains?

This is a most instructive piece of music to show you what a long way you have come. Go back and listen again to your selection of Haydn, and then to the "Classical" once again.

Now on to more Prokofiev in order to watch his development!

Recommended Listening
Love for Three Oranges
Lieutenant Kijé Suite

The opera *Love for Three Oranges,* has a ridiculous plot concerning the King (of Clubs) trying to cure his son of a depression by getting him to laugh. The Three Oranges contain three princesses, one of whom is turned into a rat before she is restored to her pristine beauty. The prince is happy, he marries, and the couple lives happily ever after. The music, however, is not ridiculous at all! Prokofiev excerpted parts of the opera, and used them in a suite called, you guessed it, *Love for Three Oranges.*

Prokofiev visited Russia in the late '20s, returned there in 1933, and began to live the comfortable life of a state-sponsored artist. In 1934, he wrote the music for the film *Lieutenant Kijé.* The plot should be dear to all bureaucrats. The setting is early nineteenth century Russia during the reign of Czar Paul I, a maniac fascinated by the military. A clerk writes the name "Kijé" by mistake on an army roster. The czar becomes curious, and a career must be invented for this clerical error. The fictitious Kijé is commissioned a lieutenant, married off, and eventually removed from the roster by means of a funeral with full military honors. Prokofiev converted the movie score into a suite.

Somehow Prokofiev doesn't leave us bereft, which is the brilliant touch in this funereal piece.

Disc Two, Track 41—Romeo and Juliet Suite No. 2, Op. 64 "Montagues and Capulets"

The music for *Romeo and Juliet* is an apotheosis of all that Prokofiev composed. When approached to write the music for the ballet, Prokofiev was reluctant. *Romeo and Juliet* had already been adapted to operatic form by fourteen composers, to say nothing of Berlioz's dramatic symphony and Tchaikovsky's overture. When he finally wrote the music, the choreographers rejected it, stating that it was undanceable. The proposed Leningrad premiere in 1937 was canceled. Finally, in 1938, a ballet company in Czechoslovakia mounted it for the first time without Prokofiev's participation. Its reception was tremendous, causing the Russians to relent. The Kirov Ballet in Leningrad presented the first Russian performance on January 10, 1940, to fervent acclaim. It subsequently assumed its present place as the prime successor to the Tchaikovsky ballets.

The orchestral score was excerpted from the ballet score, and divided into three suites. The selection on your disc is from Suite No. 2. It is entitled the "Montagues and Capulets" who are, of course, the respective families of Romeo and Juliet whom Shakespeare immortalized by having them die instead of live happily ever after. In his original score, Prokofiev had tried to promote a happy ending, but eventually bowed to Shakespeare's wisdom. Listen for the throbbing, luxurious melodies and clashing harmonies paradigmatic of Prokofiev.

I think by now you understand why the accolades of three selections have been given to Prokofiev.

CHAPTER THIRTY-EIGHT

Gershwin, George (1898–1937)

"True music must repeat the thought and inspirations
of the people and the time.
My people are Americans and my time is today."

disc two
tracks 42–43

You are already familiar with a great deal of Gershwin's music, for he is the most widely known American composer in history. His early success as a writer of popular songs is exemplified by "Swanee" (made famous when sung by Al Jolson in the musical *Sinbad*). Written when he was only nineteen, it sold a million copies. Everybody knows his folk opera *Porgy and Bess* (1935*)* just as everyone has heard the song "I Got Rhythm." Have you seen the 1937 Academy Award–winning film *Shall We Dance?* starring Fred Astaire and Ginger Rogers, with music by George Gershwin and lyrics by his brother, Ira? Gershwin is the only composer we have met whose primary field was writing for the Broadway theater, and yet he has made these august pages. Musicals like *Lady Be Good* (1924), *Strike Up the Band* and *Funny Face* (1927), and *Of Thee I Sing* (1931), which won the Pulitzer prize for drama, recall the heyday of the American musical theater.

George Gershwin was born in Brooklyn, New York, and died in Hollywood, California. His parents emigrated from Russia in 1891 to New York City's Lower East Side. George's birth in Brooklyn indicates that the family had started to ascend the economic ladder. Reflecting this even more was the arrival in their home, in 1910, of an upright piano. As expected, George learned to play it quickly, and he soon required the more expert instruction of such luminaries as Henry Cowell and Wallingford Riegger (1885–1961). At sixteen, he quit school to become a pianist for a publisher in Tin Pan Alley.

In the *OED*, a definition of **"tin pan"** is a cheap "tinny" piano. Tin Pan Alley refers to the world of composers and publishers of popular music; it is loosely applied to areas where song publishers abound. They used to be on 28th Street in Manhattan, the Brill Building at 49th Street and Broadway, and Denmark Street in London.

Disc Two, Track 43—*Rhapsody in Blue*

Gershwin wrote the score for the 1920 *George White Scandals*. The bandleader for this show was Paul Whiteman, one of the most famous personalities of the "Big Band" era. Whiteman devised the public relations gimmick of a jazz-style concert to prove to the public that jazz could be socially acceptable if dressed in symphonic clothes.

Please, please get **Ferde Grofé's Grand Canyon Suite**, the best piece of classical music he ever wrote, with an assured place in the pops concert repertoire. You will recognize portions of it, but the "Sunrise over the Canyon" is spectacular and the burros' clip-clop (once used as the theme to promote Philip Morris cigarettes) while carrying the tourists "On The Trail" is unforgettable.

He commissioned George to write a symphonic jazz-style piece. *Rhapsody in Blue*, written for two pianos, was the result. Brother Ira suggested the title. As stated earlier, a rhapsody is a free-form work most often based on folk music. The folk music here is jazz, about as delectable as any that exists. George did not have the technical background at that point to feel comfortable with its orchestration. Whiteman turned this task over to his band arranger, Ferde Grofé, whose original version demanded the instrumental capabilities found in the jazz musicians of the Whiteman band. A 1942 version arranged more for the average symphony orchestra is the one usually heard. George Gershwin was the pianist at the original concert. It was a smash hit, and established him forever as "the man who brought jazz into the concert hall."

The opening "blues" notes will make you glad he did. The initial minute and a half features a truly golden trumpet with the piano coming in for a brief appearance. This is followed by a long, completely unaccompanied solo piano part culminating in the welcome return of Grofé's inspired orchestration, of which you only get a hint. I'm ever apologetic for the truncated end. *Rhapsody in Blue* and *An American in Paris* are often paired, so that your purchase of the CD will be a "twofer" as they say about two seats for the price of one to a Broadway play.

Gershwin is reported to have asked Ravel to give him lessons on orchestration. The story soon circulated that in the course of conversation, Ravel asked Gershwin how much he made a year from his compositions. The answer was $100,000. Ravel's reply, "In that case, you give *me* lessons." Stravinsky is quoted as saying "A nice story, but I heard it about myself from Ravel a year before I met Gershwin."

Recommended Listening
An American in Paris

Gershwin was commissioned to write *An American in Paris* by Walter Damrosch, who conducted it in his first appearance with the New York Philharmonic at Carnegie Hall on December 13, 1928. Gershwin's father, Morris, must have been justifiably proud of his son, "the composer," when he said, "It's very important music—it takes twenty minutes to play." No explication is obligatory because if you can't hear the hustle and bustle of Paris with the constant honking of car horns and the din of traffic, you shouldn't be allowed to wander the streets without a companion.

Rhapsody in Blue and *An American in Paris* are milestones in the development of an independent American concert repertoire.

The immigrant family boy from Brooklyn did very well. Damrosch commissioned yet another Gershwin work worthy of your attention, the *Concerto in F* for piano. He went on to Hollywood, where his movie songs were performed by stars such as Fred and Adele Astaire, Ethel Merman, Ginger Rogers, and the incomparable Gertrude Lawrence. In 1937, he started to complain that he smelled burning charcoal and was having dizzy spells. A month later, he died during a brain tumor operation.

CHAPTER THIRTY-NINE

Poulenc, Francis (1899–1963)

"When I wrote this piece…I had in mind those frescoes by Gozzoli where the angels stick out their tongues. And also some serious Benedictine monks I had once seen reveling in a game of football."
—Poulenc on *Gloria*

disc two
tracks 44–46

Francis Poulenc was a native Parisian born to a wealthy family of pharmaceutical manufacturers (Rhone-Poulenc, France's largest). His mother was a fine pianist and her brother "Oncle Papoum" introduced young Francis to the more risqué aspects of the French theater, which are clearly evident in his music. When he was fourteen, he heard Stravinsky's *Le sacre du printemps,* and observed the polarization of musical society that it elicited. He is an exception to the majority of our French composers in that he did not go to the Conservatoire and did not win the Prix de Rome. He had little in the way of formal music education before he was dubbed a member of "Les Six," but he later felt the need to increase his formal musical knowledge, and studied under a tutor. Typical of this quest was a 1921 visit, accompanied by fellow composer Darius Milhaud, to Vienna to meet Schoenberg before traveling on to Italy to further his studies.

In terms of acceptance in the concert repertoire, Francis Poulenc has emerged as the most important member of "Les Six," clearly edging out the likes of Honegger and Milhaud, both of whom are worth your while to explore on your own.

Arthur Honegger (1892–1955) is a composer you will have to sample on your own. A good place to start is a suite made from his music to accompany the epic silent film *Napoleon* (1927). This gripping film is available on video and demonstrates the dramatic power that silent motion pictures could achieve. Beyond that, try his Symphonies No. 2 and No. 4 and his oratorio, *Le roi David.*

Poulenc was the jokester of the group, and his large elongated head calls to mind the French comedian, Fernandel. His songs are considered, by that ubi-quitous some, the greatest of anyone since Fauré, even outshining Debussy. As was the case with Bizet, in terms of stature in the musical world of this book, he properly rates only a single

Marie Laurencin (1883–1956) was a French painter known particularly for her delicate watercolors of vaguely mournful young women. She was a classmate of Georges Braque, and Gertrude Stein was one of the first to buy her work. As mentioned in our discussion of Stravinsky's *The Rite of Spring*, there was a movement in French art, starting in about 1907, known as *Les Fauves (Wild Beasts)*. They were known for their use of the very brightest colored paints on their canvasses. Since Laurencin used only delicate pastel colors, she was nick-named "La Fauvette."

Antoine Watteau (1684–1721) was a French artist whose work typified the charming and graceful style of the Rococo period. When you see a painting of a graceful clown in a beautifully wooded area, it is most likely a Watteau.

slot. He is getting more because I want you to share the pleasure I've had in choosing his pieces. By and large, the sonorities are sweet and pungent. In spite of occasional dissonances and polytonalities, his harmonies never stray from those of the nineteenth century that even to this day are more comfortable to our ears than the "modernism" of the twentieth.

Recommended Listening
Les Biches

Back in Paris, Poulenc came under the sway of the dynamic ballet producer, and our old friend, Sergei Diaghilev. Poulenc's first major orchestral work was the score for Diaghilev's ballet *Les Biches*. Marie Laurencin designed the costumes and stage sets. *Les Biches* contains very little in the way of plot, but consists of a series of Watteau-like pantomimes. It premiered in Monte Carlo in January 1924, a few days before Poulenc's twenty-fifth birthday, was an instant success, and established Poulenc's reputation internationally.

In the ten years following *Les Biches*, Poulenc consolidated his technical abilities and continued to compose, reaching a new maturity around 1935, precipitated by the death of a close friend and a relationship with a great singer, Pierre Bernac. After a spiritual awakening, he reembraced his paternal faith of Roman Catholicism, and began to compose some religiously inspired works such as *Litanies à la vierge noire* (*Prayers to the Black Virgin*.)

During World War II, Poulenc remained in occupied France, expressing his antipathy to the Germans by dedicating a composition to the Spanish revolutionary poet Federico García Lorca, and setting poems of resistance to music. After the war, he returned to Paris and found himself in the strange position of defending the now "classical" music of Stravinsky against the onslaught of a new avant-garde of composers who embraced the tenets of French composer Olivier Messiaen. Poulenc's 1947 opera

Les mamelles de Tirésias (*The Breasts of Tirésias*) is based on an old play by his friend Apollonaire. It's a farce, with suggestions of women's liberation far ahead of its time that met with great applause, and has remained in the repertoire. In 1948, Poulenc was enthusiastically received on a tour of the United States, which he repeated in 1960.

> Tiresias was a blind seer in Greek mythology. One theory as to his condition goes as follows: Hera told her husband, Zeus, that women get less pleasure from sex than men. Tiresias set the record straight by explaining to Hera that women derived ten times more pleasure than men. She became enraged and struck him blind. Zeus thereupon bestowed Tiresias with the gift of prophecy.

In 1954, Poulenc suffered from a severe depression over financial matters, but made a complete emotional recovery. He spent his last years enjoying his palatial country home at Noizay in Touraine, where he resisted the efforts of his neighbors to elect him mayor of the town. He died suddenly of a heart attack just after his sixty-fourth birthday. Incidentally, in the first movement of his Ninth Symphony, Mahler gives a musical description of his own heart attack. There are extra beats, an episode of an irregularity (fibrillation) and the searing pain—an unhappy event, but program music par excellence.

Poulenc's oeuvre is extensive, encompassing a wide range of piano works, chamber music, orchestral music, choral music—of which we will hear an example—film and theater scores, plus five books and many articles. This laughable character, the one of "Les Six" who would have been voted the least likely to succeed, has enjoyed the most enduring success in the repertoire of any of the other five!

Recommended Listening
Trio for Piano, Oboe, and Bassoon

The *Trio for Piano, Oboe, and Bassoon* dates from 1926, and is Poulenc's first important chamber work. Here you have only the last of its three movements. The melody is memorable, the rhythm makes you want to jump; the unorthodox combination of the three instruments seems perfectly integrated. A cavorting clown might be conjured up by this music.

Disc Two, Track 45—*The Bestiary,* or *The Procession of Orpheus*

It was mentioned earlier that Poulenc was a great songwriter. The entire group of six pieces in *The Bestiary* lasts four minutes. In your sample, "Le Dromadaire" ("The Camel"), you get one short song, dating from 1919, and based on a poem by the avant-garde poet, Apollinaire. Enjoy hearing "The Camel" bray while you read.

Avec ses quatre dromadaires	With his four camels
Don Pedro d'Alfaroubeira	Don Pedro d'Alfaroubeira
courut le monde et l'admira.	traveled admiringly around the world.
Il fit ce que je voudrais faire	He did just what I would do
si j'avais quatre dromadaires.	if I had four camels.

Wasn't that a delight?

Recommended Listening
Le Bal Masque

Le Bal Masque was written in 1932 for a musical entertainment organized by friends. Its music is much more than a cheerful piece of nonsense based on poems by Max Jacobs that, I must admit, are pretty nonsensical. When you buy the complete work, spend some time reading the poems, which are nutty but fun. They deal with suburban life around Paris. I don't know quite how to define it, but virtually all of Poulenc's music contains sections that wouldn't be out of place in a Broadway musical. Yet, within it, there is a depth and substance not found on Broadway. His ability to make melody has, in many minds, cast him as the Schubert of the twentieth century.

Disc Two, Track 46—*Gloria*

Your last excerpt is from a serious religious choral work, *Gloria,* written in 1959. At one point in his tutorial musical education, Poulenc was given a set of Bach choral melodies to harmonize. Poulenc claimed these exercises had a decisive influence on his future output. Once again, listen to this first section written as a religious offering by a pious composer, and think whether it would be totally out of place somewhere in a Broadway show.

I've really derived immense pleasure in browsing through Poulenc's oeuvre to select the segments for this book. Prior to this, I possessed only a casual familiarity with his music, and now suddenly feel as though there is, in explorer's terms, a whole new continent to survey. I hope you will have similar pleasure.

CHAPTER FORTY

Copland, Aaron (1900–1990)

"My discovery of music was rather like coming upon
an unsuspected city—like Paris or Rome
if you never before heard of their existence.
The excitement of the discovery was enhanced
because I came upon a few streets at a time,
but before long I began to suspect
the full extent of the city."

disc two
tracks 47–48

opland is our first composer born in the twentieth century, and our second Brooklyn native. If this book has stimulated your liking for classical music enough to proceed further—which it probably has if you've gotten this far—the very next book for you to buy is an inexpensive paperback by Aaron Copland titled *What to Listen for in Music*. While it will put the nonmusician off a bit with its discussions of "triads," "dominant fifths," and musical notation, there is also a brilliant range of common sense, nontechnical discussion that will build well upon the background you already have.

Aaron Copland was, like Gershwin, the son of immigrant Jewish parents, but his father had spent several years in England, and his mother had grown up and attended school in the Midwest and Texas. Aaron was the fifth child and seven years younger than his sister, who gave him his initial piano lessons when he was about thirteen.

Dr. Harvey Fineberg, former Dean of the School of Public Health and Provost of Harvard, has gone beyond any reasonable bond of friendship in doing a painstaking review of this manuscript. He penciled in the following handsomely composed and erudite note:

This is a remarkably late age to start. I am reminded of the sage and great scholar, Rabbi Akiva, who was reportedly illiterate until adulthood! With each passing year, I more avidly seek evidence of late-blooming genius. This leads me also to a more general reflection on the relation of age to creativity. In many people an interest in music and mathematics go together, just as interests in music and medicine seem often to reside in the same person. With few exceptions, creative advances in mathematics are a young person's game (teens and twenties) while musicians and composers seem to retain, even enhance, their creative and expressive powers well into the winter of their lives. (I think of the late piano recitals of Artur Rubinstein and Vladimir Horowitz.) All more the pity and posterity's loss, from the premature deaths of Mozart, Schubert, and a number of others described in this book. With the health advances of the 21st century (extending life expectancy at birth in the U.S. from less than fifty years to more than seventy-five years) perhaps future musical genius will more likely enjoy its fuller lifelong expression.

Copland quickly received more expert instruction, and was taken to concerts at the Brooklyn Academy of Music. He particularly remembered hearing the Polish pianist and future Polish prime minister Ignacy Paderewski play and seeing the Diaghilev ballets *Scheherazade* and *L'après-midi d'une faune*. He attended Boys' High School in Brooklyn, and was tutored in music by eminent teachers, but never went to college. In those early years, he leaned away from Beethoven and toward such composers as Musorgsky, Ravel, and Debussy.

In 1920, he set off to study music in Paris where he spent four years studying under Nadia Boulanger (1887–1979). Copland later described this as the most important experience of his musical life.

Nadia Boulanger was an extraordinarily gifted teacher, composer, and conductor from a distinguished French musical family. She also helped train the eminent American composers Elliott Carter (b. 1908) and Roy Harris (1898–1979). She was the first woman to conduct a major symphony orchestra in London (1937), and conducted the premiere performance of her friend Stravinsky's *Dumbarton Oaks Concerto* in Washington, D.C. (1938). It was her ability as a teacher that brought her the most fame. She taught at the Paris Conservatoire and the American Conservatory at Fontainebleu, of which she became director in 1950. During World War II, she taught at Radcliffe College, Wellesley College, Bryn Mawr, and the Juilliard School of Music. Her sister, Lili Boulanger (1893–1918), was the first woman to win the coveted Prix de Rome (in 1910) but her career was too soon truncated by her early death to determine whether she would have entered the first rank of composers.

The feminist movement in music points to Nadia Boulanger with appropriate pride. Frankly, I have given serious thought to including at least one work in this collection by a gifted contemporary woman composer (Ellen Taaffe Zwilich, Libby Larsen, Sofia Gubaidulina, Joan Tower). The major reason for doing so would have been because of gender (and this would have been unfair to them and to you).

Copland's Paris was that of Ravel, Stravinsky, Prokofiev, "Les Six," and the Ballet Russe, complemented by the Left Bank writers and artists who included Joyce, Hemingway, and Picasso, to name only a few. At first, his compositions were heavily influenced by Stravinsky, "Les Six," and the American jazz idiom. Following his Piano Concerto (1927) he dispensed with jazz, as was the case with the other major composers who had tested its possibilities. He then embarked upon becoming "Copland." The product was predominantly jarring rhythmic patterns and dissonances within near totally abstract forms. His music inspired a generation of American composers, who followed in his footsteps with "modern" music encompassing rigorous logical progressions that were neither understood nor liked by the public. Copland's compositions of this period were *Piano Variations* (1930) and *Statements* (1935).

Suddenly, however, he changed his style once again, now composing in a way that appealed to the standard concert-going audiences who liked a tune and wanted to comprehend what they were hearing. His output from then on places him in the forefront of American composers. To start, get *El Salon México* (1938) and three superb ballets, *Billy The Kid* (1938), *Rodeo* (1940), and *Appalachian Spring* (1944). The common denominator among the three is a spiky rhythmic quality in which dissonance is combined with catchy melodies. The music is a far cry from Mozart, Haydn, and Beethoven, and may suggest reminiscences of Poulenc. Yet it is so different that it can only be vintage Copland. Even though he is modern, Copland is not difficult.

Disc Two, Track 48—*Appalachian Spring*

Your sample is from the end of *Appalachian Spring*. Copland composed it for Martha Graham, whose company developed a new form of dance. While it is called a ballet, it is the antithesis of classical ballet. Somehow it is more passionate and yet highly controlled; the dancers are barefoot and the entire body moves. Miss Graham chose the title from the heading of a poem by Hart Crane, though the ballet really bears no relation to the subject matter of the poem itself. The principal theme is from an old Shaker melody entitled *Simple Gifts*.

Recommended Listening
Rodeo
Billy The Kid

The ballet *Rodeo* was set by the famous American dancer-choreographer Agnes de Mille. At their first meeting, Copland was skeptical of the project because the "Russian" ballet was so completely antithetical to his musical idiom. After Miss de Mille had outlined the plot to him, an uncomfortable silence pervaded the room. She remarked with a frown that, while it wasn't *Hamlet,* Martha Graham (who apparently had read Jung) felt that it might well provide "an aura of race memory." Copland doubled up in laughter and Miss de Mille looked angrier and angrier until Copland finally got himself under control. He then suggested that a ballet featuring Ellis Island might be more effective in suggesting "race memory." She told him to go to hell. The next day he called, and a most successful collaboration resulted. Listen and you will know without the least difficulty that you are at a square dance. Even so, the music is distinct from any you've heard at such a dance. I fear that dancing to the music of the raucous beginning and ending could cripple anyone but a professional dancer.

Billy the Kid was composed for the choreographer Eugene Loring. The legendary Western outlaw Billy the Kid was born William Bonney in New York City but grew up in Silver City, New Mexico. I cannot go into the entire plot, but according to an American border ballad, Billy "had a notch in his pistol for twenty-one men" before "his young manhood reached its sad end." There are parts of the music describing the "Open Prairie," "A Gun Battle," "A Celebration after Billy's Capture," "Billy's Death," and "Street in a Frontier Town."

None of these works are long. You should be able to get them all on a single compact disc. My disc also includes *Fanfare for the Common Man.* This is a splendid piece that Copland later used in the fourth movement of his Symphony No. 3. Again, if you have not already done so, pick up a copy of the paperback by Copland entitled *What to Listen for in Music.*

CHAPTER FORTY-ONE

Shostakovich, Dmitry (1906–1975)

"Even before the war, in Leningrad, there wasn't a single family
who hadn't lost someone...I had to write a requiem for all those
who had died, who had suffered...I had to describe
the horrible extermination machine and express protest against it."
—on his Seventh Symphony,
(from *Testimony*, page 135)

disc two
tracks 49–51

Shostakovich is to me the greatest composer of the twentieth century, although Stravinsky is often given this accolade. This view of Shostakovich is dominant. Therefore, it was particularly shocking to come upon this opinion expressed by respected music critic B. H. Haggin: "Worst of all, by far, is Shostakovich—I heard a reworking of some of Prokofiev's writing by as low-grade and vulgar a mind and taste as ever had communicated itself to me through an artistic medium—crude, derivative, inane, banal, and pretentious." Listen and make up your own mind. I am told that Haggin disliked 99.9 percent of twentieth century music.

Shostakovich's fifteen symphonies and chamber music (fifteen string quartets among many other combinations) rival Beethoven's output in majesty and creativity—the ultimate compliment for any composer. Unlike Prokofiev, who spent considerable time living outside of Russia, and Stravinsky, who defected, Shostakovich spent his entire adult life under the stifling and brutal rule of the USSR, alternately as a cultural hero or in disgrace. He must have lived a life of fear, waiting for the knock on the door and the ultimate denunciation, but he survived the Russian Revolution, World War II, and the Stalinist massacres. It is no surprise that his musical voices are predominantly savage or mournful, usually with a ruthless pulse and a preference for large-scale musical forms. No one but a psychotic would choose this music for the proverbial desert island. No matter, it is great!

Dmitry Shostakovich was born in St. Petersburg one year after the bloody uprising of 1905 that eventually led to the decisive October Revolution of 1917, placing him in history as the first important musical child of the revolution. His father was an engineer and serious amateur musician; his mother was a professional pianist who began his lessons when he was nine years old. At the age of thirteen, he was admitted to the Petrograd Conservatory where he remained for twelve years. The principal of the school was the composer Alexander Glazunov (1865–1936), who may be categorized as falling into the tail end of the Russian nationalist school.

> You would do well to listen to Glazunov's *The Seasons*, as it contains the delight-ful "Waltz of the Cornflowers and Poppies." I'm also particularly fond of his Symphony No. 1, composed when he was seventeen years old. And I absolutely guarantee that you will be delighted by the Violin Concerto in A Minor, Op. 82.

During these school years, Shostakovich helped support his widowed mother by accompanying silent films on the piano. As he neared graduation, he was torn between devoting his energy to a career as a concert pianist or as a composer. As it turned out, the decision was made for him by the success of the graduation piece he composed at the age of nineteen, the Symphony No. 1 in F Minor, Op. 10. It was an immediate sensation and was played by major symphony orchestras throughout Europe and the United States. A minority of musicologists still consider it to be the best of Shostakovich's symphonic works. On the other hand, our selection, Symphony No. 5, puts us with the majority, as demonstrated by nineteen different CD recordings listed in OPUS as compared to ten for the Symphony No. 1. Obviously, such a statistic is meaningless; get both and drop me a line as to your preference!

In 1936, Shostakovich ran afoul of Stalin, who described his opera *Lady Macbeth of the Mzensk District* as "chaos." At the end of the first act, Stalin is said to have stormed out of the opera house in a rage over the "degenerate" nature of the music, specifically the sexual intercourse scene, vividly illustrated in the orchestration by trombone glissandos. A glissando is a rapid sliding back and forth, sometimes slowly. Immediately thereafter, three criteria were decreed for Soviet opera: 1) a socialist theme must be the subject; 2) the music must be "realistic," based on Russian folk-song, and have no glaring atonalities; 3) the plot must have a happy ending with the state eulogized. (Maybe Stalin wasn't such a prude. In the U.S. at that time, an exposed breast was forbidden in films, and the novel *Lady Chatterley's Lover* was still being smuggled in.) An almost instantaneous attack appeared in *Pravda*. This was no laughing matter to Shostakovich because it could have meant he would lose his job, the publication and performance of his compositions would cease, and the niceties of life that he enjoyed such as the apartment, the chauffeur-driven car, and the *dacha* would be taken from him. In the worst case, it could have meant imprisonment.

To rehabilitate himself, Shostakovich composed the Fifth Symphony in celebra-tion of the anniversary of the October Revolution. It premiered a year after the *Pravda* attack, and the "perks" remained.

The description given by Mstislav Rostropovich (who was then giving the party line), the great cellist, now an American, who was a student at the Moscow Conservatory when Shostakovich taught there, is worthy of quotation:

> The applause went on for an entire hour. People were in an uproar, and ran up and down the streets of Leningrad till the small hours, embracing and congratulating each other on having been there. They had understood the message that forms the "lower bottom," the outer hull, of the Fifth Symphony; the message of sorrow, suffering, and isolation; stretched on the rack of Inquisition, the victim still tries to smile in his pain. The shrill repetitions of the "A" at the end of the symphony are to me like a spear-point jabbing in the wounds of a person on the rack. The hearers of the first performance could identify with that person. Anybody who thinks the finale is glorification is an idiot—yes, it is a triumph for idiots.

In 1937, Shostakovich was appointed to the faculty of the Leningrad Conservatory, where he remained during the early months of the attack by the German army in 1941. During these months, he composed his Seventh Symphony, dedicated to Leningrad and known by that name. Its tremendous success was bolstered by the patriotic outpourings of a population standing up valiantly to an unparalleled siege of a major city, but it doesn't measure up to the Fifth Symphony in musical quality and emotional power. To celebrate victory and the war's end, he wrote the Ninth Symphony. This work elicited negative comment because of its totally unexpected, light-hearted nature.

Following World War II, Shostakovich taught at both the Moscow and Leningrad conservatories. During the Stalinist post-war era, viselike strictures were placed on artistic creativity, culminating in 1948 at a notoriously repressive conference where many of the leading figures of Soviet art, including Shostakovich, were stripped of their titles and publicly disgraced. This repression waxed and waned as administrations changed, but the plight of the Soviet composer was never a happy one. An example is the fate of Shostakovich's Thirteenth Symphony (1962) based on five poems of Yevgeny Yevtushenko. One of these, *Babi Yar*, concerned the massacre of Jews in Kiev during World War II. Despite the sponsorship of the artistic bureaucracy and the fact that its composition was a joint effort of the leading composer and the premier poet of the USSR, word was passed that Khrushchev didn't approve. As a result, it received exactly two performances.

Many have speculated about what Shostakovich might have composed had he lived in a free society, and to what degree he compromised his artistic integrity. In point of fact, he was an avowed Communist and participated in political matters. So what? The music is what counts. In fact, Shostakovich has the distinction of being the first composer to have his music beamed to earth from outer space. On April 12, 1961, Yuri Gagarin, the first space traveler, sang to Mission Control a Shostakovich song, "My homeland hears, my homeland knows where in the skies her son soars on." Of the "modern" composers, his music is easily accessible and pays rich dividends if you give it a chance. The First Piano Concerto (1933) is a good place to start your exploration because the piano partly shares the stage with a trumpet, and the accompaniment is restricted to a string orchestra. The First Violin Concerto is superb; pay particular attention to the last movement, which is great fun and bears the label "Burlesque." If you listen to the CD of Rostropovich doing Shostakovich's First Cello Concerto, you will hear both the result of an historic student-teacher relationship, and a performance by a brilliant cellist.

Disc Two, Track 50—Symphony No. 5 in D Minor, Op. 47

You will have to listen to the entire symphony to fully appreciate the Rostropovich comment, but no apology is needed for the stirring emotions invoked by its second movement. I find it to be quite as rousing as Beethoven's "Eroica." Keep in mind that Beethoven had only the threat of an invasion by Napoleon; Shostakovich had Stalin at his front door!

The interpretation of music has no absolutes, as it is influenced by what we bring to it. In this instance, I come armed with a picture of the behemoth totalitarian state and the individual's existence within it. Shostakovich spells it out simply and then executes the concept brilliantly.

The tremendous marching chords that open the movement and recur throughout represent the state. The individual is depicted by the solo passages. Try and resolve the remainder of the movement with this formulation in mind. As I hear it, at times the individuality is maintained. More often, the individuals march collectively to the tune of the state, sometimes fervently and at other times unhappily. You will get more enjoyment, particularly in meaty works like this one, if you come up with your own formulations of what the composers are attempting to say.

Of all Shostakovich's luminous music, the two accomplishments that stand highest are the fifteen symphonies and fifteen string quartets. You have listened to an excerpt of the Fifth Symphony; now you will sample a string quartet. Somehow the string quartet form is more apolitical than the symphony or concerto, giving me the impression that they represent the unencumbered Shostakovich. I've selected the beginning of the fourth movement of String Quartet No. 8 in C Minor. This quartet has five movements, the last two of which are slow (largo). Forget interpretation; this music will connect directly with your nervous system.

You have been introduced to Shostakovich's longhaired mien. For a completely different persona and a boisterous good time, treat yourself to his *Jazz Suites Numbers 1 and 2*. He did a charming takeoff of the song "Tea for Two" in his *Tahiti Trot*. As mentioned earlier but worth repeating, you will delight in the Piano Concerto No. 1 in C Minor, Op. 35 for some perfectly wonderful trumpet playing (yes, I did say Piano Concerto) and musical jokes (on Haydn and Beethoven, no less). Talent is talent!

Shostakovich, Dmitry

Bernstein, Leonard (1918–1990)

"My life is, I think, dedicated to communication,
to sharing the wonder of experience with other people."

disc two
tracks 52–53

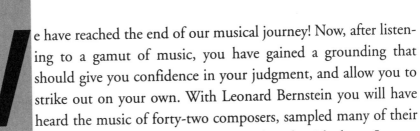

We have reached the end of our musical journey! Now, after listening to a gamut of music, you have gained a grounding that should give you confidence in your judgment, and allow you to strike out on your own. With Leonard Bernstein you will have heard the music of forty-two composers, sampled many of their works, and learned enough about their lives to begin to identify with them. I regret the chorus of composers that I had to neglect and whose music you must investigate on your own. The "contemporary" composer group has been omitted deliberately because they might have discouraged you. If you feel ready for the adventure, have a go at Cage, Carter, Crumb, Lutosławski, Pärt, Schnittke, and Tippett.

Thirty-five years ago, none of the composers named above were even categorized by Aaron Copland in his book, *What to Listen for in Music,* which I have repeatedly urged upon you. He has a simple classification based upon his opinion of the difficulties of understanding the music of individual composers. It is satisfying that a good many of the "modern" composers in his list are by now old friends of ours.

Very easy:	Shostakovich and Khachaturian, Francis Poulenc and Erik Satie, early Stravinsky and Schoenberg, Virgil Thomson.
Quite approachable:	Prokofiev, Villa-Lobos, Ernest Bloch, Roy Harris, William Walton, Malipiero, and Britten.
Fairly difficult:	Late Stravinsky, Béla Bartók, Milhaud, Chávez, William Schuman, Honegger, Hindemith, Walter Piston.
Very tough:	Middle and late Schoenberg, Alban Berg, Anton Webern, Varèse, Dallapiccola, Krenek, Roger Sessions, sometimes Charles Ives.

Putting Leonard Bernstein in this distinguished "last place" was an easy decision for me. He conducted the first concert I ever attended. It was held at the Lewisohn

Stadium in New York City, and my recollection is that he conducted Beethoven's Fifth Symphony, but I remember Bernstein himself much more vividly than the music. He had all but reached the Frank Sinatra level of teenage idolatry. Nothing was held back as he went through the contortions of conducting. Every part of his body moved. There was a great baseball player of the time, Mel Ott, who, when he swung at a ball, kicked his left foreleg up and out to the side. I was certain that "Lenny" had seen him play and had adapted that motion, among many others, to his conducting gyrations.

Few conductors have charisma enough to capture and control an audience the way Bernstein did, whether from the conductor's podium, the university lectern, or in front of a television camera teaching music appreciation. The twenty-five Young People's Concerts that he hosted for television for over two decades ranged from Bach to jazz, rock, and Broadway.

In submitting this book to publishing houses, there were the inevitable rejections (something that I was not used to in my life as a surgeon and professor of surgery). One editor said, "Very frankly, the only books on music appreciation that make money are by Leonard Bernstein." The composer/conductor combination is a rarity in our time, but in the past there was Mendelssohn, Berlioz, and Mahler. Bernstein was undoubtedly their equal as a conductor, but not as a composer. Nonetheless, he has given us some fine music.

Leonard Bernstein was born in Lawrence, Massachusetts, in 1918. He studied music at Harvard University with a concentration in piano, which he had begun to play when he was ten. He pursued postgraduate studies at the Curtis Institute in Philadelphia, and during the summers at Tanglewood under Serge Koussevitzky.

The big break came on November 13, 1943. He was assistant conductor of the New York Philharmonic Orchestra. Bruno Walter, a guest conductor, became indisposed the evening before a major Sunday afternoon concert that was to be nationally broadcast. At that time, the Sunday afternoon concerts drew a huge audience. No home television existed with its Sunday afternoon professional football games. Bernstein, without rehearsal, took over and performed flawlessly in his début before a major orchestra and the nation. Such events are the stuff of legends. From then on, Bernstein rose like a rocket. He succeeded Koussevitzky as the head of the conducting department at Tanglewood. From 1957 to 1969, he was musical director and chief conductor of the New York Philharmonic. On stepping down, he was given the title of Laureate Conductor for Life. He conducted virtually every major orchestra in the world, and became a world-renowned personality from his television appearances and books; he had the great honor of delivering the Charles Elliot Norton lectures at his alma mater, Harvard.

From a *New York Times* editorial on 16 November 1943:

There are many variations of the six best stories in the world: the young corporal takes over the platoon when all the officers are down; the captain, with the dead admiral at his side, signals the fleet to go ahead; the young actress, fresh from Corinth or Ashtabula, steps into the star's role; the junior clerk, alone in the office, makes the instantaneous decision that saves the firm from ruin. The adventure of Leonard Bernstein, twenty-five-year-old assistant conductor of the Philharmonic, who blithely mounted the podium at Carnegie Hall Sunday afternoon when Conductor Bruno Walter became ill, belongs in the list...

Bernstein resurrected the works of Mahler and recorded his entire symphonic output; doing so was no small task. I advised you earlier to get his complete recordings of the Beethoven symphonies. He was responsible for the premier performances of innumerable major works, including those of Ives, Messiaen, and Britten. While one can debate the greatness of conductors, there is no question that he did more to introduce classical music to the public than any other individual in our time. A portion of West 65th Street, adjacent to New York City's Lincoln Center, has since been named Leonard Bernstein Place.

Parallel to his career of conductor and pianist, he was also a composer. His First Symphony won the New York Music Critics' Circle award as the best new American orchestral work of 1943–44. His first ballet music, *Fancy Free*, led to the long-running Broadway musical, *On The Town*. In the 1960s, his Symphony No. 3 and *Chichester Psalms* were notable, along with *Mass,* commissioned by Jacqueline Kennedy Onassis as a memorial to the assassinated president. Most of his nontheatrical works deal with a "crisis in faith." Bernstein had a wife and three children, but was a homosexual. One must wonder if the spiritual nature of his serious works was motivated by the conflicts he encountered by living in the closet for most of his career.

In the year 2001, eleven years after his death, Bernstein received the ultimate accolade—the U.S. Postal Service issued a postage stamp in his honor with his picture displayed on it.

Disc Two, Track 53—Overture to *Candide*

Candide is based on the 1759 satirical novel by Voltaire, in which the young Candide travels with his girlfriend, Cunégonde, believing in "the best of all possible worlds" only to unearth evil and mayhem. The Bernstein musical (1956) was initially a failure with a book written by the dramatist Lillian Hellman and the poet, Richard Wilbur. The libretto was rewritten and new lyrics were added. The second version (1973) ran for 740 performances. The Overture has become a concert hall staple. Just as Voltaire wrote a parody on life, Bernstein's Overture to *Candide* is said to be a caricature of the music of Jacques Offenbach (1819–1880, known as "the Mozart of the Champs-Élysées") and Gilbert and Sullivan. I hear an overly frenetic version of Offenbach's "Gaite Parisienne" with some cats meowing, but don't pick up echoes of the Savoy Theater. Do you?

Recommended Listening
Symphonic Dances from *West Side Story*

West Side Story is a Broadway musical based on the Romeo and Juliet story transposed to the gangs of 1950s New York. Its melodies are captivating, and there is nothing more to say.

"Lenny," as everybody affectionately called him, was perhaps the greatest teacher of musical appreciation to the general public. It is to be hoped that his many radio and television lectures will be resurrected.

e have come such a long way in musical history that some perspective is in order. The value of dividing history into periods is that it allows for useful generalizations; periods blend into one another so that the given dates are approximate.

In the Middle Ages and during the Renaissance, music was a servant of the church. Restraint and religiosity are characteristic. The harmonies and tonal system familiar to our ears were developed in a rudimentary way. The mass was to the Renaissance audience what the symphony was to the eighteenth century audience, and the opera to the nineteenth.

The Baroque Period, roughly 1600 to 1750, a handmaiden of the aristocracy, began the development of musical forms and developed beautifully filigreed music, mostly polyphonic, that could be listened to with great ease despite its complexity. Symmetry, orderliness, bouquets of melodies, joyfulness, and lots of notes are its traits.

Music, which was essentially a decorative art in the Baroque period, acquired the ability to touch the deepest emotions in the Classical period. Its dates are generally given as 1750 to 1830; it can be thought of as starting at the death of Bach (1750) and extending to the death of Beethoven (1827).

During the Classical period, music developed that was pleasant to our ears, and forms were wrought that were readily understandable. The forms provided a sense of stability and did not tax the psyche other than to interest us intellectually so that we could better appreciate what was going on. Classical period music provides pure, undiluted pleasure, and most people still make it their first choice today. It improved on the Baroque in that there was a single story line and could be more intuitively understood.

Then Beethoven came along. He began his career in the Classical period, and though for the most part he observed its forms, he bent them to his own use and, in mid-career, knocked Classicism out of the ballpark. He ushered in Romanticism, and presaged Modern music by a century in his late string quartets. It is not hyperbole to compare Beethoven's impact on music to Einstein's on physics.

The Romantic period, or Romanticism, overlaps the Classical period. The dates given are from the late eighteenth century to the early years of the twentieth. Romanticism stressed the dominance of emotion over reason, of stimulus and feeling over form and order. New value was placed on innovation and experimentation, mutation, and novelty. The creation of pictures, the telling of stories, and the presence of nature assumed dominance; plumbing the soul and recreation of individual (as opposed to generic) torments and orgasmic behavior were its fodder. Poetry, literature, drama, art, and, again, nature, became its source materials and often were included in its substance. Love was important above all. Expression shaped form in the Romantic period as opposed to the Classical period in which form shaped expression, although the structural elements of Classicism were by no means discarded. Just as a painter doesn't want his work to be considered derivative of another painter's style, the Romantic composers strove for individualism. This desire dovetailed well with the rise of nationalism. Native folk materials incorporated into the style were a surefire solution. You would never confuse Smetana with Musorgsky as you might easily have done with Haydn and Mozart, or Bach and Vivaldi.

The Modern era is more difficult to define, but is usually dated from after the first decade of our just-passed century. Time and distance perceptions changed. No longer were there long flowing melodies. Attention spans became shorter. Just as the physics of Newton became archaic, the orderly and comfortable were thrown out in favor of entirely new sound combinations. Rhythm became ever more important with silences often having more consequence than notes. Give it a chance, but there is no disgrace in acquiring more knowledge of the Baroque, Classic, and Romantic periods first, with even some earlier music as well.

You have had sufficient exposure and background to proceed on your own. Congratulations. And now…

Bon Voyage!

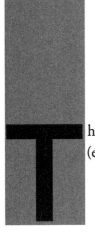

The following is a list of works most frequently repeated in my collection (each is well worth owning, but not necessarily in three or four versions):

Bach	Toccata and Fugue in D Minor
Borodin	*On the Steppes of Central Asia*
Brahms	*Variation on a Theme by Haydn*
Chausson	Symphony in B-flat
Debussy	*Afternoon of a Faun*
Delius	*On Hearing the First Cuckoo in Spring*
Elgar	*Enigma Variations*
	Pomp and Circumstance
Grieg	Suite Nos. 1 and 2 from *Peer Gynt*
Khachaturian	"Sabre Dance"
Liszt	Hungarian Rhapsody No. 2
	Mephisto Waltz
Massenet	"Meditation" from *Thais*
Mozart	Andante for Flute and Orchestra in C Major, K. 315
	Concerto for Flute, Harp, and Orchestra, K. 299
	"Eine kleine Nachtmusik," K. 525
	Sinfonia Concertante in E-flat Major for Violin, Viola, and Orchestra, K. 364
Pachelbel	Canon
Ravel	*Bolero*
	Pavane pour une infante défunte
Rimsky-Korsakov	*Scheherazade*
Saint-Saens	"The Swan" from *Carnival of the Animals*
Tchaikovsky	*1812 Overture*
	Variations on a Rococo Theme for Cello and Orchestra

Your collection of compact discs will soon become unmanageable unless you catalog them. I know people who arrange composers or types of music together and locate them that way. The fallacy of their method is that one disc can have multiple composers or types of music. My system, which has worked well, is to give each compact disc a number which I affix to the top front of the disc case on a quarter-inch round label (a standard item in stationery stores). I arrange the discs next to one another in numeric order. The end result is a composer file listing all the works broken into categories such as symphonies, concertos, etc. Preceding each work is the number of the disc on which it appears. Using this method, the contents of a single compact disc will often end up in multiple composer files.

Although you can use an index card file, you will find it easy to set up a database on a computer. It takes a bit of time to enter the data as each new disc is acquired, but the ability of finding what you want immediately is worth the effort. The one bit of advice is to keep the database simple (CD#, composer, and name of selection are quite enough). An extra dividend is that a printout of what you own can be taken to the music store. Remember to save the sales slip so that you can return your mistakes.

RESOURCES

Haas, Karl. *Inside Music*. New York: Doubleday, 1984.

Kramer, Jonathan. *Listen to the Music*. New York: Schirmer Books, 1988.

Latham, Alison, ed. *The Oxford Companion to Music*. Oxford: Oxford University Press, 2002.

Sadie, Stanley, ed. *The New Grove Dictionary of Music and Musicians*. 2nd edition. New York: Macmillan, 2001.

Staines, Joe, ed. *The Rough Guide to Classical Music*, London: Rough Guides Ltd., 2001.

ABOUT THE AUTHOR

Author **Julius H. Jacobson II, MD,** is an internationally known vascular surgeon. He is widely regarded as the father of microsurgery for his pioneering work in the reconstruction of small blood vessels. This has directly led to coronary bypass surgery and the re-implantation of limbs and digits. About half of all neurosurgical operations employ the technique.

Dr. Jacobson is a graduate of the Johns Hopkins School of Medicine, and trained at the Columbia Presbyterian Hospital. He is now Director Emeritus of Vascular Surgery and Distinguished Service Professor of Surgery at the Mount Sinai Medical Center in New York City. He has five degrees, two of them honorary, but alas, none of them in music, one of his greatest loves.

ABOUT THE NARRATOR

Brigitte Lacombe

Narrator **Kevin Kline** is an Academy and Tony Award–winning actor whose films include: *The Big Chill, A Fish Called Wanda, Dave, In & Out, Sophie's Choice,* and *Life as a House.* His stage performances include *Pirates of Penzance, Hamlet* (PBS), *Richard III, Henry V, Ivanov,* and *The Seagull.*